Human-Centered Learning Design in the AI Era

Andi Asrifan
Universitas Negeri Makassar, Indonesia

IGI Global
Scientific Publishing
Publishing Tomorrow's Research Today

Vice President of Editorial Melissa Wagner
Director of Acquisitions Mikaela Felty
Director of Book Development Jocelynn Hessler
Production Manager Mike Brehm
Cover Design Jose Rosado

Published in the United States of America by
IGI Global Scientific Publishing
701 East Chocolate Avenue
Hershey, PA, 17033, USA
Tel: 717-533-8845
Fax: 717-533-7115
Website: https://www.igi-global.com E-mail: cust@igi-global.com

Library of Congress Cataloging-in-Publication Data

Names: Asrifan, Andi, 1985- editor
Title: Human-centered learning design in the AI era / Edited by Andi Asrifan.
Description: Hershey, PA : IGI Global Scientific Publishing, [2026] | Includes bibliographical references and index. | Summary: "The book outlines a plan to reimagine higher education for a human-centered, technology-driven world. It discusses how innovative curriculum design that supports these goals can help higher education institutions adapt to this paradigm change"-- Provided by publisher.
Identifiers: LCCN 2025029132 (print) | LCCN 2025029133 (ebook) | ISBN 9798337357867 hardcover | ISBN 9798337357874 paperback | ISBN 9798337357881 ebook
Subjects: LCSH: Artificial intelligence--Educational applications | Student-centered learning | Education, Higher--Curricula | Educational change
Classification: LCC LB1028.43 .H845 2026 (print) | LCC LB1028.43 (ebook)
LC record available at https://lccn.loc.gov/2025029132
LC ebook record available at https://lccn.loc.gov/2025029133

British Cataloguing in Publication Data
A Cataloguing in Publication record for this book is available from the British Library.

Table of Contents

Detailed Table of Contents

The diverse applications of AI in education are streamlining and individualising the academic landscape. Educational resources are now universally accessible via smart devices and systems, transforming learning. Students can acquire knowledge without attending physical classes due to their computer and Internet access. The impact of learners' general satisfaction with their experience utilizing the AI-driven platform encompasses their perceived value and efficacy in facilitating their learning. The study aims to investigate the impact of the engagement level of the AI-driven platform relative to conventional learning approaches. This study utilised a quantitative data analysis methodology primarily focusing on numerical data, to analyze the repercussions of building international AI-powered learning platforms. The findings indicate that most EFL students perceive AI platforms positively, acknowledging their significant contribution to learning. Students recognize the efficacy of AI in enhancing learning and accept its unique benefits over conventional educational approaches

This study examines the amalgamation of artificial intelligence (AI), pedagogical tactics, and psychological concepts to establish comprehensive learning environments that facilitate students' cognitive, emotional, and social growth. Holistic learning prioritizes the entire learner by accommodating varied requirements, motivations, and intelligences. Artificial intelligence technology, including adaptive learning systems, emotional monitoring tools, and collaborative platforms, facilitate individualized, inclusive, and engaging educational experiences. The study examines the theoretical foundations, design principles, ethical issues, and optimal methods for integrating AI with constructivist, humanistic, and socio-emotional learning frameworks. Case examples illustrate how AI can improve student autonomy, well-being, and achievement when integrated with psychological principles. The results underscore the significance of user-centered design, professional development, and stakeholder involvement in maintaining inclusive, technology-driven, and human-centered educational institutions.

This chapter examines the amalgamation of mathematics and physical education within the interdisciplinary STEAM (Science, Technology, Engineering, Arts, and Mathematics) framework. Integrating mathematical ideas like geometry, statistics, and probability into physical activities can elevate student engagement, critical thinking, and practical application. The study emphasizes effective tactics such as project-based learning, movement analysis, fitness data monitoring, and gamified activities that enhance both academic and physical literacy. Collaborative learning environments enhance the cultivation of communication and problem-solving

This chapter examines the transformative impact of artificial intelligence (AI) on students' mental health and well-being, addressing the urgent need for innovative solutions in response to escalating mental health challenges among this demographic. In recent years, mental health issues among students have surged due to a combination of factors, including increasing academic pressures, socio-economic disparities, and the pervasive influence of digital technologies. These challenges create a complex array of psychological and emotional difficulties that necessitate timely and effective interventions.AI technologies, particularly those leveraging natural language processing (NLP) and machine learning (ML), are emerging as scalable and accessible tools for mental health support in educational settings. Unlike traditional therapeutic methods, which often face geographical, financial, and logistical constraints, AI-powered tools provide round-the-clock assistance to users, transcending barriers of time and location.

Preface

INTRODUCTION

As we stand at the crossroads of technological innovation and educational reform, *Human-Centered Learning Design in the AI Era* offers timely insights into how artificial intelligence can be harnessed to redefine learning in a way that places the human experience at its core. In this rapidly evolving landscape, AI's influence on higher education is no longer a distant possibility—it is an immediate reality. This book provides an in-depth exploration of AI's potential to enhance student well-being, improve critical thinking, personalize learning, and support multidisciplinary collaboration.

Targeted toward educators, policymakers, researchers, curriculum developers, and edtech innovators, this volume offers both a conceptual roadmap and practical strategies for integrating AI-driven solutions into educational systems. Contributors to this book examine not only the capabilities of emerging technologies but also the ethical, societal, and pedagogical implications of their implementation. Whether you are a teacher looking to refine your instructional methods, a policymaker seeking to draft inclusive and equitable AI policies, or an entrepreneur exploring new frontiers in education technology, this book speaks directly to your role in shaping the future of education.

Our vision aligns with the ambitions of Society 5.0—a human-centered society that balances technological advancement with social responsibility and sustainability. Through case studies, theoretical frameworks, and evidence-based recommendations, this work empowers readers to lead transformative change. It underscores the urgent need to craft learning environments that are inclusive, adaptive, and deeply attuned to the diverse needs of learners in the digital age.

Human-Centered Learning Design in the AI Era is not just a scholarly contribution; it is a call to action. It is an invitation to join a collective movement to reimagine education in the AI age—one where innovation supports equity, where data serves human dignity, and where learning becomes a catalyst for sustainable progress.

ORGANIZATION OF THE BOOK

Chapter 1: Collaborative AI for Global Education Networks: Building International AI-Powered Learning Platforms

This chapter introduces the transformative power of collaborative AI in expanding global access to education. By examining the development and implementation of AI-driven learning platforms, the authors reveal how technology enables students—especially English as a Foreign Language (EFL) learners—to experience personalized, accessible, and effective learning without the constraints of physical classrooms. Employing a quantitative methodology, the chapter presents compelling evidence of student satisfaction and engagement, highlighting the potential of AI to outperform traditional approaches in fostering meaningful educational experiences. This work offers a foundational perspective on how international AI-powered networks can drive equity and innovation in global learning.

Chapter 2: Creating Holistic Learning Environments: Integrating AI, Education, and Psychological Principles

Rooted in a vision of education that honors the whole student, this chapter explores the integration of AI with pedagogical and psychological theories to create inclusive and supportive learning environments. Drawing from humanistic and socio-emotional learning frameworks, the authors advocate for adaptive technologies that promote cognitive, emotional, and social development. The chapter underscores the importance of user-centered design and institutional collaboration in achieving meaningful educational outcomes. Through practical examples and ethical considerations, it calls for a human-centered approach to AI adoption that prioritizes student well-being and institutional inclusivity.

Chapter 3: Bridging Disciplines: Integrating Mathematics and Physical Education Through STEAM

This chapter exemplifies the possibilities of cross-disciplinary learning by demonstrating how mathematics can be taught through physical education using the STEAM model. By embedding mathematical concepts like geometry and statistics into physical activity, educators can increase student engagement, motivation, and applied comprehension. The authors emphasize project-based learning, movement tracking, and gamified strategies that promote holistic literacy—both academic and physical. With strong case examples and best practices, this chapter champions STEAM as a dynamic framework for cultivating critical thinking, teamwork, and lifelong learning skills.

Chapter 4: Designing for People: Integrating Human-Centric Approaches in Technology Management

Human-centered design takes center stage in this chapter's analysis of ethical and empathetic technology development. By tracing the roots of user-centered approaches and applying them to emerging technologies such as AI, AR/VR, and IoT, the authors build a robust framework for inclusive and responsive design. They explore accessibility, data ethics, and AI bias while advocating for iterative prototyping and interdisciplinary collaboration. Through compelling case studies, the chapter showcases how organizations can embed empathy and ethical responsibility into their design processes—reinforcing that technological progress must always serve human needs.

Chapter 5: Integrating Artificial Intelligence and Design Thinking: Enhancing Students' Practical Skills

Design thinking, celebrated for its creativity and human-centered methodology, finds a new ally in artificial intelligence. This chapter investigates how generative AI tools like ChatGPT and Gemini can augment the design thinking process across educational and professional settings. While AI brings efficiency and scalability to this iterative model, the chapter raises critical questions about how technology can support—but not replace—the deeply human elements of empathy and ideation. It offers practical insights into leveraging AI without diluting the experiential essence of design thinking, emphasizing a hybrid model of human-AI collaboration.

Chapter 6: Dimensions of Cognitive Processes: Integrating Concepts, Decision-Making, Reasoning, and Creativity in Learning

This chapter offers a comprehensive exploration of the cognitive dimensions that shape learning and problem-solving. From concept formation and decision-making to reasoning, intelligence, and emotion, the authors highlight how each facet influences educational outcomes. The chapter underscores the importance of cultivating creativity and emotional intelligence alongside traditional academic skills. Using qualitative analysis and literature reviews, the authors propose integrative teaching strategies that respond to the complexity of human cognition, presenting educators with a blueprint for nurturing well-rounded, reflective, and capable learners.

Chapter 7: Transforming Workforce Development Through AI-Driven Education Networks: A Pathway to Sustainable Economic Growth

In response to growing skills gaps and labor market volatility, this chapter presents AI-powered education as a key driver of workforce development and economic resilience. The authors examine how machine learning, predictive analytics, and natural language processing can align educational outcomes with industry demands. Through case studies and curriculum strategies, the chapter outlines best practices for collaboration among educators, businesses, and policymakers. It also addresses critical issues such as equity, data privacy, and accessibility—emphasizing lifelong learning and inclusive innovation as foundations for a thriving future economy.

Chapter 8: Impact of AI on Students' Mental Health and Well-Being

Confronting the mental health crisis among students, this chapter explores how AI can serve as an accessible, scalable solution for emotional support and psychological resilience. The authors detail how AI tools—particularly those using natural language processing and machine learning—can deliver 24/7 assistance and circumvent common barriers to traditional mental health services. This chapter articulates a compelling case for the ethical and thoughtful integration of AI in educational ecosystems, encouraging schools to leverage technology to support student well-being while maintaining sensitivity to privacy, agency, and emotional nuance.

CONCLUSION

As we conclude this volume, *Human-Centered Learning Design in the AI Era*, we are reminded that the future of education does not rest solely in technological advancement, but in our collective commitment to keeping humanity at the heart of innovation. The chapters presented here illustrate a shared vision—one where artificial intelligence empowers learners, supports educators, and transforms educational systems to be more inclusive, adaptive, and effective.

From reimagining global learning networks and integrating psychological principles into AI-enhanced environments, to designing ethical, human-centric technologies and addressing students' mental health with intelligent tools, this book highlights a wide spectrum of possibilities for educational transformation. It is through this interdisciplinary and human-centered approach that we can truly harness the potential of AI to support lifelong learning, promote equity, and prepare students for the complexities of Society 5.0.

This work is both a reflection of current progress and a roadmap for future action. We hope it inspires educators, researchers, designers, and policymakers to lead with intention, to innovate responsibly, and to design learning systems that are as compassionate as they are advanced. Together, we can shape an educational landscape where technology enhances—not replaces—the human experience.

Andi Asrifan
Universitas Negeri Makassar, Indonesia

Chapter 1
Collaborative AI for Global Education Networks:
Building International AI-Powered Learning Platforms

Sukmawati Sukmawati
https://orcid.org/0000-0003-1434-3453
Universitas Megarezky, Makassar, Indonesia

Sunarlia Limbong
Politeknik Ilmu Pelayaran (PIP) Makassar, Indonesia

Yulini Rinantanti
Universitas Cenderawasih, Jayapura, Indonesia

Asdar Asdar
https://orcid.org/0000-0002-3277-0283
Universitas Bosowa, Makassar, Indonesia

Sujarwo Sujarwo
Universitas Megarezky, Makassar, Indonesia

ABSTRACT

The diverse applications of AI in education are streamlining and individualising the academic landscape. Educational resources are now universally accessible via smart devices and systems, transforming learning. Students can acquire knowledge without attending physical classes due to their computer and Internet access. The impact of learners' general satisfaction with their experience utilizing the AI-driven platform

DOI: 10.4018/979-8-3373-5786-7.ch001

encompasses their perceived value and efficacy in facilitating their learning. The study aims to investigate the impact of the engagement level of the AI-driven platform relative to conventional learning approaches. This study utilised a quantitative data analysis methodology primarily focusing on numerical data, to analyze the repercussions of building international AI-powered learning platforms. The findings indicate that most EFL students perceive AI platforms positively, acknowledging their significant contribution to learning. Students recognize the efficacy of AI in enhancing learning and accept its unique benefits over conventional educational approaches

INTRODUCTION

Technology has evolved into a necessary component of daily life in this digital era, influencing people's interactions, employment, and learning within the larger society. With the fast development of digital tools and platforms, many industries have been changed; education is one of the most affected ones (Nurhikmah H et al., 2024). Of these advancements, educational technology has become an indispensable tool for the teaching and learning process. From virtual classrooms to language learning apps to artificial intelligence-driven feedback systems, these technologies cover a broad spectrum of tools that improve the accessibility and efficiency of language training. Consequently, including technology into language instruction not only modernizes conventional methods but also creates new paths for interactive and customized learning environments (Sasabone et al., 2022). Particularly in language teaching, educational technology has many benefits that enhance and promote student involvement as well as the development of competency (Wahid et al., 2025).

Dynamic and immersive experiences that traditional approaches could lack are created in part by multimedia content, real-time communication platforms, gamified learning settings, and adaptive learning systems. These resources let students track their development over time and practice listening, speaking, reading, and writing in real-world settings under instant feedback. Furthermore, technology closes geographical and cultural gaps so that students may interact with different language communities all around and with native speakers. Thus, careful application of educational technologies in language learning not only improves skill development but also motivates, encourages autonomy, and raises global awareness among students (Amaliah et al., 2022; Aderamo et al., 2024; Sukmawati et al., 2023; Limbong et al., 2022; Imran & Sulviana, 2022). Smart technologies improve productivity and innovation in these sectors and influence our daily lives, affecting how we shop, travel, manage finances, and consume media. The digital revolution is transforming all facets of our lives, prompting businesses and educational institutions to reassess their methodologies for teaching and learning (Sujarwo et al., 2023). This extensive integration underscores the increasing importance of AI in crafting a more intelligent, interconnected future (Pokrivcakova, 2019).

As a result of the rapid development of computing technology, the implementation of artificial intelligence in education (AIED) has become more accessible than ever before. The term "AIED" refers to the incorporation of artificial intelligence technologies into educational settings to improve the teaching, learning, and decision-making processes. These systems take advantage of artificial intelligence's capacity to imitate human intelligence, which enables them to conclude, make judgments, and make predictions that benefit a variety of stakeholders in the education sector (Choukaier, 2024).

When implemented, AI-based learning systems give students customized support by evaluating their learning activities, strengths, and weaknesses to provide them with particular direction, feedback, and resources. Utilizing this customized approach, students can progress at their own speed, therefore tackling special difficulties and generating the greatest potential learning results for them. A great tool for teachers, artificial intelligence education and development (AIED) helps to automate administrative tasks, including grading, tracking student achievement, and producing insights that direct classroom practices and lesson design. Apart from the classroom, AIED helps legislators and officials since it provides data insights that can be used. These realizations enable one to create policies and initiatives in line with educational trends and needs, so promoting equity and effectiveness on a broad basis. Artificial intelligence-powered predictive analytics, for instance, can find students who are at risk early on and enable quick interventions meant to improve retention and success rates.

AIED also encourages innovation in instructional strategies, including intelligent tutoring systems that offer real-time, interactive help or adaptive learning systems that dynamically change the complexity of materials depending on student performance. These two instances show how artificial intelligence helps teachers to be creative. Artificial intelligence education (AIED) has the potential to democratize education by combining these skills with the scalability of modern technology. This will allow excellent learning resources to be accessible to a broader global audience. The implementation of AIED, on the other hand, is not without its difficulties, including protecting data privacy, avoiding algorithmic biases, and maintaining inclusivity across a wide range of socioeconomic and cultural situations (Hutson et al., 2022). To address these concerns, rigorous design, ethical considerations, and continual refinement are required. This is necessary to realize AIED's revolutionary potential while protecting its users.

Artificial intelligence (AI) has been progressively incorporated into other domains, including education. In recent years, personalized learning platforms utilizing AI algorithms have developed as a potential educational strategy (Carrió-Pastor, 2016). These platforms can offer learners tailored feedback, suggestions, and assistance depending on their educational progress and objectives (Folgieri et al., 2024). AI's diverse educational applications render the academic landscape more streamlined and individualized (Lopez-Fierro et al., 2024). Educational resources are now universally available via smart devices and systems, revolutionizing learning. Students can learn without attending physical classes as long as they can access computers and the Internet. AI assists educational institutions in digitizing administrative functions, enabling teachers to enhance student engagement (Asdar et al., 2024; Hasyim et al., 2024; Limbong et al., 2024).

Artificial Intelligence (AI) is an expeditiously advancing technological domain capable of transforming all facets of human social interactions. In education, AI has created innovative instructional methods that are currently being evaluated in diverse environments. Education officials anticipate the effects of AI on the educational sector to devise informed and pertinent remedies (Tang & Foley, 2022). Artificial intelligence increasingly integrates into our daily lives, significantly influencing education and quickly upgrading traditional methodologies. Artificial Intelligence (AI) is increasingly influential in creating novel learning systems, aiming to transform the educational system (Abdulah et al., 2024).

Building a worldwide learning platform driven by artificial intelligence calls for strategic execution and meticulous planning if one is to achieve scalability, inclusivity, and efficacy concurrently. Scalability guarantees that the platform can handle an increasing number of users without compromising performance, therefore enabling a wide range of audiences all across the world. Being inclusive helps one to satisfy the needs of students from all socioeconomic, cultural, and linguistic backgrounds. This will guarantee that every pupil may access learning materials equally. Effective delivery of high-quality, customized learning opportunities that support involvement, knowledge retention, and skill development is the secret.

By means of innovative artificial intelligence technologies like adaptive learning algorithms and support for numerous languages, a platform like this may meet particular needs of individual students and simultaneously eliminate language barriers.

In addition, the platform will resonate with a worldwide audience if it is designed with user-friendly interfaces and encourages collaboration between people of different cultural backgrounds. An emphasis on ethical AI techniques, data security, and constant feedback loops further strengthens the legitimacy and functionality of the platform, thereby transforming it into a tool that may revolutionize the educational landscape worldwide (Özdere, 2023). This advancement signifies increasing awareness of AI's capacity to modify educational processes by implementing novel tools and techniques. The uses of AI in learning are beyond conventional limits, facilitating enhanced instruction, improved learning experiences, and increased accessibility (Tammets & Ley, 2023). AI can deliver prompt feedback, adjust the learner's pace, and create interactive and engaging educational environments customized to individual competence levels and learning styles (Choukaier, 2024). Artificial Intelligence is an interdisciplinary field encompassing natural and social sciences (Fraidan, 2024).

LITERATURE REVIEW

Collaborative Teaching and AI

In the continuously changing landscape of education, collaborative teaching and artificial intelligence (AI) are two revolutionary aspects that, when coupled, have the potential to build learning environments that are both innovative and effective by combining their respective strengths (Choukaier, 2024). Planning, delivering, and evaluating instruction is considered collaborative teaching, which involves numerous educators working together. This encourages a culture of shared accountability and allows educators to combine their various teaching styles and areas of expertise. Addressing the specific requirements of each student and encouraging collaboration among teachers improves the overall quality of the educational experience.

Either as a self-directed study tool or complement to traditional language teaching approaches, artificial intelligence-driven language learning applications can offer a variety of instructional tools and exercises meant to help students improve their vocabulary, grammar, and speaking skills. Some applications let students improve their communication skills in a virtual reality using interactive chats with virtual language teachers. The use of artificial intelligence in language acquisition can change our attitude to learning languages (Alharbi, 2023). It offers a customized and adaptable approach for language acquisition so that students may focus on the parts of the language they find most challenging and go at their speed. AI-driven language learning tools should be used to complement traditional language teaching approaches; they cannot replace human teachers. Artificial intelligence (AI), on the other hand, presents tools and systems that might revolutionize teacher cooperation and instruction. Artificial intelligence (AI) allows teachers to automate tedious tasks like grading, customize their paths of education for each student, and access data-driven insights that could guide their work. Additionally, systems that AI powers will facilitate communication and collaboration among educators, thereby simplifying the process of working together in both traditional and online classrooms (Roy & Putatunda, 2023).

AI-Powered Personalized Learning Platforms

Artificial intelligence (AI)-driven individualized learning platforms are transforming educational delivery by prioritizing the learner in the educational experience (Folgieri et al., 2024). Utilizing advanced algorithms, these platforms evaluate comprehensive data regarding each student's performance, preferences, and learning behaviors. This data-centric methodology allows the AI to discern knowledge deficiencies, anticipate forthcoming learning obstacles, and tailor the curriculum to successfully address individual requirements (Khamis, 2024). The platforms can dynamically modify the difficulty, structure, and content of educational materials to align with a learner's abilities and preferences. For instance, visual learners may be provided with more infographics and films, whilst others might gain from text-based explanations or interactive hands-on modules. This customization enhances comprehension and cultivates motivation by aligning the learning process with the student's individual style.

Furthermore, AI-driven solutions offer immediate feedback and real-time progress monitoring, enabling students to assume control of their educational paths. Educators derive advantages from these platforms, which provide actionable insights and recommendations to enhance student support.

These platforms enhance the learning experience by establishing a personalized and responsive environment, thereby mitigating the inefficiencies and frustrations commonly linked to conventional, uniform educational methods. This transformation in personalized education guarantees that each student can realize their complete potential, rendering education more equal, engaging, and successful worldwide.

Complex algorithms at the heart of these systems monitor and evaluate students' behavioral patterns, academic achievement, and learning styles. Artificial intelligence recognizes patterns and adjusts the real-time curriculum, pace, and difficulty level (Folgieri et al., 2024). This therefore ensures that every student gets an education catered to their ability, so it helps them to overcome challenges and hasten their development in fields of excellence.

Adaptive Learning Paths

Artificial intelligence (AI) modifies the sequence and complexity of courses based on a student's success, ensuring that the student has mastered the material before moving on to the next level. Through the implementation of adaptive learning systems, which dynamically modify the sequence and level of difficulty of courses based on a student's performance, artificial intelligence (AI) is bringing about a transformation in the educational system (Hamamra et al., 2024). This innovative technique ensures students fully comprehend fundamental ideas before moving on to more difficult material. It facilitates longer retention of the material and improved understanding among students. Using real-time data, artificial intelligence systems assess every student's strength, weaknesses, and learning speed constantly.

When a student shows extraordinary mastery in a topic, the platform advances to more challenging content to keep interest and inspire development. Conversely, should difficulties arise, artificial intelligence offers focused assistance in the form of additional resources, alternate explanations, or customized remedial exercises to cover any voids and improve understanding.

Intelligent Feedback

A growth mindset can be developed by intelligent feedback—that is, quick, focused comments that help students fix errors and support fundamental ideas. A basic element of modern educational technology, intelligent feedback, lets students get quick, targeted responses to their performance. This type of comment not only helps students quickly fix their errors but also reinforces basic ideas, therefore enhancing their memory and comprehension. Given intelligent feedback, students are urged to see mistakes as opportunities for learning rather than failures, since it resolves flaws in real-time. This motivates students to adopt a growth mindset—that is, the conviction that, with diligence and tenacity, their skills could develop. When students have such an attitude, they are more likely to be driven to take on challenges, accept comments, and keep on when faced with problems (Pokrivcakova, 2019). Intelligent feedback systems help teachers simplify the feedback process, thereby allowing them to interact with each student in a way that is both consistent and unique. In an environment built by the mix of technology and pedagogy, students might feel enabled to reach their best potential.

Data-Driven Insights

Data-driven insights give teachers practical knowledge about class and personal performance, therefore guiding their decisions about their field of work. Data-driven insights are revolutionizing education since they provide teachers and students with actionable numbers they can apply to guide decisions. These revelations help one to better understand the learning processes and effects by gathering and analyzing data related to student performance, interaction, and behavior (Redmond et al., 2018). Data-driven insights can help teachers by offering a whole picture of group and personal development, pointing up areas of strength and weakness, and spotting trends.

This allows teachers to change their courses, provide especially targeted interventions, and enhance classroom strategies to meet the various educational needs of their students. Students are encouraged in self-awareness and self-regulation through tailored comments grounded in statistics. Eventually, better results and more motivation follow from their capacity to track their development, set goals, and take ownership of their learning process. Data-driven insights leverage analytics' ability to convert unprocessed data into significant activity. This thus stimulates education's creativity and quality. They open the path for a more flexible, effective, and inclusive learning ecosystem that would help every initiative participant.

Engaging Content Delivery

Gamification, interactive simulations, and multimedia components—all of which help to make learning more dynamic and appealing—help to drive this process (Morales et al., 2016). New techniques, including gamification, interactive simulations, and multimedia components, are driving learning to be more dynamic, interesting, and pleasurable. Modern education is starting to feature these technologies rather more often. These approaches draw students in and help them to grasp challenging concepts by using technology's ability.

Gamification makes it possible to include elements reminiscent of games into the educational process. These components consist of points, badges, leaderboards, and challenges. Competition and prizes can motivate individuals, encourage active involvement, and cultivate a sense of success. Through interactive simulations, learners can experiment, explore, and apply their knowledge in realistic circumstances. These immersive experiences allow for hands-on participation. This set of tools helps to bridge the gap between theory and practice by rendering intangible ideas more concrete and simpler to understand (Abu Bakar et al., 2018).

By including visual, audio, and interactive components, multimedia components, such as movies, animations, and infographics, can appeal to a wide range of learning styles. Students who have diverse preferences and requirements might benefit from this multisensory approach when it comes to improving their knowledge, retention, and accessibility. Not only does the incorporation of these dynamic components make education more successful, but it also makes it a source of inspiration and excitement for students, who can, in turn, play an active role in their own learning path.

Accessibility and Equity

These platforms frequently feature available alternatives in several languages, assistive technologies, and offline access, which ensures that they are inclusive of learners from a variety of backgrounds.

By overcoming the constraints of approaches that are universally applicable, personalized learning platforms that are powered by artificial intelligence give students the ability to take responsibility for their own education (Creely, 2024).

Not only do they improve academic performance, but they also cultivate abilities in critical thinking, self-regulation, and learning that continue throughout one's life. These tools offer instructors a vital support system, enabling them to concentrate on mentoring and creating more in-depth learning experiences for their students.

AI-driven personalized learning platforms can revolutionize the integration of education and artificial intelligence. These systems tailor educational experiences based on individual learners' needs, preferences, and performance by applying advanced algorithms and machine-learning techniques (Fraidan, 2024). AI enables instructors to customize education, promote engagement, and optimize assignments while students benefit from advanced technologies that enrich their learning experiences. (Han et al., 2024). This deliberate integration facilitates individualized, efficient, and significant learning experiences while maintaining core principles such as empathy, creativity, and critical thinking (Makeleni et al., 2023).

Challenges and Opportunities of AI

Including artificial intelligence (AI) in many different disciplines, especially education, presents both possibilities and challenges in many spheres. These components must be adequately addressed if we are to maximize artificial intelligence's advantages and lower the possible risks. Examining the possibilities and difficulties artificial intelligence offers, mostly in the domain of education.

Challenges of AI

Artificial intelligence in education poses Privacy and security issues, and artificial intelligence systems frequently rely on enormous volumes of personal data, including student performance, behavior, and learning preferences. Ensuring this data against breaches and guaranteeing it will be used ethically presents a major challenge. Maintaining student privacy depends on following data protection laws, including GDPR. Unfairness and prejudice mean that how objective AI systems are depends on the data used to train them. Should artificial intelligence systems be taught on biased datasets, they could either reinforce or even exacerbate current inequalities, therefore affecting already marginalized populations. Should this happen in the context of education, it could lead to unfair assessments or biased learning paths. Essential is addressing bias in artificial intelligence and guaranteeing fair use of teaching resources. Lack of openness means many artificial intelligence systems, especially those using deep learning techniques, have the potential to run as "black boxes," meaning their decision-making processes are difficult for humans to understand.

Teachers, students, or legislators may find it challenging to assess whether judgments taken by artificial intelligence software are fair and accurate due to a lack of openness. It can also make consumers less likely to trust platforms driven by instructional artificial intelligence. Artificial intelligence needs to be applied in classrooms; thus, teachers and students have to be able to adapt to new tools. Students may have trouble connecting with artificial intelligence-driven learning systems, and teachers might not have the expertise or training required to successfully include artificial intelligence into their classroom experiences. This lack of digital literacy could limit the influence of education grounded in artificial intelligence. Automating grading or admissions, among other educational decisions, raises moral questions about responsibility and the place of human judgment in the educational system. Decisions made entirely by artificial intelligence without appropriate supervision could overlook the particular circumstances or learning needs of a pupil, therefore causing possible damage.

Advantages of AI

Using artificial intelligence, adaptive learning systems can be developed that personalize educational content according to a student's learning style, strengths, and limitations. This individualized approach has the potential to greatly improve student engagement and academic performance by delivering resources and comments that are specifically customized to the student (Guo & Wang, 2024). Improved tools powered by artificial intelligence, such as intelligent tutoring systems, virtual teaching assistants, and language translation services, can provide students with real-time support, enhancing their comprehension of difficult ideas. Moreover, by means of virtual or augmented reality (VR/AR) applications, artificial intelligence can enable immersive learning experiences, so transforming learning into more dynamic and interesting process (Redmond et al., 2018).

Obligations In the educational sector, artificial intelligence could be able to automate a great range of administrative tasks including material management, tracking attendance, and grading. This advantage lets teachers spend more of their crucial time on pedagogy and student contact. AI tools can also help find trends in student data, so giving teachers information they can use to enhance their teaching strategies. Particularly in underdeveloped or inaccessible areas, artificial intelligence could help to make education more easily available. By giving students all around access to top-notch educational resources, using virtual classrooms, and utilizing artificial intelligence-driven platforms to get customized learning help, one can close the disparity in educational possibilities

Artificial intelligence allows for collecting and analyzing huge volumes of data regarding student performance, learning outcomes, and teaching effectiveness (Fraidan, 2024)This method, driven by data, assists policymakers and educators in making well-informed decisions, recognizing patterns, and developing solutions supported by evidence to enhance educational policies and practices. Artificial intelligence could greatly help in the lifetime of learning and skill development. By offering flexible, on-demand learning opportunities and customized feedback, artificial intelligence platforms can help people keep improving their skills in response to rising job market needs. This promotes continuous education for the entirety of an individual's career because it allows for continuous learning.

Review of Previous Studies on AI in Language Learning

Some studies stated that an AI-driven personalized learning platform is a viable method for augmenting self-directed learning and facilitating personal and professional development (Folgieri et al., 2024). Mentor AI presents significant potential to transform professional development by addressing the constraints of conventional mentorship, with advantages including accelerated career advancement, skill enhancement, greater work-life balance, and increased employee satisfaction, engagement, and retention (Bagai & Mane, 2023). The AI-driven tools facilitate the development of a complex educational environment that allows for personalized learning, flexible teaching, and inclusive management (Pokrivcakova, 2019). Perceived ease of use significantly and positively impacts students' behavioral intention to use AI through their attitude toward AI rather than through perceived usefulness (Wu et al., 2024).

With the ability to address individual needs through personalization and systemic difficulties through scalable and flexible solutions, artificial intelligence is positioned to be a disruptive force in both the educational and professional realms (Jia & Stan, 2021). To be successful, however, it is necessary to build tools that are easy to use, to guarantee accessibility, and to address ethical concerns. This will pave the way for implementation that is both sustainable and impactful. Artificial intelligence has the potential to revolutionize education and professional growth if it is implemented with careful consideration. As a result of its ability to address individual demands through personalization and systemic challenges through scalability, it provides novel answers to problems that have persisted for a long time. On the other hand, the success of this endeavor is contingent upon responsible design, equal access, and a balanced integration that emphasizes the enhancement of human potential rather than decreasing it.

Objectives of Study

1) To assess the impact of EFL learners' satisfaction with their experience utilizing the AI-driven platform, encompassing their perceived value and efficacy in facilitating their learning.
2) Investigating the impact of the engagement level of the AI-driven platform relative to conventional learning approaches.

Hypothesis

H1: Learners using the AI-powered platform will show significant performance improvement compared to those using traditional learning methods.
H2: The AI platforms will exhibit elevated student satisfaction and engagement levels.

METHOD

Research Design

This study utilized a quantitative data analysis methodology, primarily focusing on numerical data, to analyze the repercussions of building international AI-powered learning platforms. The research consisted of questionnaires and surveys so students could provide feedback on the development of worldwide learning platforms powered by artificial intelligence. The use of inferential statistics to determine the significance of observed changes in the student's existing knowledge and abilities. The pre-experimental approach is suitable for investigating the effects of the AI-driven learning platform on participants' performance and educational experiences. The study's duration ranges from 4 to 6 weeks, contingent upon the intricacy of the content and platform. Participants will utilize the AI-driven learning platform to organize assignments, lectures, or modules pertinent to their educational goals. The platform will track user engagement, including duration of use, activities accomplished, and frequency of interactions. Students' perspectives regarding acquiring general knowledge in artificial intelligence were disclosed using the data obtained from the Likert Scale questionnaire with five points. In this particular study, the methods of data analysis that were utilized included percentage analysis, mean analysis, and theme analysis (Creswell, 2013).

Participants

Researchers typically employ a single-group pre-test and post-test design in a pre-experimental design including 56 EFL students from two private universities, Universitas Bosowa and Universitas Megarezky. This arrangement entails evaluating participants before and after the intervention, devoid of a control group, enabling the assessment of the intervention's impact on the identical cohort of EFL students.

Research Instruments

The subsequent research instruments will facilitate the methodical collection of data for the study:

Standardized Pre-Test and Post-Test. To assess educational outcomes prior to and after to the intervention. Multiple-choice inquiries, analytical tasks, or performance-oriented exercises. Consistent with the course objectives or learning abilities aimed at by the AI-driven platform. Guarantee the reliability and validity of tests by conducting a pilot with a small cohort before comprehensive implementation. Evaluate baseline knowledge against enhancements following the intervention. Questionnaire for Survey

To evaluate user perceptions, satisfaction, engagement, and perceived efficacy. Closed-ended inquiries: Likert scale (1 to 5) for quantitative assessment. User contentment, Platform functionality, and Participation. Enhancement in educational results recognized. Collect self-reported data regarding learner experiences and insights.

Questionnaire

The researchers created a 5-point Likert Scale questionnaire to examine students' assessments of their general knowledge of AI platforms. The questionnaire employed a 5-point Likert Scale of 10 items, each offering five response options: strongly disagree (1 point), disagree (2 points), neither agree nor disagree (3 points), agree (4 points), and strongly agree (5 points). The items of the questionnaire are shown as follows.

To determine if learners utilizing the AI-powered platform exhibit significant performance enhancement relative to those employing conventional learning methods, questionnaires must measure multiple variables, including perceived learning efficacy, engagement, usability, and satisfaction.

1) How would you assess your overall comprehension of the course material before utilizing the platform?

2) How would you evaluate your comprehensive grasp of the course material after utilizing the platform?
3) Did you perceive that the platform tailored the educational content to suit your requirements?
4) To what extent did the input from the AI enhance your comprehension?
5) How captivating did you perceive the AI-driven platform compared to conventional learning techniques?
6) Did the platform incentivize you to fulfill learning activities punctually?
7) How effortless was it to traverse and utilize the AI-driven platform?
8) How often did you utilize the platform compared to conventional methods?
9) How satisfied are you with your overall experience utilizing the AI-driven platform?
10) Would you endorse this platform for educational purposes?
11) Do you believe the AI-driven platform is superior to conventional learning methods? What are the reasons for or against it?

The evaluation of the AI-driven learning platform is arranged around fundamental questions meant to investigate learners' experiences, involvement, and platform impact on their knowledge and general satisfaction. Initially asked to assess their grasp of the course content both before and after using the platform, participants provide comments on supposed improvements in clarity. Emphasizing the personalizing qualities of the AI system, we evaluate the platform's ability to adapt instructional content to fit specific needs. Questions probe how the feedback and input of artificial intelligence enhanced students' knowledge and the degree of platform participation as compared to more traditional learning environments. Students are encouraged to evaluate whether the platform incentivized the timely completion of learning tasks, highlighting its possible impact on punctuality and task management.

The study also assesses the platform’s usability by evaluating the ease of users navigate and utilize its features. Moreover, learners provide insights into the frequency of their platform utilization relative to traditional techniques, illuminating adoption rates and preferences. Satisfaction levels are evaluated via inquiries regarding the overall experience, and participants are queried on their willingness to suggest the platform for educational use. Ultimately, learners are prompted to evaluate the platform against conventional learning approaches, articulating arguments for or against its superiority. These responses provide significant insights into the platform’s efficacy, user experience, and potential for wider deployment in educational contexts.

DATA COLLECTION AND ANALYSIS

Comparison of Pre-Test and Post-Test Results

Employ paired t-tests to analyze the pre-test and post-test scores within the groups (AI-powered versus traditional). An independent samples t-test was performed to evaluate the difference in score improvement between the experimental and control groups.

Engagement Metrics

Examine engagement data through descriptive statistics (e.g., means, medians) to discern usage patterns. Employ correlation analysis to investigate the relationships between engagement measures (e.g., time invested) and learning results.

Survey Feedback

Compute percentages and averages for Likert-scale inquiries to evaluate user happiness, perceived learning efficacy, and usability. Utilize SPSS analysis to investigate the impact of various variables (e.g., age, prior experience) on learner outcomes.

FINDINGS AND DISCUSSION

This study aims to investigate the effect of learners' general satisfaction with their experience utilizing the AI-driven platform, encompassing their perceived value and efficacy in facilitating their learning, and to assess the allure and engagement level of the AI-driven platform relative to conventional learning approaches.

EFL Students' Satisfaction

A substantial number of learners had a favorable experience with the AI-driven platform. More than 60% of participants expressed general satisfaction with its performance, especially its engagement and user-friendly interface.

Figure 1. EFL students' satisfaction with using AI platforms

This graph demonstrates the general sentiment of EFL students on their use of the AI platform, emphasizing its beneficial effect on their learning experience and their inclination towards AI-driven approaches as opposed to conventional learning techniques. It visibly underscores the elevated satisfaction levels and the platform's efficacy in augmenting student engagement and motivation.

Perceived Value of the Platform

Students state that the site is an essential resource for improving their education. Approximately 74% of participants indicated that the AI system's tailored information and adaptive feedback enhanced their comprehension of the material more profoundly and efficiently than conventional techniques.

Figure 2. Perceived value of the platform

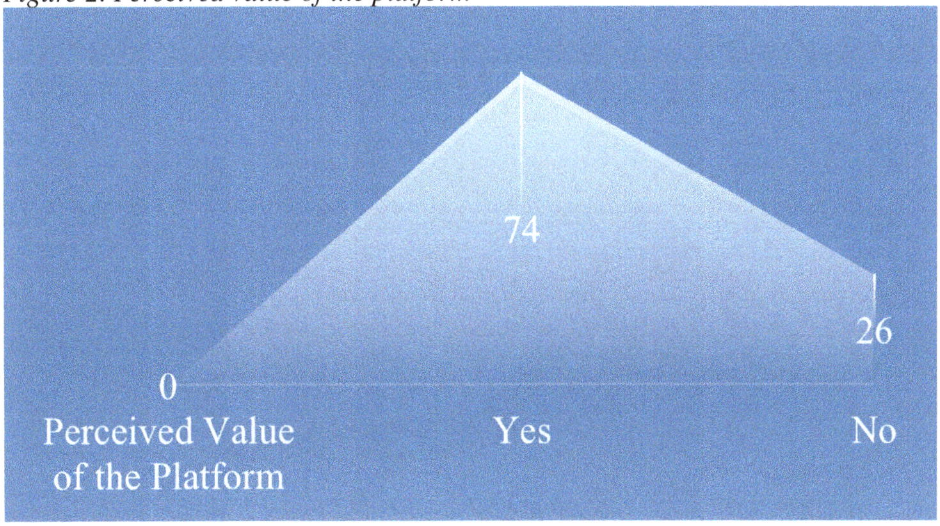

The research indicates that a majority of individuals regard the platform as valuable, with 74 out of 100 respondents affirming this by saying "Yes." This signifies a favorable reaction or acknowledgment of the platform's worth among the majority of users. Conversely, 26 respondents (or 26%) perceive the platform as lacking value, constituting a lesser proportion.

Efficacy in Facilitating Learning

EFL Students indicated considerable enhancement in their understanding of the course content following their utilization of the platform. Approximately 65% of participants said that the AI-driven advice elucidated challenging ideas, particularly via tailored feedback.

Figure 3. Efficacy in facilitating learning

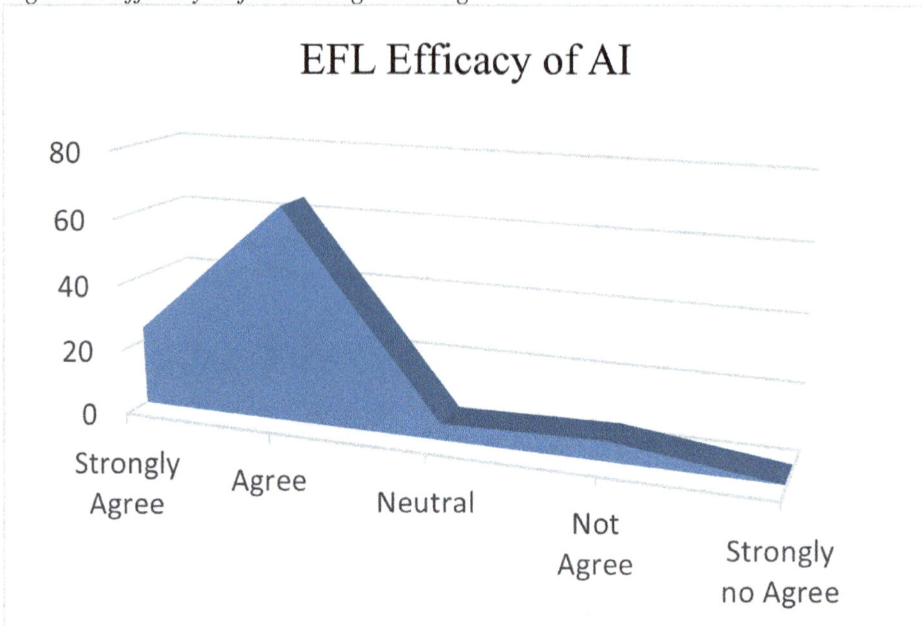

With 24 people strongly agreeing, most of the participants—65 out of 100—concur that the platform helps learning rather well. This shows a general positive view on the ability of the platform to improve learning. Six people show disagreement; none of them indicate strong dissent, suggesting that most users view the site as helpful for learning; only a small number of users raise issues. Only five people remain neutral, which emphasizes that most users have a clear opinion on the efficiency of the site, either positive or negative. According to the statistics, learning on the platform is mostly seen as successful. Still, a small portion of users express doubt or disapproval.

Comparison with Traditional Learning Methods

pointing to the ability to get immediate feedback and tailored learning paths, most students—about 69%—preferred the AI-powered platform over conventional approaches. These elements, they felt, made their educational process faster and more fun than traditional, teacher-led instruction. While the AI-driven platform provided insightful analysis and instantaneous assistance, some students pointed out that for more complicated or nuanced learning questions they still felt the need of human interaction. About twenty percent of the respondents wanted a combination of artificial intelligence and conventional education approaches.

Figure 4. AI platforms vs traditional learning

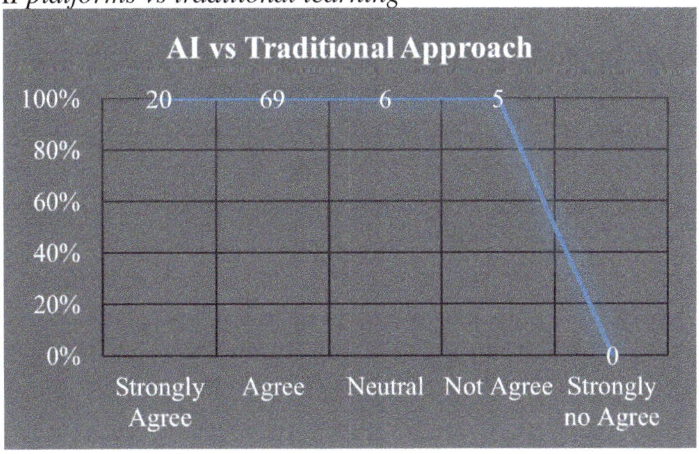

Most respondents (69 out of 100) state that AI platforms are successful or superior to traditional learning methods, with an additional 20 persons expressing strong agreement. A limited quantity (6) maintains neutrality, indicating an absence of a strong stance on the issue. Only five students disagreed, although none vehemently opposed, indicating that most respondents regard AI platforms more favorably than conventional learning approaches. The data indicates that AI platforms are predominantly regarded favorably, with most participants considering them successful or beneficial compared to conventional learning methods.

According to the statistics, participants view AI-powered learning systems favorably; most of them agree their advantages over more conventional teaching methods. These systems were hailed for their ability to offer a customized learning environment, changing materials and support to meet the particular needs of every student. Participants noted that the AI systems provide instantaneous feedback, therefore improving understanding of complex concepts and enabling more effective progress using instructional resources.

Moreover, the platforms were lauded for their dynamic and engaging attributes, which were perceived as better than the static and generalized characteristics of traditional approaches. Numerous learners indicated increased motivation and concentration as the AI platforms fostered a dynamic learning environment customized to their speeds and preferences. The participants underlined how easily AI-driven learning could be accessed and how it would help them to study at their comfort and pace without sacrificing the content quality. Those with different learning styles especially benefited from this adaptability since it made the platforms easily available and user-friendly. The results show a consensus that by making education more personalized, effective, and impactful, AI-powered platforms improve the learning process and have the ability to transform it. The positive comments point to a strong case for more artificial intelligence technology inclusion in learning settings.

Virtual language tutors can include learners in interactive conversations, replicate real-life situations, and offer feedback on pronunciation and language application (Alotaibi & Alshehri, 2023). AI in education enhances the quality of both learning and instruction. The AI-driven tools facilitate the development of an advanced educational environment characterized by personalized learning, flexible teaching, and inclusive management. They can assist learners in acquiring the knowledge and skills demanded by our technology-driven society (Pokrivcakova, 2019). AI learning systems may evolve into increasingly potent and invaluable instruments for language acquisition. Their integration is essential for enhancing the efficacy and efficiency of learning user experience solutions (Rebolledo Font De La Vall & González Araya, 2023).

Mentor AI presents significant potential to transform professional development by addressing the constraints of conventional mentorship. This platform employs modern AI technologies, machine learning, and natural language understanding to provide tailored, accessible, and scalable mentorship experiences for a variety of professionals. Advantages encompass augmented career advancement, skill enhancement, work-life equilibrium, and heightened employee satisfaction, engagement, and retention (Bagai & Mane, 2023). Mobile AI-driven educational applications are crucial in the investigation of technology-enhanced learning amidst the convergence of media and technology. This study is pertinent and enhances the discourse regarding the influence of usage context and gratifications on technology users' attitudes and behavioral intentions (Chang et al., 2022).

Furthermore, AI-powered tools enable personalized, adaptable, and inclusive learning in education and professional development. Virtual instructors simulate real-life situations, provide interactive feedback, and improve language learning. For a society driven by technology, these tools enhance the user experience. Mentor AI uses AI and machine learning to offer scalable, customized mentoring, so improving professional development and satisfaction. Mobile artificial intelligence apps also affect attitudes and intents for technologically advanced learning.

SOLUTIONS AND RECOMMENDATIONS

Emphasizing ongoing enhancement allows the platform to progress and adjust to its users' evolving requirements and anticipations. This continuous enhancement guarantees that the platform remains pertinent, accessible, and proficient in providing the optimal experience. Consistent updates informed by user feedback and technology progress will boost functionality and signify a dedication to addressing the changing requirements of the learning environment. This responsiveness cultivates confidence among users, strengthening their conviction that the platform is continually enhancing its service.

Addressing consumer issues simultaneously is crucial for preserving a favorable user experience. All platforms will encounter hurdles or obstacles; nevertheless, how these issues are addressed is truly significant (Vall & Araya, 2023). By attentively listening to users, comprehending their challenges, and offering solutions, the platform can mitigate frustrations before they escalate into disengagement. Employing technical help or direct connection, encouraging user involvement and support will strengthen the relationship with the platform and transform occasional users into active ones. Furthermore, encouraging adoption by awareness and training is crucial to guarantee that more users understand the value of the platform and feel confident in using it to its best capability. Tutorials, seminars, and ongoing support added to effective onboarding will help users become comfortable with the features of the platform. Users who understand the benefits will probably include them in their professional or educational activities. Awareness campaigns can underscore the platform's worth, drawing in new users and bolstering its trust.

With the implementation of these initiatives, the platform will transform into a resource that users trust and depend on for their learning and growth (Bagai & Mane, 2023). Enhanced user happiness stemming from ongoing enhancements, adequate support, and the requisite knowledge for optimal platform utilization would inherently result in more efficacy. A content user base is more inclined to interact with the platform consistently, fostering user retention and expansion. This will establish a feedback loop that fosters additional innovations, enabling the platform to maintain competitiveness in a swiftly evolving environment.

In the long term, expanding the user base entails not merely augmenting numbers but also diversifying the input and insights that drive the platform's growth. An expanded and diverse user base presents greater chances for innovation, adaptation, and competitive advantage. By consistently enhancing, heeding user feedback, and guaranteeing accessibility and value for all, it will uphold its status as a reliable, essential resource in the educational or professional development sector.

FUTURE RESEARCH DIRECTIONS

The proposed future research directions present considerable opportunities to improve AI platforms and their incorporation into educational settings, augmenting the learning experience. Researchers can gain a great understanding of the ways in which artificial intelligence influences student involvement, motivation, and achievement by focusing on elements including long-term educational outcomes, user experience among different demographics, and the effect of social interaction in AI-driven platforms. Understanding the ethical, privacy, and scalability concerns related to artificial intelligence platforms will help ensure these tools' responsible and inclusive development, guaranteeing their accessibility and efficacy for all users, regardless of background or technical expertise.

Furthermore, looking at the convergence of artificial intelligence with customized learning paths, individualized learning trajectories, and hybrid educational frameworks might provide important insights on properly combining AI's benefits with conventional pedagogical approaches. This all-encompassing strategy will help future studies to enable teachers to more successfully include artificial intelligence tools into their classrooms, so improving support for different learning needs. Through analysis of these several characteristics, scientists can improve the creation of artificial intelligence systems more sensitive to the particular needs of teachers and students, as well as more efficient. These platforms will adapt to various learning situations, ensuring AI maintains a revolutionary role in education while cultivating an environment where learners feel encouraged, motivated, and empowered. This research will ultimately enhance the next generation of AI tools, rendering them invaluable in education, augmenting the learning experience, and fostering innovation in the domain.

CONCLUSION

The study highlights a favorable view among EFL students concerning using AI-driven learning tools. These platforms improve comprehension, provide individualized instructional information, and provide rapid, personalized feedback and engagement, which most students prefer. These elements are considered an advantage over motivation. This customization is often credited with improving learning effectiveness and enjoyment. Few students acknowledged qualms about AI platforms, but their issues did not overwhelm the overall enthusiasm for this technology. The majority of students want to see AI tools integrated into school, and many want to see them evolve. The results indicate a considerable confidence shift towards AI-driven learning solutions, indicating their expanding importance in education. Students increasingly see these technologies as essential parts of a modern, innovative learning ecosystem that meets various demands and improves education. The positive response suggests readiness for wider application and ongoing growth of AI technology in learning contexts.

REFERENCES

Abdulah, D. M., Zaman, B. A., Mustafa, Z. R., & Hassan, L. H. (2024). Artificial Intelligence Integration in Academic Writing: Insights from the University of Duhok. *ARO (Koya)*, *12*(2), 194–200. DOI: 10.14500/aro.11794

Abu Bakar, N. F., Yusof, A. F. A., Iahad, N., & Ahmad, N. (2018). The Implementation of Gamification in Massive Open Online Courses (MOOC) Platform. In Abdullah, N., Wan Adnan, W. A., & Foth, M. (Eds.), *User Science and Engineering* (Vol. 886, pp. 183–193). Springer Singapore., DOI: 10.1007/978-981-13-1628-9_17

Aderamo, A. T., Olisakwe, H. C., Adebayo, Y. A., & Esiri, A. E. (2024). AI-powered pandemic response framework for offshore oil platforms: Ensuring safety during global health crises. Comprehensive Research and Reviews in Engineering and Technology, 2(1), 044-063.

Alharbi, W. (2023). AI in the Foreign Language Classroom: A Pedagogical Overview of Automated Writing Assistance Tools. *Education Research International*, *2023*, 1–15. DOI: 10.1155/2023/4253331

Alotaibi, N. S., & Alshehri, A. H. (2023). Prospers and Obstacles in Using Artificial Intelligence in Saudi Arabia Higher Education Institutions—The Potential of AI-Based Learning Outcomes. *Sustainability (Basel)*, *15*(13), 10723. DOI: 10.3390/su151310723

Amaliah, N., Limbong, S., Syam, N. I., Room, F., & Bashar, K. (2022). Using Technology as Learning Media to Enrich ESP Students' Speaking Skill for Indonesian Higher Education Students. IJOLEH. *International Journal of Education and Humanities*, *2*(1), 43–51.

Asdar, A., Hamsiah, A., Sujarwo, S., Lutfin, N., & Sukmawati, S. (2024). Integrative Approach for Reading Comprehension Espousing Information Communication Technology Literacy. [IJERE]. *International Journal of Evaluation and Research in Education*, *13*(6), 4384. DOI: 10.11591/ijere.v13i6.29461

Bagai, R., & Mane, V. (2023). Designing an AI-Powered Mentorship Platform for Professional Development: Opportunities and Challenges. *International Journal of Computer Trends and Technology*, *71*(4), 108–114. DOI: 10.14445/22312803/IJCTT-V71I4P114

Carrió-Pastor, M. L. (Ed.). (2016). *Technology Implementation in Second Language Teaching and Translation Studies: New Tools, New Approaches*. Springer Singapore., DOI: 10.1007/978-981-10-0572-5

Chang, Y., Lee, S., Wong, S. F., & Jeong, S. (2022). AI-powered learning application use and gratification: An integrative model. *Information Technology & People, 35*(7), 2115–2139. DOI: 10.1108/ITP-09-2020-0632

Choukaier, D. (2024). Integrating AI In English Language Pedagogy: Innovations And Outcomes In Teaching English As Second /Foreign Language. *Educational Administration: Theory and Practice, 30*(5), 3811–3822. https://doi.org/Doi: DOI: 10.53555/kuey.v30i5.3538

Creely, E. (2024). Exploring the Role of Generative AI in Enhancing Language Learning: Opportunities and Challenges. *International Journal of Changes in Education, 1*(3), 158–167. DOI: 10.47852/bonviewIJCE42022495

Creswell, J. W. (2013). *Educational research: Planning, conducting, and evaluating quantitative and qualitative research* (Fourth Indian edition). PHI Learning Private Limited.

Folgieri, R., Gil, M., Bait, M., & Lucchiari, C. (2024). AI-Powered Personalised Learning Platforms for EFL Learning: Preliminary Results: *Proceedings of the 16th International Conference on Computer Supported Education*, 255–261. DOI: 10.5220/0012672000003693

Fraidan, A. A. (2024). Integrating AI-Powered Library Systems to Enhance Research and Learning in English Language Departments: A Case Study of Faculty and Student Perceptions. *Library Progress International, 44*(3), 12058–12065.

Guo, Y., & Wang, Y. (2024). Exploring the Effects of Artificial Intelligence Application on EFL Students' Academic Engagement and Emotional Experiences: A Mixed-Methods Study. *European Journal of Education, 12812*. Advance online publication. DOI: 10.1111/ejed.12812

Hamamra, B., Mayaleh, A., & Khlaif, Z. N. (2024). Between tech and text: The use of generative AI in Palestinian universities - a ChatGPT case study. *Cogent Education, 11*(1), 2380622. DOI: 10.1080/2331186X.2024.2380622

Han, A., Zhou, X., Cai, Z., Han, S., Ko, R., Corrigan, S., & Peppler, K. A. (2024). Teachers, Parents, and Students' perspectives on Integrating Generative AI into Elementary Literacy Education. *Proceedings of the CHI Conference on Human Factors in Computing Systems*, 1–17. DOI: 10.1145/3613904.3642438

Hasyim, N., Arismunandar, , Butarbutar, R., Ramli, A. M., & Malik Nur, I. D. (2024). Mind Mapping of Teachers' Readiness for Online Teaching and Learning: A Reflective Study of Urban and Suburban Areas. *Cogent Education, 11*(1), 2292864. DOI: 10.1080/2331186X.2023.2292864

Hutson, J., Jeevanjee, T., Graaf, V. V., Lively, J., Weber, J., Weir, G., Arnone, K., Carnes, G., Vosevich, K., Plate, D., Leary, M., & Edele, S. (2022). Artificial Intelligence and the Disruption of Higher Education: Strategies for Integrations across Disciplines. *Creative Education, 13*(12), 3953–3980. DOI: 10.4236/ce.2022.1312253

Imran, M. C., & Sulviana, S. (2022). Using BBC Web-Based Learning Courses to Improve Vocational High School (VHS) Students' Speaking Skill. Education. *Language and Culture Journal*, *2*(1), 94–100.

Jia, P., & Stan, C. (2021). Artificial Intelligence Factory, Data Risk, and VCs' Mediation: The Case of ByteDance, an AI-Powered Startup. *Journal of Risk and Financial Management, 14*(5), 203. DOI: 10.3390/jrfm14050203

Khamis, R. (2024). *AI-Powered Learning Experience Platforms: Investigating Personalized Learning in the Workplace: A Case of an International Company in Sweden.*

Limbong, S., Nursyam, Asdar, Palayukan, N., & Tandibura, F. (2024). Synchronous Online Reading toward Digital Literacy and Higher-Order Thinking Skills Supporting Cadets' Self-Regulated Learning. *XLinguae, 17*(4), 317–335. DOI: 10.18355/XL.2024.17.04.19

Limbong, S., Jabu, B., & Basri, M. (2022). The Impact of Synchronous Learning of Marlins in Teaching Maritime English. *Journal of Learning and Development Studies, 2*(3), 06–13. DOI: 10.32996/jlds.2022.2.3.2

Lopez-Fierro, S., Kollar, I., & Nguyen, H. (2024). Making Human-AI Contributions Transparent in Qualitative Coding. *17th International Conference on Computer-Supported Collaborative Learning (CSCL).* ISLS Annual Meeting 2024 June 10-14, 2024 Learning as a Cornerstone of Healing, Resilience, and Community. DOI: 10.22318/cscl2024.352932

Makeleni, S., Mutongoza, B. H., & Linake, M. A. (2023). Language Education and Artificial Intelligence: An Exploration of Challenges Confronting Academics in Global South Universities. *Journal of Culture and Values in Education, 6*(2), 158–171. DOI: 10.46303/jcve.2023.14

Morales, M., Amado-Salvatierra, H. R., Hernández, R., Pirker, J., & Gütl, C. (2016). A Practical Experience on the Use of Gamification in MOOC Courses as a Strategy to Increase Motivation. In Uden, L., Liberona, D., & Feldmann, B. (Eds.), *Learning Technology for Education in Cloud – The Changing Face of Education* (Vol. 620, pp. 139–149). Springer International Publishing., DOI: 10.1007/978-3-319-42147-6_12

Nurhikmah, H., & Ramli, A. M. (2024). Teachers' Readiness in Online Learning: Digital Literacy-Self-Efficacy, Pedagogical Competence, Attitude, Infrastructure, and Management Support. *Electronic Journal of e-Learning*, *22*(8), 93–105. DOI: 10.34190/ejel.22.8.3358

Özdere, M. (2023). The Integration of Artificial Intelligence in English Education: Opportunities and Challenges. [LET Journal]. *Language Education & Technology*, *3*(2), 137–172.

Pokrivcakova, S. (2019). Preparing teachers for the application of AI-powered technologies in foreign language education. *Journal of Language and Cultural Education*, *7*(3), 135–153. DOI: 10.2478/jolace-2019-0025

Rebolledo Font De La Vall, R., & González Araya, F. (2023). Exploring the Benefits and Challenges of AI-Language Learning Tools. *International Journal of Social Sciences and Humanities Invention*, *10*(01), 7569–7576. DOI: 10.18535/ijsshi/v10i01.02

Redmond, P., Heffernan, A., Abawi, L., Brown, A., & Henderson, R. (2018). An Online Engagement Framework for Higher Education. *Online Learning : the Official Journal of the Online Learning Consortium*, *22*(1). Advance online publication. DOI: 10.24059/olj.v22i1.1175

Roy, D., & Putatunda, T. (2023). From Textbooks to Chatbots: Integrating AI in English literature classrooms of India. *Journal of E-Learning and Knowledge Society*, 65-73 Pages. DOI: 10.20368/1971-8829/1135860

Sasabone, L., Limbong, S., Pongpalilu, F., Soepriadi, & Jubhari. (2022). Utilizing WhatsApp As An Educational Technology Tool In Improving Students' Speaking For ESP Instruction. *EDULEC : Education, Language, and Culture Journal*, *2*(2). https://doi.org/DOI: 10.56314/edulec.v2i2

Sujarwo, S., Asdar, A., Sabillah, B. M., Sukmawati, S., Akhiruddin, A., & Muh. Syata, W. (2023). Innovation In English Language Learning Model Based Digital Literacy To Construct Young Learners' Character. *Ethical Lingua. Journal of Language Teaching and Literature*, *10*(2). Advance online publication. DOI: 10.30605/25409190.640

Sukmawati, S., Syam, N. I. S., Jubhari, Y. J., Mardiani, M., Sasabone, L., & Sujarwo, S. (2023). Implementation of Technology on English for Specific Purposes (ESP) Students in Communicative Language Teaching Approach. *Ethical Lingua: Journal of Language Teaching and Literature*, *10*(1). Advance online publication. DOI: 10.30605/25409190.566

Tammets, K., & Ley, T. (2023). Integrating AI tools in teacher professional learning: A conceptual model and illustrative case. *Frontiers in Artificial Intelligence*, *6*, 1255089. DOI: 10.3389/frai.2023.1255089 PMID: 38130325

Tang, J., & Foley, J. (2022). A Case Study on the Effectiveness of Applying Content and Language Integrated Learning in an Artificial Intelligence English Reading Course. *Arab World English Journal*, *13*(3), 236–253. DOI: 10.24093/awej/vol13no3.15

Wahid, A., Afni, N., & Sujarwo, S. (2025). Promoting Learners' Autonomy through Metacognitive, Higher-Order Thinking Skills and Digital Literacy of Indonesian Private Universities. *Educational Process International Journal*, *16*(1). Advance online publication. DOI: 10.22521/edupij.2025.16.204

Wu, H., Wang, Y., & Wang, Y. (2024). "To Use or Not to Use?" A Mixed-Methods Study on the Determinants of EFL College Learners' Behavioral Intention to Use AI in the Distributed Learning Context. *International Review of Research in Open and Distance Learning*, *25*(3), 158–178. DOI: 10.19173/irrodl.v25i3.7708

Chapter 2
Creating Holistic Learning Environments: Integrating AI, Education, and Psychological Principles

Abdul Kadir
https://orcid.org/0000-0001-8989-4423
Universitas Muhammadiyah Palopo, Indonesia

Sjafri Sairin
Universitas Muhammadiyah Palopo, Indonesia

Abd Madjid
Universitas Muhammadiyah Palopo, Indonesia

Mohammad Syifa Amin Widigdo
Universitas Muhammadiyah Palopo, Indonesia

Syamsul Alam Ramli
Universitas Muhammadiyah Palopo, Indonesia

Andi Asrifan
https://orcid.org/0000-0002-9934-6129
Universitas Negeri Makassar, Indonesia

ABSTRACT

This study examines the amalgamation of artificial intelligence (AI), pedagogical tactics, and psychological concepts to establish comprehensive learning environments that facilitate students' cognitive, emotional, and social growth. Holistic learning prioritizes the entire learner by accommodating varied requirements, motivations, and intelligences. Artificial intelligence technology, including adaptive learning systems, emotional monitoring tools, and collaborative platforms, facilitate individualized, inclusive, and engaging educational experiences. The study examines the theoretical foundations, design principles, ethical issues, and optimal methods for integrating AI with constructivist, humanistic, and socio-emotional learning frameworks. Case examples illustrate how AI can improve student autonomy, well-being, and achievement when integrated with psychological principles. The results

DOI: 10.4018/979-8-3373-5786-7.ch002

underscore the significance of user-centered design, professional development, and stakeholder involvement in maintaining inclusive, technology-driven, and human-centered educational institutions.

UNDERSTANDING HOLISTIC LEARNING

Definition and Importance of Holistic Learning

Holistic learning is an educational theory that highlights the interrelation of multiple facets of a learner's experience, including cognitive, emotional, social, and physical dimensions (Ramaila, 2025). In contrast to conventional educational paradigms that frequently emphasize rote memorization and standardized assessments, holistic learning aims to cultivate the entire individual. This method acknowledges that effective learning transpires when students are engaged academically, emotionally, and socially, hence promoting a more holistic comprehension of knowledge and its application in real-world scenarios.

Holistic education fundamentally seeks to foster a learning environment that acknowledges and addresses the varied requirements of every student. It urges educators to acknowledge the distinct backgrounds, experiences, and learning modalities of their pupils, therefore fostering inclusivity and equity within the classroom. Holistic education facilitates the exploration of student interests and the development of critical thinking, creativity, and emotional intelligence through the integration of several pedagogical approaches, including experiential learning, collaborative projects, and reflective practices (Estrada et al., 2021).

The importance of holistic learning cannot be emphasized. Studies indicate that adolescents participating in holistic educational approaches exhibit superior academic performance, increased motivation, and improved emotional well-being (Amores-Valencia et al., 2022). This method facilitates knowledge acquisition while simultaneously imparting crucial life skills, like problem-solving, resilience, and effective communication. Holistic learning settings cultivate a sense of belonging and community in the classroom, establishing a supportive climate where students feel esteemed and encouraged to engage in risk-taking in their education.

Furthermore, in the contemporary, swiftly evolving world, the capacity to adjust and excel in many circumstances is essential. Holistic education equips students to navigate the intricacies of contemporary life by fostering critical thinking regarding their experiences and the surrounding environment (Miseliunaite et al., 2022). Through the integration of social, emotional, and cognitive learning, students enhance their self-awareness and social responsibility, so becoming more adept at overcoming problems and positively impacting society.

In conclusion, holistic learning is an essential methodology that not only augments academic achievement but also fosters the whole growth of persons. In examining the amalgamation of artificial intelligence and psychological concepts in education, it is crucial to acknowledge the fundamental significance of holistic learning in establishing effective and meaningful educational environments. By emphasizing the holistic learner, we may cultivate a generation of individuals who are not only informed but also empathetic, versatile, and active citizens.

Theoretical Foundations

The theoretical underpinnings of holistic learning are fundamentally anchored in various critical psychological theories that highlight the interrelation of cognitive, emotional, and social aspects of education (Ozberk, 2025). Constructivism, a prominent theory, was developed by theorists including Jean Piaget and Lev Vygotsky. Constructivism asserts that learners actively build their comprehension and knowledge of the world via experiences and interactions. This viewpoint urges educators to establish learning settings that promote hands-on activities, collaborative projects, and reflective practices, thus enhancing comprehension and retention of information.

Another notable hypothesis is Howard Gardner's Multiple Intelligences, which contests the conventional concept of a solitary intelligence assessed through standardized testing. Gardner posited that individuals exhibit several intelligences, encompassing linguistic, logical-mathematical, spatial, musical, bodily-kinesthetic, interpersonal, intrapersonal, and naturalistic (Okwuduba et al. 2021). This approach advocates for holistic education to accommodate varied learning styles, enabling students to utilize their strengths and interact with knowledge in personally meaningful ways. By acknowledging and fostering many intelligences, educators may cultivate more inclusive and effective educational settings.

The historical development of holistic education can be linked to numerous intellectual trends. The early 20th-century progressive education movement, advocated by individuals such as John Dewey, prioritized experiential learning and the significance of linking education to real-world experiences (Meyer and Seaman, 2021). Dewey championed an educational framework that promotes critical thinking and social accountability, establishing the foundation for comprehensive methodologies.

During the latter half of the 20th century, the humanistic education movement evolved, with theorists like Carl Rogers and Abraham Maslow highlighting the significance of emotional and psychological well-being in the learning process (Elfert, 2023). Their research emphasized the necessity of a supportive and loving environment in which students feel secure to articulate themselves and investigate their identities.

The incorporation of these theories into holistic education has resulted in a more thorough comprehension of learning as a multifaceted process. Contemporary educators recognize that effective instruction must encompass not only academic competencies but also emotional intelligence, social skills, and personal development (Gimbert et al., 2023). This comprehensive viewpoint is crucial in equipping pupils for the intricacies of the contemporary world, where cooperation, flexibility, and emotional fortitude are vital.

The theoretical foundations of holistic learning are derived from a diverse array of psychological theories and historical movements, highlighting the necessity of considering the entire learner. As we delve deeper into the amalgamation of AI and psychological concepts in education, these fundamental theories will inform the creation of creative and effective holistic learning environments.

Components of a Holistic Learning Environment

Establishing a comprehensive learning environment entails multiple interrelated elements that together promote a rewarding educational experience (Ramaila2025). The components encompass the physical environment, emotional and social aspects, and cognitive involvement, each significantly contributing to the comprehensive development of learners.

Physical Space

The physical atmosphere of a classroom area profoundly influences student engagement and well-being. A comprehensive learning environment must be crafted to be adaptable, welcoming, and supportive of diverse educational activities (Niemi, 2021). This entails the integration of natural light, ergonomic seating configurations, and spaces designated for both solitary and collaborative tasks. Educational environments must be furnished with resources that promote experiential learning, including technological instruments, artistic materials, and manipulatives that accommodate various learning modalities. By establishing a dynamic and exciting physical environment, educators may foster curiosity, creativity, and a sense of belonging in children.

Emotional and Social Dimensions

The emotional and social aspects are essential for cultivating a comprehensive learning environment. Students flourish when they perceive safety, respect, and value inside their educational environment. Establishing robust relationships among students and between students and educators is crucial for fostering trust and facilitating open communication (Zheng, 2022). Implementing methods such as restorative circles, peer mentorship, and cooperative learning can improve social interactions and emotional support. Furthermore, the integration of social-emotional learning (SEL) programs facilitates the development of essential abilities in students, including empathy, self-awareness, and conflict resolution, which are crucial for their personal and academic achievement. By emphasizing emotional and social aspects, instructors can cultivate a supportive environment that motivates students to embrace risks and actively participate in their learning.

Cognitive Engagement

Cognitive engagement denotes the mental investment and exertion that students dedicate to their learning experiences. A comprehensive learning environment must foster critical thinking, problem-solving, and creativity by motivating students to investigate intricate, real-world challenges (Weng et al., 2022). This can be accomplished via project-based learning, inquiry-driven activities, and interdisciplinary methods that integrate several subject domains. Educators can leverage technology, including artificial intelligence and interactive platforms, to deliver tailored learning experiences that engage students at their respective levels of ability. By promoting cognitive engagement, educators enable students to actively participate in their learning, facilitating a deeper comprehension of subject and its significance in their life.

In summary, a holistic learning environment is defined by a meticulously crafted physical setting, robust emotional and social connections, and avenues for cognitive engagement. By incorporating these components, educators may cultivate a comprehensive and supportive environment that fosters holistic development, equipping students for success in their academic endeavors and future lives. As we further investigate the amalgamation of AI and psychological concepts in education, these fundamental elements will direct the creation of creative and effective holistic learning environments.

THE ROLE OF ARTIFICIAL INTELLIGENCE IN EDUCATION

Introduction to AI in Educational Contexts

Artificial Intelligence (AI) denotes the emulation of human cognitive functions by technology, especially computer systems. These processes encompass learning, reasoning, problem-solving, perception, and language comprehension. In educational settings, AI has become a revolutionary instrument, facilitating tailored learning experiences, improving administrative efficiency, and offering vital insights into student performance and engagement (Bahroun et al., 2023).

The uses of AI in education are many and complex. A significant application is in the creation of adaptive learning systems that customize educational content to address the specific needs of pupils (Gligorea et al. 2023). These systems evaluate data regarding student performance and learning preferences, facilitating the personalization of classes, exams, and feedback. Platforms such as DreamBox and Smart Sparrow employ AI algorithms to dynamically modify task complexity, ensuring that learners are adequately pushed without becoming overwhelmed. This tailored method not only increases student involvement but also fosters a more profound comprehension of the content.

A notable application of AI in education pertains to administrative activities. AI-driven solutions can automate repetitive tasks such as grading, scheduling, and attendance monitoring, allowing educators to concentrate more on instruction and student engagement (Kavitha et al.). Furthermore, AI can facilitate the identification of at-risk kids by scrutinizing patterns in academic performance and behavior, so enabling prompt interventions and support.

Contemporary advancements in AI technology are transforming the educational scene. Machine learning, a kind of artificial intelligence, is being employed to examine extensive educational data (Bozkurt et al. 2021). This skill enables educators to acquire insights regarding effective pedagogical practices, curricular efficacy, and student learning results. Moreover, natural language processing (NLP) technologies are improving communication between students and educational platforms, facilitating more dynamic and intuitive learning experiences. Instruments like chatbots and virtual teaching assistants are more prevalent, offering students immediate assistance and resources.

The use of AI in education is promoting the emergence of immersive learning experiences via technologies like virtual reality (VR) and augmented reality (AR) (Gandedkar et al., 2021). These tools enable students to interact with knowledge innovatively, promoting greater comprehension through experiential learning.

In summary, artificial intelligence is assuming an increasingly crucial role in education by delivering tailored learning experiences, optimizing administrative operations, and furnishing useful insights into student performance. As we explore the amalgamation of AI with educational methodologies and psychological theories, it is crucial to evaluate how these innovations might improve comprehensive learning environments, thereby equipping students for success in a constantly changing world.

Personalized Learning through AI

Personalized learning has arisen as a revolutionary method in education, enabling instruction to be customized to address the distinct requirements, preferences, and interests of each student (Kaswan et al. 2024). Artificial Intelligence (AI) is essential in enabling individualized learning via adaptive learning systems and data-driven insights, hence enhancing the educational experience's engagement and effectiveness.

Adaptive Learning Systems

Adaptive learning systems employ AI algorithms to continuously evaluate and react to individual student performance in real-time. These systems are engineered to modify the content, tempo, and complexity of educational materials in accordance with the learner's advancement and comprehension (Gligorea et al. 2023). Platforms such as Knewton and DreamBox Learning evaluate students' interactions and results, allowing them to offer tailored pathways that align with each learner's strengths and weaknesses.

Adaptive systems personalize the learning experience, ensuring that students are neither disengaged by overly simplistic content nor overwhelmed by excessively difficult material. This customized method not only improves engagement but also cultivates a growth mentality, allowing students to progress at their own pace and obtain immediate feedback (Strielkowski et al. 2024). Consequently, students are more inclined to assume responsibility for their education, resulting in enhanced motivation and academic achievement.

Data-Driven Insights for Individualized Learning Paths

Besides adaptive learning systems, AI utilizes data-driven insights to formulate personalized learning trajectories for pupils. Through the collection and analysis of extensive educational data—ranging from assessment scores to learning behaviors—AI can discern patterns and trends that guide instructional decisions (Salas-Pilco et al., 2022). This data-centric methodology enables educators to acquire a profound comprehension of each student's educational trajectory, facilitating the development of tailored interventions and support mechanisms.

AI can identify pupils who may be struggling with particular concepts or skills, leading educators to offer supplementary resources or tailored assistance. Moreover, predictive analytics can anticipate future performance, enabling educators to proactively mitigate possible issues before they intensify (Kim et al., 2022). This information enables educators to make informed decisions that address the different needs of their pupils, ensuring that no learner is overlooked.

Furthermore, AI-driven systems can provide resources and learning activities customized to individual preferences and learning modalities (Ezzaim et al. 2024). By aligning educational material with students' preferences, AI cultivates a more interesting and pertinent learning experience, promoting deeper discovery and inquiry.

In conclusion, AI-driven personalized learning is transforming education by offering adaptive learning systems and data-informed insights tailored to the distinct requirements of each student. In our ongoing examination of AI's integration with educational methodologies and psychological theories, it is crucial to acknowledge the capacity of personalized learning to foster comprehensive learning environments that enhance student achievement and well-being.

Ethical Considerations and Challenges

The increasing integration of Artificial Intelligence (AI) in education presents several ethical considerations and problems that must be addressed to enable responsible and equitable usage of these technologies (Nguyen et al. 2023). The two primary concerns are privacy and data security, together with equitable access to AI capabilities.

Privacy Concerns and Data Security

A significant ethical concern about AI in education is the acquisition and administration of student data. Adaptive learning systems and AI-driven platforms depend on extensive data to operate efficiently (Kumar et al., 2024). This data frequently encompasses sensitive personal information, including academic performance, learning behaviors, and demographic facts. The possibility of data breaches presents considerable threats to student privacy, eliciting apprehensions around access to this information and its utilization.

Educational institutions must adhere to data protection standards, including the Family Educational Rights and Privacy Act (FERPA) in the United States, which regulates the confidentiality of student education records (Zimmerle, 2021). Moreover, transparency in data collection methodologies is essential. Educational institutions and technology providers must explicitly convey the methods of data collection, storage, and utilization, together with the safeguards implemented to protect this information. Neglecting to resolve these privacy issues may result in a lack of confidence among kids, parents, and educators, hence compromising the efficacy of AI tools in educational environments.

Equity in Access to AI Tools

A notable difficulty is guaranteeing equitable access to AI tools and resources. Although AI can improve tailored learning experiences, unequal access to technology may intensify pre-existing educational gaps. Students from economically disadvantaged origins or marginalized groups may be deficient in essential technology, internet access, or technical assistance to fully utilize AI-driven educational platforms (Johnson & Davis, 2024). The digital gap might obstruct their educational possibilities and sustain cycles of deprivation.

To mitigate these equity issues, educational institutions and policymakers must prioritize initiatives that ensure equitable access to technology. This may encompass activities such as supplying gadgets to disadvantaged children, enhancing internet connectivity in underprivileged regions, and giving training for educators and families on the efficient utilization of AI tools (Shaheen, 2022). Moreover, it is imperative to acknowledge the cultural significance of AI applications, ensuring their design accommodates the varied requirements of all pupils.

In conclusion, whereas the incorporation of AI in education provides substantial advantages, it also introduces ethical dilemmas that require meticulous consideration. Mitigating privacy issues and guaranteeing fair access to AI resources are essential measures in cultivating a responsible and inclusive educational setting. In our examination of the convergence of AI, education, and psychological principles, it is essential to emphasize ethical considerations to establish comprehensive learning environments that serve all learners effectively.

PSYCHOLOGICAL PRINCIPLES IN LEARNING

Understanding Learner Diversity

Comprehending learner diversity is crucial for developing effective educational settings that address the distinct requirements of every student. Cognitive styles and learning preferences profoundly affect how individuals assimilate information, interact with content, and ultimately achieve success in their educational endeavors (Almulla & Al-Rahmi, 2023). By acknowledging and addressing these disparities, educators may cultivate more inclusive and effective educational environments.

The Impact of Cognitive Styles and Learning Preferences

Cognitive styles define the favored methods by which individuals think, learn, and address challenges. Learning styles can differ significantly among students, with some excelling in analytical work and others thriving in creative or practical activities (Güner & Erbay, 2021). For example, certain learners may like visual aids and diagrams, whereas others could derive greater benefit from auditory explanations or kinesthetic activities. Comprehending these cognitive styles is essential, since it enables educators to customize their instructional methods to suit diverse learning preferences.

Learning preferences, frequently linked to theories like Howard Gardner's Multiple Intelligences, underscore the variability among learners. Gardner delineated multiple separate intelligences, including as linguistic, logical-mathematical, spatial, and interpersonal, among others (Tugberk & Sirin, 2024). Understanding that students have diverse talents allows educators to create classes that engage a broader spectrum of intelligences, thus improving student motivation and comprehension.

Strategies for Accommodating Diverse Learners

To effectively support different learners, educators can employ many tactics that foster inclusivity and participation. One option is differentiated instruction, which entails customizing instructional strategies, resources, and evaluations to accommodate the diverse needs of students. For instance, educators may offer many methods for pupils to exhibit their comprehension, including written reports, presentations, or creative projects (Goyibova et al. 2025). This adaptability enables students to utilize their strengths while simultaneously encouraging the acquisition of new skills.

An additional effective technique is the implementation of cooperative learning groups, wherein students collaboratively engage in tasks. This method fosters social interaction and enables learners to leverage each other's varied abilities and viewpoints. By cultivating a feeling of community and collaboration, educators may establish an environment in which all students feel esteemed and supported (Lakkala et al. 2021).

The integration of technology can improve the support for different learners. AI-driven educational technologies can tailor resources and feedback to accommodate individual learning styles (Gibson et al. 2023). This technology can detect areas where students require further support, facilitating customized treatments that address their unique requirements.

In conclusion, comprehending learner variability is essential for establishing comprehensive learning environments. By acknowledging the influence of cognitive styles and learning preferences, educators can adopt successful techniques to cater to varied learners. This method promotes academic achievement while cultivating a sense of belonging and engagement, ultimately equipping kids for lifetime learning and success in a varied environment.

Motivation and Engagement

Motivation and engagement are essential elements of effective learning, impacting students' readiness to engage in educational activities and their overall academic achievement (Lin et al., 2023). Comprehending the psychological principles underlying motivation, especially theories like Self-Determination Theory (SDT), can yield significant insights on cultivating a more engaged and motivated student.

Theories of Motivation

Self-Determination Theory, formulated by Edward Deci and Richard Ryan, asserts that motivation is influenced by three essential psychological needs: autonomy, competence, and relatedness. Autonomy denotes the aspiration for self-governance and authority over one's educational process (Autin et al. 2022). Students are more likely to be engaged and motivated when they perceive autonomy in their educational activities. Competence entails the necessity of feeling competent in one's endeavors; pupils are driven when they believe they can achieve success and acquire new abilities.

Ultimately, relatedness underscores the significance of social ties and a sense of belonging; learners exhibit heightened motivation when they perceive a connection with their peers and educators.

These needs underscore the importance of intrinsic motivation, which originates from the learner and is fueled by personal interest, curiosity, and the pleasure derived from the learning experience. Conversely, extrinsic motivation depends on external incentives or demands, which may not foster enduring engagement or profound learning.

Techniques to Foster Intrinsic Motivation in Learners

Educators can employ various successful ways to foster intrinsic desire in kids. One method is to offer possibilities for selection and independence in educational activities (Guay, 2022). Permitting students to select project themes, determine their learning trajectories, or establish personal objectives can augment their sense of ownership and commitment to their education.

Establishing a nurturing and affirmative classroom atmosphere is crucial. Educators can cultivate a growth attitude by commending effort and perseverance instead of just emphasizing results (Namaziandost et al. 2024). This method aids pupils in recognizing that problems present possibilities for development, fostering resilience and a readiness to tackle arduous activities.

Integrating real-world relevance into lessons can augment motivation. Students' attention and engagement tend to rise as they observe the practical applications of their study. Project-based learning, in which students engage with genuine problems or projects, can successfully link academic information to real-world contexts, enhancing the significance of learning (Zhang, 2022).

Ultimately, encouraging collaboration and social engagement among students can improve relatedness, hence enhancing intrinsic motivation. Collaborative activities, dialogues, and peer evaluation opportunities enable learners to engage with one another, exchange ideas, and assist each other's educational progress.

In summary, comprehending motivation and engagement via psychological principles, such as Self-Determination Theory, is crucial for developing comprehensive learning environments. By employing strategies that cultivate intrinsic drive, educators can improve student engagement, resulting in more significant and successful learning experiences. This emphasis on motivation fosters academic achievement and cultivates a lasting passion for studying.

Emotional and Social Learning

Emotional and social learning (ESL) is integral to education, impacting kids' holistic development, academic achievement, and interpersonal abilities (Lau and Shea 2024). By incorporating emotional intelligence and cultivating supportive learning communities, educators can establish environments that enhance cognitive development as well as emotional and social well-being.

The Role of Emotional Intelligence in Education

Emotional intelligence (EI) denotes the capability to identify, comprehend, and regulate one's own emotions, with the ability to empathize with others and maneuver through social intricacies (Saxena, 2025). In the realm of education, emotional intelligence is essential for cultivating constructive interactions among students and between students and educators. Studies indicate that students possessing elevated emotional intelligence typically achieve superior academic performance, display enhanced leadership abilities, and exhibit more resilience when confronted with difficulties.

Integrating emotional intelligence into the curriculum can facilitate the development of self-awareness, self-regulation, motivation, empathy, and social skills in pupils. Educators can promote this development by providing specific education on emotional literacy, guiding children to understand and express their emotions constructively (Vila et al. 2021). Engaging in role-playing, discussing emotional experiences, and reflective journaling can improve students' comprehension of their own emotions and those of their peers, so cultivating a more compassionate classroom atmosphere.

Building a Supportive Learning Community

Establishing a supportive learning community is crucial for fostering emotional and social learning. An affirmative classroom atmosphere fosters student risk-taking, self-expression, and peer engagement (Monteiro et al., 2021). Educators may foster this climate by setting explicit standards for behavior and communication, prioritizing respect, diversity, and collaboration.

An effective technique for fostering a supportive community is the implementation of social-emotional learning (SEL) programs that emphasize the cultivation of interpersonal skills and emotional competencies. These programs frequently incorporate exercises that foster collaboration, dispute resolution, and proficient communication. Integrating SEL into the curriculum enables educators to provide students with the necessary tools to navigate social encounters and cultivate meaningful connections (Demirdis, 2025).

Moreover, cultivating a sense of belonging in the classroom is essential. Students who sense a connection to their peers and educators are more inclined to participate in the learning process. Collaborative activities, including group projects and peer mentoring, can enhance connections and foster a feeling of community. Consistent check-ins and transparent communication between instructors and students foster trust and support, enabling students to comfortably express their views and concerns.

In conclusion, emotional and social learning constitutes an essential element of comprehensive education. By prioritizing emotional intelligence and fostering supportive learning communities, educators may cultivate environments that develop the entire learner. This emphasis not only improves academic performance but also cultivates vital life skills, equipping students to succeed in their personal and professional endeavors.

INTEGRATING AI WITH PSYCHOLOGICAL PRINCIPLES

Designing AI-Enhanced Learning Experiences

The incorporation of Artificial Intelligence (AI) in education offers promising prospects to improve learning experiences. To ensure that these technologies adequately address the demands of varied learners, it is imperative to implement user-centered design concepts in the development of educational AI tools (Cen et al., 2023). This chapter examines these ideas and presents case studies of effective AI integration in educational environments.

Principles of User-Centered Design in Educational AI Tools

User-centered design (UCD) emphasizes comprehending the needs, preferences, and behaviors of end users, specifically students and educators, during the creation process. The fundamental principles of User-Centered Design (UCD) encompass empathy, usability, and iterative design (Almenara et al. 2024).

1. Empathy: Comprehending the varied backgrounds, learning modalities, and emotional requirements of pupils is essential. Developers must interact with people via interviews, surveys, and observations to collect insights that guide the design process. This compassionate methodology guarantees that AI solutions are customized to tackle genuine obstacles encountered by learners.
2. Usability: Educational AI technologies must be user-friendly and easily navigable. An intuitive interface improves the learning experience by reducing cognitive load and enabling students to concentrate on content instead of technical challenges. Usability testing with real users can pinpoint areas for enhancement and confirm that the technology aligns with user expectations.
3. Iterative Design: The design approach must be iterative, incorporating ongoing feedback and refinement. By consistently evaluating prototypes with students and educators, developers can modify them according to user feedback, thereby guaranteeing that the final product effectively facilitates learning objectives.

Case Studies of Successful AI Integration

Numerous case studies exemplify the effective incorporation of AI in educational environments, highlighting the influence of user-centered design concepts.

Knewton, an AI-driven platform, exemplifies personalized learning by tailoring information according to individual student performance. Knewton offers customized recommendations that improve engagement and comprehension by assessing data on learners' strengths and shortcomings (Dutta et al. 2024). The platform's design embodies user-centered concepts by integrating feedback from both students and instructors to enhance its features and usability regularly.

Another instance is Carnegie Learning's MATHia, an intelligent tutoring system that employs AI to provide customized mathematics training. MATHia adjusts in real-time to students' responses, offering hints and feedback to assist them in navigating problem-solving procedures (Bhardwaj2024). MATHia's design prioritizes usability and empathy, guaranteeing that students have necessary support while cultivating a sense of autonomy in their learning process.

In summary, creating AI-enhanced learning experiences necessitates adherence to user-centered design principles that emphasize the requirements of students and instructors. Through the use of empathy, the assurance of usability, and the practice of iterative design, developers may produce effective educational AI systems that accommodate varied learners. The case studies of Knewton and MATHia illustrate how deliberate incorporation of AI can result in significant enhancements in educational outcomes, hence fostering the development of comprehensive learning environments.

Enhancing Emotional and Social Learning through AI

The incorporation of Artificial Intelligence (AI) in education presents promising opportunities for the advancement of emotional and social learning (ESL) (AlTwijri & Alghizzi, 2024). Utilizing AI tools for social interaction and collaboration, alongside monitoring and enhancing emotional well-being, educators may cultivate more inclusive and supportive learning environments that promote both academic and personal development.

AI Tools for Social Interaction and Collaboration

AI-driven solutions can markedly improve prospects for social engagement and collaboration among students. Platforms like Microsoft Teams and Google Classroom incorporate AI functionalities that enhance collaborative efforts and communication, enabling learners to work together effortlessly, irrespective of their geographical location (Kovari, 2025). These technologies frequently incorporate features such as intelligent chatbots that facilitate group task management, meeting scheduling, and reminder provision, thereby enhancing the collaborative process.

Furthermore, AI can facilitate the development of virtual learning environments that replicate authentic social interactions (Dai & Ke, 2022). AI-powered virtual reality (VR) systems facilitate student participation in immersive collaborative activities, enhancing cooperation and communication abilities. In these environments, learners can engage in social interactions within a secure and regulated context, thereby enhancing their confidence and proficiency in managing social dynamics.

AI can be employed to form individualized learning groups based on students' interests and abilities, fostering collaboration among peers with shared passions. AI tools can foster connections among students, so augmenting their sense of belonging and community, which is vital for emotional and social learning.

Monitoring and Supporting Emotional Well-Being with AI

Besides facilitating social connection, AI can significantly contribute to the monitoring and enhancement of students' emotional well-being. AI-driven platforms can evaluate data from many sources, including student interactions, engagement metrics, and physiological markers (e.g., heart rate variability) to determine emotional states (Qasmi and Fatima 2024). For instance, systems such as Woebot, a mental health chatbot, deliver prompt emotional assistance to students by utilizing AI to facilitate conversations, providing coping skills and resources customized to individual need.

Moreover, AI can assist educators in identifying kids who may be experiencing emotional or social difficulties by evaluating behavioral and engagement patterns. For example, if a student's engagement in conversations diminishes or their assignment submissions become inconsistent, AI systems can alert educators to examine these alterations more closely (Vistorte et al. 2024). This proactive strategy facilitates prompt interventions, guaranteeing that pupils have necessary help prior to the escalation of issues.

In conclusion, the use of AI in augmenting emotional and social learning offers substantial prospects for fostering helpful educational settings. By employing AI tools for social engagement and cooperation, alongside monitoring emotional well-being, instructors can cultivate a comprehensive approach to learning that meets both the academic and emotional requirements of students. This emphasis on emotional and social learning enhances individual well-being and fosters a pleasant, inclusive classroom atmosphere, thereby equipping students for success in their personal and professional endeavors.

Assessing the Impact of AI on Learning Outcomes

As the use of Artificial Intelligence (AI) in education proliferates, it is crucial to evaluate its influence on learning outcomes accurately. Comprehending the impact of AI tools on student performance, engagement, and overall educational experiences is essential for enhancing these technologies and ensuring they address the varied demands of learners (Eltahir & Babiker, 2024). This section examines measures for assessing the efficacy of AI in education and underscores the significance of longitudinal studies and prospective research avenues.

Metrics for Evaluating Effectiveness

To assess the efficacy of AI-augmented learning experiences, various indicators may be utilized (Islam et al. 2024). Quantitative metrics may encompass academic performance indicators, including test scores, grades, and assignment and course completion rates. These measurements offer a clear evaluation of the extent to which AI tools enhance students' academic performance.

Moreover, engagement measures are essential for comprehending the influence of AI on student motivation and participation. This may encompass statistics regarding time allocated to learning platforms, frequency of engagement with AI technologies, and involvement in collaborative activities. Evaluating engagement levels can assist educators in ascertaining whether AI systems provide a sense of participation and dedication among students (Almusaed et al., 2023).

Qualitative measures, like student comments and surveys, are crucial in evaluating the efficacy of AI systems. Collecting perspectives from students regarding their experiences with AI-driven learning can highlight strengths and places for enhancement that quantitative data alone may not disclose (Zhou et al., 2021). Moreover, assessing emotional and social results via self-reported metrics of well-being and interpersonal connections can yield a more thorough comprehension of AI's influence on holistic learning.

Longitudinal Studies and Future Research Directions

Although early evaluations of AI's efficacy are significant, longitudinal studies provide a more profound insight into its enduring effects on learning outcomes. These studies monitor students over prolonged durations, enabling researchers to examine patterns in academic achievement, engagement, and emotional well-being (Salmela-Aro et al. 2021). By analyzing the impact of AI on students over time, educators can discern patterns and make informed judgments regarding the ongoing incorporation of AI tools in educational environments.

Future studies should investigate the intricate impacts of AI on various learner demographics. Examining the interplay of socioeconomic position, cultural background, and learning difficulties with AI tools can promote inclusivity and equity in these technologies (Lin et al., 2024). Furthermore, studies must investigate the ethical ramifications of AI in education, specifically with data privacy and the potential biases inherent in AI systems.

In conclusion, evaluating the influence of AI on educational achievements necessitates a comprehensive strategy incorporating both quantitative and qualitative indicators. Longitudinal studies and continuous research will be crucial for comprehending the enduring impacts of AI on education. By emphasizing effective evaluation techniques and investigating future research avenues, educators may leverage AI's potential to establish comprehensive learning environments that foster academic achievement and personal development for all students.

CREATING AND SUSTAINING HOLISTIC LEARNING ENVIRONMENTS

Practical Strategies for Educators

Establishing and maintaining comprehensive learning environments necessitates deliberate tactics that incorporate Artificial Intelligence (AI) and psychological principles into curriculum development and teaching methodologies (Vistorte et al. 2024). By concentrating on these domains, educators may develop engaging, inclusive, and successful learning experiences that meet the varied requirements of all students.

Curriculum Design that Incorporates AI and Psychological Principles

An essential strategy for educators is to develop courses that utilize AI tools while integrating psychological learning principles. This commences with the alignment of learning objectives to the varied cognitive types and learning preferences of students (Halkiopoulos & Gkintoni, 2024). Educators can employ AI-driven platforms that customize content according to individual performance, enabling students to advance at their own speed. This tailored method not only improves engagement but also reinforces the psychological notion of autonomy, motivating students to assume responsibility for their learning.

Furthermore, including project-based learning (PBL) into the curriculum helps enhance teamwork and critical thinking. AI tools can enhance project-based learning by supplying resources, monitoring progress, and delivering real-time feedback (Yu, 2024). By involving students in significant, real-world projects, educators may facilitate the development of crucial skills such as problem-solving, collaboration, and communication, while also adhering to the principles of social and emotional learning.

Furthermore, integrating components of emotional intelligence into the curriculum is essential. Activities that foster self-awareness, empathy, and relationship development can be incorporated into diverse subjects (Vila et al. 2021). Literature conversations may concentrate on character motives and emotional responses, whereas science projects might promote teamwork and collaborative problem-solving. By integrating emotional and social learning into the curriculum, educators foster a comprehensive strategy that cultivates the entire student.

Professional Development for Educators in Holistic Practices

Continuous professional development for educators is crucial for the efficient implementation of these initiatives. Training programs must prioritize the incorporation of AI tools and psychological principles inside pedagogical methods (Sims and Fletcher-Wood 2021). Workshops and seminars equip educators with the requisite knowledge and abilities to effectively apply AI, assuring their proficiency in data interpretation, instructional adaptation, and technological leverage to improve learning outcomes.

Furthermore, cultivating a collaborative culture among educators can enhance the exchange of best practices and new techniques for comprehensive education (Ahsan, 2025). Professional learning communities (PLCs) function as forums for educators to confront issues, exchange accomplishments, and collaborate devise solutions that cater to the varied needs of their students.

Educators should be motivated to participate in reflective activities that evaluate the efficacy of their teaching techniques and the influence of AI technologies on student learning. Through ongoing assessment and enhancement of their methodologies, educators can maintain comprehensive learning environments that adjust to the changing requirements of their pupils.

In summary, effective solutions for establishing and maintaining holistic learning environments necessitate deliberate curriculum design that integrates AI and psychological principles, coupled with comprehensive professional development for instructors. By emphasizing these qualities, educators may develop engaging, inclusive, and successful learning environments that enable all students to excel academically and personally.

Community and Stakeholder Engagement

Establishing and maintaining holistic learning environments transcends the classroom; it necessitates the active involvement of parents, community members, and other stakeholders in the educational process (Koul & Nayar, 2021). Through cooperation and partnership cultivation, instructors may augment learning experiences and facilitate the development of well-rounded pupils.

Involving Parents and Community in the Learning Process

Involving parents and the community in the educational process is crucial for establishing a conducive learning environment. Parents are instrumental in their children's education, and their engagement can profoundly influence student motivation and success (Lerner et al. 2022). Educational institutions can promote parental involvement via consistent communication, workshops, and events that educate parents about the curriculum and the significance of comprehensive education.

Schools might provide family nights in which parents engage in interactive learning activities with their children. These events can offer parents insights into the educational methodologies employed, including the incorporation of AI tools and psychological principles. By cultivating a knowledge of how these factors enhance student learning, parents are more inclined to promote these habits at home (Gonzalez-DeHass et al. 2022).

Furthermore, educational institutions can create parent-teacher associations (PTAs) or advisory committees to engage parents in decision-making processes (Muro, 2024). This inclusion cultivates a sense of ownership and investment within the school community, establishing a collaborative atmosphere where parents feel empowered to share their insights and resources.

Community involvement is of equal significance. Educational institutions can collaborate with local entities, enterprises, and nonprofit organizations to develop learning opportunities that transcend the classroom environment. Community service programs offer students practical experiences that link academic knowledge to social challenges, promoting civic duty and empathy (O'Neill & Short, 2025). Engaging with local experts can enhance the curriculum by incorporating varied perspectives and resources into the educational setting.

Building Partnerships with Tech Companies and Educational Institutions

In a progressively technology-oriented world, establishing collaborations with technology firms and educational institutions is essential for improving comprehensive learning environments (Ghanbaripour et al. 2024). Partnering with technology companies helps guarantee that instructors access the most recent AI technologies and resources that enhance individualized learning experiences. These collaborations can also offer professional development opportunities for educators, arming them with the necessary skills to properly incorporate technology into their instructional methodologies.

Moreover, collaborations with higher education institutions can establish avenues for students to participate in advanced learning opportunities (Sajja et al., 2024). Initiatives like dual enrollment, mentorships, and internships can familiarize students with collegiate curriculum and professional environments, thereby equipping them for future academic and career endeavors. By linking pupils with nearby colleges and institutions, schools may cultivate a culture of ambition and success.

In summary, contact with the community and stakeholders is vital for establishing and maintaining comprehensive learning environments. Engaging parents and the community in the educational process, alongside fostering collaborations with technology firms and academic institutions, enriches learning experiences and promotes the cultivation of well-rounded individuals. By promoting cooperation and involvement, educators may establish a strong support network that enables students to excel academically and personally.

Future Trends and Innovations

As education progresses, new technologies and innovations are transforming the dynamics of teaching and learning. These developments not only improve the educational experience but also redefine the role of educators in cultivating comprehensive learning environments (Makda, 2025). Comprehending these tendencies is crucial for equipping pupils for the future and guaranteeing that educational methodologies remain pertinent and efficacious.

Emerging Technologies in Education

Emerging technologies are crucial in revolutionizing educational methodologies. Artificial Intelligence (AI) leads in facilitating personalized learning experiences tailored to particular student requirements (George & Wooden, 2023). AI-driven platforms may assess student performance data, customize instructional materials, and deliver real-time feedback, facilitating a personalized learning experience that enhances engagement and comprehension of information.

Furthermore, virtual reality (VR) and augmented reality (AR) are increasingly being adopted in educational environments. These immersive technologies facilitate interactive learning experiences, enabling students to investigate intricate concepts through practical engagement (Lampropoulos et al. 2022). For instance, virtual reality can immerse students in historical locations or scientific settings, enhancing comprehension and retention of information through experiential learning. As these technologies become increasingly available, their incorporation into the curriculum will undoubtedly broaden, offering students novel methods to interact with knowledge.

A notable trend is the increasing implementation of gamification in education.

Incorporating game design aspects into educational sessions can augment motivation and engagement (Piñero et al. 2022). Gamified learning systems promote risk-taking, peer collaboration, and the cultivation of problem-solving abilities within an engaging and dynamic setting. This method is consistent with psychological concepts of motivation and engagement, enhancing the enjoyment and efficacy of learning.

The Evolving Role of Educators in a Tech-Enhanced Learning Landscape

As technology progresses, the function of educators is transforming from conventional knowledge dispensers to facilitators of learning. In a technology-driven educational environment, instructors are accountable for assisting students in utilizing digital resources, cultivating critical thinking, and encouraging ethical technology use (Kaakandikar et al., 2025). This transition necessitates that educators are proficient in both instructional methodologies and technical instruments.

Professional development will be crucial for educators to adjust to these changes. Continuous training in developing technologies, data analysis, and individualized learning methodologies will enable instructors to proficiently incorporate AI and other tools into their instruction. Furthermore, educators must foster emotional intelligence and social learning skills to assist kids in acquiring interpersonal skills and resilience in a progressively digital environment.

In conclusion, forthcoming trends and breakthroughs in education, propelled by rising technology, are transforming the learning environment. As AI, VR, AR, and gamification gain prominence, educators must adjust to their transforming roles as facilitators and guides in the educational process. By adopting these changes and emphasizing professional development, educators may establish and maintain comprehensive learning environments that equip students for success in a dynamic and linked world.

CONCLUSION

The amalgamation of artificial intelligence (AI) with educational methodologies and psychological theories presents a robust avenue for creating genuinely comprehensive learning environments. These environments emphasize academic success alongside emotional well-being, social connectivity, and learner independence. By adopting AI technologies—such as adaptive learning systems, emotion-detection tools, and collaborative platforms—educators may enhance personalized education, accommodate varied learning styles, and cultivate inclusive classrooms that honor individual diversity.

The study emphasizes that successful execution involves more than mere technological adoption. It requires a foundation in constructivist, humanistic, and socio-emotional theories to guarantee that AI technologies augment rather than supplant the human elements of teaching and learning. Ethical considerations, such as data protection, equitable access, and algorithmic transparency, must be addressed to foster confidence and promote responsible innovation.

Moreover, establishing and maintaining holistic learning environments necessitates comprehensive strategies: developing AI-informed curricula, investing in ongoing professional development for educators, including families and communities, and forging collaborations with technology providers. These interrelated initiatives facilitate the connection between technical progress and significant educational reform.

In conclusion, AI can serve as a catalyst—not a substitute—for learner-centered education when matched with robust psychological concepts. The future of education depends on utilizing intelligent technologies to foster knowledge acquisition, emotional intelligence, critical thinking, and social responsibility. Well-designed and ethically executed holistic learning environments equip students for academic achievement as well as for lifelong learning and adaptive, compassionate interaction with the world.

REFERENCES

Ahsan, M. J. (2025). Cultivating a culture of learning: The role of leadership in fostering lifelong development. [HTML]. *The Learning Organization*, *32*(2), 282–306. DOI: 10.1108/TLO-03-2024-0099

Almenara, A. P., Elich, J. H., & Saltiveri, T. G. (2024). Past, present and future of user-centred design methodologies that empathise with the user and generate better accessible experiences. from theory to practice. In Future Perspectives on Human-Computer Interaction Research: Towards the Year 2030 (pp. 17-43). Cham: Springer Nature Switzerland. [HTML]

Almulla, M. A. & Al-Rahmi, W. M. (2023). Integrated social cognitive theory with learning input factors: The effects of problem-solving skills and critical thinking skills on learning performance sustainability. Sustainability. mdpi.com

Almusaed, A., Almssad, A., Yitmen, I., & Homod, R. Z. (2023). Enhancing student engagement: Harnessing "AIED"'s power in hybrid education—A review analysis. Education Sciences. mdpi.com

AlTwijri, L. & Alghizzi, T. M. (2024). Investigating the integration of artificial intelligence in English as foreign language classes for enhancing learners' affective factors: A systematic review. Heliyon. cell.com

Amores-Valencia, A., Burgos, D., & Branch-Bedoya, J. W. (2022). Influence of motivation and academic performance in the use of Augmented Reality in education. A systematic review. [frontiersin.org]. *Frontiers in Psychology*, *13*, 1011409. DOI: 10.3389/fpsyg.2022.1011409 PMID: 36304863

Autin, K. L., Herdt, M. E., Garcia, R. G., & Ezema, G. N. (2022). Basic psychological need satisfaction, autonomous motivation, and meaningful work: A self-determination theory perspective. [HTML]. *Journal of Career Assessment*, *30*(1), 78–93. DOI: 10.1177/10690727211018647

Bahroun, Z., Anane, C., Ahmed, V., & Zacca, A. (2023). Transforming education: A comprehensive review of generative artificial intelligence in educational settings through bibliometric and content analysis. Sustainability. mdpi.com

Bhardwaj, R. (2024, May). AI Integrated Model Design for Education System for Analytical Computation (Mathematics). In 2024 4th International Conference on Advance Computing and Innovative Technologies in Engineering (ICACITE) (pp. 1412-1417). IEEE. [HTML]

Bozkurt, A., Karadeniz, A., Baneres, D., Guerrero-Roldán, A. E., & Rodríguez, M. E. (2021). Artificial intelligence and reflections from educational landscape: A review of AI studies in half a century. [mdpi.com]. *Sustainability (Basel)*, *13*(2), 800. DOI: 10.3390/su13020800

Cen, C., Luo, G., Li, L., Liang, Y., Li, K., Jiang, T., & Xiong, Q. (2023). User-Centered software design: user interface redesign for Blockly–Electron, artificial intelligence educational software for primary and secondary schools. Sustainability. mdpi.com

Dai, C. P. & Ke, F. (2022). Educational applications of artificial intelligence in simulation-based learning: A systematic mapping review. Computers and Education: Artificial Intelligence. sciencedirect.com

Demirdis, B. (2025). Integrating Digital Literacy to Enhance Emotional and Social Skills in Education. In Innovative Educational Frameworks for Future Skills and Competencies (pp. 1-38). IGI Global Scientific Publishing. [HTML]

Dutta, S., Ranjan, S., Mishra, S., Sharma, V., Hewage, P., & Iwendi, C. (2024, February). Enhancing educational adaptability: A review and analysis of AI-driven adaptive learning platforms. In 2024 4th International Conference on Innovative Practices in Technology and Management (ICIPTM) (pp. 1-5). IEEE. [HTML]

Elfert, M. (2023). Humanism and democracy in comparative education. Comparative Education. tandfonline.com

Eltahir, M. E. & Babiker, F. M. E. (2024). The influence of artificial intelligence tools on student performance in e-learning environments: Case study. Electronic Journal of e-Learning. academic-publishing.org

Estrada, M., Monferrer, D., Rodríguez, A., & Moliner, M. (2021). Does emotional intelligence influence academic performance? The role of compassion and engagement in education for sustainable development. Sustainability. mdpi.com

Ezzaim, A., Dahbi, A., Aqqal, A., & Haidine, A. (2024). AI-based learning style detection in adaptive learning systems: A systematic literature review. [HTML]. *Journal of Computers in Education*, •••, 1–39. DOI: 10.1007/s40692-024-00328-9

Gandedkar, N. H., Wong, M. T., & Darendeliler, M. A. (2021). Role of virtual reality (VR), augmented reality (AR) and artificial intelligence (AI) in tertiary education and research of orthodontics: An insight. [HTML]. *Seminars in Orthodontics*, *27*(2), 69–77. DOI: 10.1053/j.sodo.2021.05.003

George, B. & Wooden, O. (2023). Managing the strategic transformation of higher education through artificial intelligence. Administrative Sciences. mdpi.com

Ghanbaripour, A. N., Talebian, N., Miller, D., Tumpa, R. J., Zhang, W., Golmoradi, M., & Skitmore, M. (2024). A Systematic Review of the Impact of Emerging Technologies on Student Learning, Engagement, and Employability in Built Environment Education. [mdpi.com]. *Buildings (Basel, Switzerland), 14*(9), 2769. DOI: 10.3390/buildings14092769

Gibson, L., Obiakor, F. E., & Obi, S. O. (2023). Using technology to enhance learning for students from culturally and linguistically diverse backgrounds. In *Using technology to enhance special education* (pp. 199–214). Emerald Publishing Limited. [HTML] DOI: 10.1108/S0270-401320230000037012

Gimbert, B. G., Miller, D., Herman, E., Breedlove, M., & Molina, C. E. (2023). Social emotional learning in schools: The importance of educator competence. [sagepub.com]. *Journal of Research on Leadership Education, 18*(1), 3–39. DOI: 10.1177/19427751211014920

Gligorea, I., Cioca, M., Oancea, R., Gorski, A. T., Gorski, H., & Tudorache, P. (2023). Adaptive learning using artificial intelligence in e-learning: A literature review. [mdpi.com]. *Education Sciences, 13*(12), 1216. DOI: 10.3390/educsci13121216

Gonzalez-DeHass, A. R., Willems, P. P., Powers, J. R., & Musgrove, A. T. (2022). Parental involvement in supporting students' digital learning. [HTML]. *Educational Psychologist, 57*(4), 281–294. DOI: 10.1080/00461520.2022.2129647

Goyibova, N., Muslimov, N., Sabirova, G., Kadirova, N., & Samatova, B. (2025). Differentiation approach in education: Tailoring instruction for diverse learner needs. [sciencedirect.com]. *MethodsX, 14*, 103163. DOI: 10.1016/j.mex.2025.103163 PMID: 39897653

Guay, F. (2022). Applying self-determination theory to education: Regulations types, psychological needs, and autonomy supporting behaviors. Canadian Journal of School Psychology. sagepub.com

Güner, P., & Erbay, H. N. (2021). Prospective mathematics teachers' thinking styles and problem-solving skills. [HTML]. *Thinking Skills and Creativity, 40*, 100827. DOI: 10.1016/j.tsc.2021.100827

Halkiopoulos, C. & Gkintoni, E. (2024). Leveraging AI in e-learning: Personalized learning and adaptive assessment through cognitive neuropsychology—A systematic analysis. Electronics. mdpi.com

Islam, A., Ali, R., Singh, G., Islam, B., Islam, A., & Hossain, S. (2024, May). An Evaluation of AI-Enhanced Collaborative Learning Platforms. In 2024 International Conference on Communication, Computer Sciences and Engineering (IC3SE) (pp. 207-211). IEEE. [HTML]

Johnson, D. L. & Davis, C. G. (2024). Bridging the gap for underserved populations: Personalized AI solutions for college access and learning support. New Directions for Higher Education. wiley.com

Kaakandikar, R. M., Sakhare, A. A., & Prasad, N. (2025). Innovative Approaches to Teaching and Learning in the 21st Century: Leveraging Technology for Enhanced Outcomes. In New Technological Applications in the Flipped Learning Model (pp. 37-70). IGI Global Scientific Publishing. [HTML]

Kaswan, K. S., Dhatterwal, J. S., & Ojha, R. P. (2024). AI in personalized learning. In *Advances in technological innovations in higher education* (pp. 103–117). CRC Press. [HTML] DOI: 10.1201/9781003376699-9

Kavitha, R. K., Krupa, C. R., & Kaarthiekheyan, V. AI-Powered Digital Solutions for Smart Learning: Revolutionizing Education. In Cybersecurity and Data Science Innovations for Sustainable Development of HEICC (pp. 213-227). CRC Press. [HTML]

Kim, J., Lee, H., & Cho, Y. H. (2022). Learning design to support student-AI collaboration: Perspectives of leading teachers for AI in education. Education and information technologies. springer.com

Koul, S., & Nayar, B. (2021). The holistic learning educational ecosystem: A classroom 4.0 perspective. [HTML]. *Higher Education Quarterly*, *75*(1), 98–112. DOI: 10.1111/hequ.12271

Kovari, A. (2025). A systematic review of AI-powered collaborative learning in higher education: Trends and outcomes from the last decade. Social Sciences & Humanities Open. sciencedirect.com

Kumar, Y., Marchena, J., Awlla, A. H., Li, J. J., & Abdalla, H. B. (2024). The AI-Powered Evolution of Big Data. Applied Sciences. mdpi.com

Lakkala, S., Galkienė, A., Navaitienė, J., Cierpiałowska, T., Tomecek, S., & Uusiautti, S. (2021). Teachers supporting students in collaborative ways—An analysis of collaborative work creating supportive learning environments for every student in a school: Cases from Austria, Finland, Lithuania, and Poland. [mdpi.com]. *Sustainability (Basel)*, *13*(5), 2804. DOI: 10.3390/su13052804

Lampropoulos, G., Keramopoulos, E., Diamantaras, K., & Evangelidis, G. (2022). Augmented reality and virtual reality in education: Public perspectives, sentiments, attitudes, and discourses. [mdpi.com]. *Education Sciences, 12*(11), 798. DOI: 10.3390/educsci12110798

Lau, W. S., & Shea, M. (2024). Empowering English learners in the classroom through culturally responsive social-emotional teaching practices. [HTML]. *Journal of Multilingual and Multicultural Development, 45*(7), 2880–2897. DOI: 10.1080/01434632.2022.2078337

Lerner, R. E., Grolnick, W. S., Caruso, A. J., & Levitt, M. R. (2022). Parental involvement and children's academics: The roles of autonomy support and parents' motivation for involvement. [HTML]. *Contemporary Educational Psychology, 68*, 102039. DOI: 10.1016/j.cedpsych.2021.102039

Lin, M. P. C., Liu, A. L., Poitras, E., Chang, M., & Chang, D. H. (2024). An exploratory study on the efficacy and inclusivity of AI technologies in diverse learning environments. Sustainability. mdpi.com

Lin, W., Zaman, S. I., Jamil, S., & Khan, S. A. (2023). Students engagement in distant learning: How much influence do the critical factors have for success in academic performance? [HTML]. *Psychology in the Schools, 60*(7), 2373–2394. DOI: 10.1002/pits.22858

Makda, F. (2025). Digital education: Mapping the landscape of virtual teaching in higher education–a bibliometric review. Education and Information Technologies. springer.com

Meyer, J., & Seaman, J. (2021). Beyond experiential learning cycles. Outdoor environmental education in higher education: International perspectives, 75-87. [HTML]

Miseliunaite, B., Kliziene, I., & Cibulskas, G. (2022). Can holistic education solve the world's problems: A systematic literature review. Sustainability. mdpi.com

Monteiro, V., Carvalho, C., & Santos, N. N. (2021). Creating a supportive classroom environment through effective feedback: Effects on students' school identification and behavioral engagement. Frontiers in Education. frontiersin.org

Muro, J. A. (2024). "The PTA intimidates": Racially segregated parent organizations in a dual immersion school. [HTML]. *Race, Ethnicity and Education, 27*(1), 55–74. DOI: 10.1080/13613324.2023.2192915

Namaziandost, E., Behbahani, H. K., & Naserpour, A. (2024). Peer support in language learning: Mitigating anxiety, enhancing achievement, cultivating growth mindsets, and increasing enjoyment. [researchgate.net]. *Journal of Applied Learning and Teaching*, *7*(2), 296–313.

Nguyen, A., Ngo, H. N., Hong, Y., Dang, B., & Nguyen, B. P. T. (2023). Ethical principles for artificial intelligence in education. [springer.com]. *Education and Information Technologies*, *28*(4), 4221–4241. DOI: 10.1007/s10639-022-11316-w PMID: 36254344

Niemi, K. (2021). 'The best guess for the future?'Teachers' adaptation to open and flexible learning environments in Finland. Education Inquiry. tandfonline.com

O'Neill, G. & Short, A. (2025). Relevant, practical and connected to the real world: what higher education students say engages them in the curriculum. Irish Educational Studies. tandfonline.com

Okwuduba, E. N., Nwosu, K. C., Okigbo, E. C., Samuel, N. N., & Achugbu, C. (2021). Impact of intrapersonal and interpersonal emotional intelligence and self-directed learning on academic performance among pre-university science students. Heliyon, 7(3). cell.com

Ozberk, E. H. (2025). *Learning Theories in Psychology From Philosophical Roots to Educational Measurement*. Exploring Adult Education Through Learning Theory. [HTML]

Piñero Charlo, J. C., Belova, N., Quevedo Gutiérrez, E., Zapatera Llinares, A., Arboleya-García, E., Swacha, J., López-Serentill, P., & Carmona-Medeiro, E. (2022). Preface for the special issue “trends in educational gamification: Challenges and learning opportunities”. [mdpi.com]. *Education Sciences*, *12*(3), 179. DOI: 10.3390/educsci12030179

Qasmi, F., & Fatima, S. K. (2024, June). Enhancing education and well-being through artificial intelligence: opportunities and challenges. In International Conference on Breaking Barriers with Generative Intelligence (pp. 154-164). Cham: Springer Nature Switzerland. [HTML] DOI: 10.1007/978-3-031-65996-6_13

Ramaila, S. M. (2025). Fostering Holistic Development: The Integral Role of Educators in Nurturing Student Growth and Learning. In Former Educators' Roles in Supporting Student Growth and Learning (pp. 117-146). IGI Global Scientific Publishing. [HTML]

Sajja, R., Sermet, Y., Cikmaz, M., Cwiertny, D., & Demir, I. (2024). Artificial intelligence-enabled intelligent assistant for personalized and adaptive learning in higher education. Information. mdpi.com

Salas-Pilco, S. Z., Xiao, K., & Hu, X. (2022). Artificial intelligence and learning analytics in teacher education: A systematic review. Education Sciences. mdpi.com

Salmela-Aro, K., Tang, X., Symonds, J., & Upadyaya, K. (2021). Student engagement in adolescence: A scoping review of longitudinal studies 2010–2020. [wiley.com]. *Journal of Research on Adolescence*, *31*(2), 256–272. DOI: 10.1111/jora.12619 PMID: 33991151

Saxena, K. (2025). *Emotive Intelligence and Interpersonal Skills: Key Drivers of Leadership Effectiveness and Personal Competence*. Pacific Business Review International. [HTML]

Shaheen, N. L. (2022). Technology accessibility: How US K-12 schools are enacting policy and addressing the equity imperative. [HTML]. *Computers & Education*, *179*, 104414. DOI: 10.1016/j.compedu.2021.104414

Sims, S., & Fletcher-Wood, H. (2021). Identifying the characteristics of effective teacher professional development: A critical review. *School Effectiveness and School Improvement*, *32*(1), 47–63. ucl.ac.uk. DOI: 10.1080/09243453.2020.1772841

Strielkowski, W., Grebennikova, V., Lisovskiy, A., Rakhimova, G., & Vasileva, T. (2024). AI-driven adaptive learning for sustainable educational transformation. Sustainable Development. wiley.com

Tugberk, C., & Sirin, S. (2024). *Beyond Intelligence: The Life and Work of Howard Gardner*. The Palgrave Handbook of Educational Thinkers. [HTML]

Vila, S., Gilar-Corbí, R., & Pozo-Rico, T. (2021). Effects of student training in social skills and emotional intelligence on the behaviour and coexistence of adolescents in the 21st century. [mdpi.com]. *International Journal of Environmental Research and Public Health*, *18*(10), 5498. DOI: 10.3390/ijerph18105498 PMID: 34065560

Vistorte, A. O. R., Deroncele-Acosta, A., Ayala, J. L. M., Barrasa, A., López-Granero, C., & Martí-González, M. (2024). Integrating artificial intelligence to assess emotions in learning environments: A systematic literature review. [frontiersin.org]. *Frontiers in Psychology*, *15*, 1387089. DOI: 10.3389/fpsyg.2024.1387089 PMID: 38966729

Weng, X., Chiu, T. K. F., & Tsang, C. C. (2022). Promoting student creativity and entrepreneurship through real-world problem-based maker education. Thinking Skills and Creativity. sciencedirect.com

Yu, H. (2024). Enhancing creative cognition through project-based learning: An in-depth scholarly exploration. Heliyon. cell.com

Zhang, R. (2022). Design of an authentic project-based learning course using project management approach. [HTML]. *International Journal of Fashion Design, Technology and Education*, *15*(1), 57–66. DOI: 10.1080/17543266.2021.1992799

Zheng, F. (2022). Fostering students' well-being: The mediating role of teacher interpersonal behavior and student-teacher relationships. Frontiers in psychology. frontiersin.org

Zhou, J., Gandomi, A. H., Chen, F., & Holzinger, A. (2021). Evaluating the quality of machine learning explanations: A survey on methods and metrics. Electronics. mdpi.com

Zimmerle, J. C. (2021). Safe, sound, and private: Promoting data protection for students. [HTML]. *Computers in the Schools*, *38*(1), 1–18. DOI: 10.1080/07380569.2021.1882203

Chapter 3
Bridging Disciplines:
Integrating Mathematics and Physical Education Through STEAM

Saman Saman
https://orcid.org/0000-0003-4743-9275
Universitas Muhammadiyah Palopo, Indonesia

Fajri Hamzah
Universitas Muhammadiyah Palopo, Indonesia

Binsar Hasudungan Sihombing
Universitas Muhammadiyah Palopo, Indonesia

Samsinar Samsinar
Universitas Muhammadiyah Palopo, Indonesia

ABSTRACT

This chapter examines the amalgamation of mathematics and physical education within the interdisciplinary STEAM (Science, Technology, Engineering, Arts, and Mathematics) framework. Integrating mathematical ideas like geometry, statistics, and probability into physical activities can elevate student engagement, critical thinking, and practical application. The study emphasizes effective tactics such as project-based learning, movement analysis, fitness data monitoring, and gamified activities that enhance both academic and physical literacy. Collaborative learning environments enhance the cultivation of communication and problem-solving abilities. The integration demonstrates not just an enhancement of mathematical comprehension but also the advancement of comprehensive health education. Case studies and exemplary practices demonstrate that this methodology improves moti-

DOI: 10.4018/979-8-3373-5786-7.ch003

vation, retention, and student autonomy, establishing STEAM as a transformative paradigm for 21st-century education.

INTRODUCTION TO STEAM EDUCATION

Understanding STEAM

In recent years, the educational environment has transformed to adopt a more integrated approach to learning, resulting in the concept of STEAM—an acronym for Science, Technology, Engineering, Arts, and Mathematics (Li, 2024). This interdisciplinary framework promotes students' ability to integrate diverse subjects, cultivating a comprehensive comprehension of intricate concepts and real-world issues.

STEAM integrates the arts into the conventional STEM framework, highlighting creativity and invention as vital elements for achievement in the 21st century.

The significance of transdisciplinary learning is paramount. Contemporary issues necessitate collaborative problem-solving that surpasses the confines of specific disciplines (Christensen et al., 2021). A project on renewable energy may encompass scientific principles, technology applications, engineering designs, mathematical computations, and creative displays to convey findings effectively. This connection not only augments student involvement but also equips them for future occupations that increasingly necessitate cross-disciplinary skills.

In physical education, including mathematics into the STEAM framework offers distinctive chances to enhance student experiences (Damaševičius & Zailskaitė-Jakštė, 2023). Mathematics is frequently regarded as an isolated, abstract discipline; nonetheless, it is essential for comprehending movement, performance measurements, and the science of sports. For instance, principles of geometry can be employed to examine the trajectories of balls in many sports, whereas statistics can assist students in assessing their performance and establishing attainable objectives. By integrating these subjects, educators can establish a dynamic learning environment that highlights the significance of mathematics in daily activities and sports.

Furthermore, the incorporation of STEAM into physical education fosters critical and creative thinking among pupils. They acquire the ability to implement mathematical concepts in practical situations, so improving their problem-solving abilities and cultivating a greater respect for both disciplines (Juškevičienė et al., 2021). This method enhances mathematical competence while fostering confidence and independence in pupils as they observe the concrete results of their education.

This chapter examines the connections of mathematics and physical education, revealing creative ideas and practical examples that demonstrate the efficacy of STEAM. By adopting this interdisciplinary methodology, we can motivate the forthcoming generation of scholars to transcend conventional limits and cultivate the competencies essential for success in a more intricate globe (Bass et al. 2023). By integrating mathematics and physical education, we are cultivating well-rounded individuals prepared to confront future problems.

The Role of Mathematics in Physical Education

Mathematics is essential in improving physical education, acting as a fundamental instrument that informs multiple facets of sports and fitness (Alvarez-Vargas et al. 2023). Integrating mathematical principles into physical education enables educators to enhance students' comprehension of the mechanics of athletic performance, refine their analytical skills, and cultivate a better respect for the science of movement.

Mathematics significantly aids physical education by facilitating the study of performance data. Metrics including velocity, distance, and duration are crucial for assessing athletic performance (Lee & Lee, 2021). For example, when students engage in track and field competitions, they can employ mathematical formulas to ascertain their average speed by dividing the distance traveled by the time elapsed. This not only assists them in assessing their performance but also motivates them to establish attainable objectives for enhancement. Furthermore, by examining data longitudinally, students can see trends and patterns that might guide their training regimens and techniques.

A crucial mathematical subject in physical education is geometry, essential for comprehending the spatial relationships inherent in sports. In basketball, players must understand angles and trajectories when shooting the ball. Students can utilize geometric principles to evaluate the ideal shooting angles that enhance their score probabilities (Uwamahoro et al. 2021). In soccer, comprehending the field's geometry aids players in making smart judgments about positioning and passing. These geometric applications not only improve students' athletic abilities but also strengthen their comprehension of mathematical principles.

Statistics are essential in sports analytics. Through the collection and analysis of data regarding team performance, players and coaches can make informed decisions to improve their strategy (Ashford et al., 2021). A basketball coach may evaluate shooting percentages from various court locations to identify the most effective strategies. Students may do analogous studies utilizing statistical tools to assess their performance or that of their colleagues, thus cultivating critical thinking and data literacy abilities.

Moreover, probability principles might be utilized to comprehend the possibility of diverse outcomes in athletics (Gredin et al. 2023). Students may compute the probability of winning a game using historical performance data, so augmenting their comprehension of risk and decision-making in competitive contexts.

In conclusion, mathematics is essential to physical education, equipping pupils with the skills to analyze, strategize, and enhance their athletic performance. By integrating these disciplines, educators can cultivate a more enriching learning environment that enhances students' physical abilities while fostering their mathematical comprehension, equipping them for success both in sports and in life.

MATHEMATICAL CONCEPTS IN SPORTS

Statistics and Data Analysis

Statistics and data analysis are crucial elements in sports, equipping athletes, coaches, and analysts with the means to assess performance, formulate strategies, and make educated decisions (Torres-Ronda et al. 2022). Collecting and evaluating sports performance data enables individuals to acquire useful insights into their strengths and limitations, thereby improving their athletic talents. This chapter examines the importance of statistical principles, including averages, medians, and modes, and their application in the realm of sports.

Gathering sports performance data entails quantifying diverse parameters, such points scored, distances traversed, or recorded times. A track coach may collect data on athletes' sprint timings over multiple weeks to assess progress. By aggregating this data, trainers can discern trends, establish benchmarks, and customize training programs to address the unique requirements of each athlete (Pashaie et al. 2024). The systematic collecting of data facilitates performance evaluation and promotes a culture of accountability and goal-setting among pupils.

Comprehending averages is essential in sports statistics. The mean, or average, is determined by aggregating all data points and dividing by the total number of observations (Khorana et al. 2023). For instance, if a basketball player accumulates 20, 25, and 30 points in three games, the mean score is calculated as $(20 + 25 + 30) / 3 = 25$. This average serves as a valuable metric for assessing the player's standard performance, facilitating comparisons with teammates or adversaries. It is crucial to acknowledge that averages can occasionally be deceptive, especially in instances involving extreme numbers, referred to as outliers.

In these circumstances, the median serves as a significant statistical metric. The median denotes the central value of a dataset when organized in ascending order (Rainio et al., 2024). In the preceding example, if a player accumulates scores of

20, 25, 30, and 50 points throughout four games, the median score is calculated as 25 + 30 divided by 2, resulting in 27.5. This metric offers a more precise representation of standard performance, particularly in the presence of outliers, as it is less influenced by extreme results.

The mode, defined as the most commonly occurring number in a data set, also contributes to sports statistics (Du & Yuan, 2021). For example, if a soccer player achieves goals in the sequence: 1, 2, 2, 3, 4, the mode is 2, signifying that this is the predominant performance level. Comprehending the mode enables trainers to discern consistent performance trends and discover areas for enhancement.

In conclusion, statistics and data analysis are essential for assessing sports performance. Through the collection and analysis of data, athletes can get insights into their performance measures, while statistical concepts such as averages, medians, and modes serve as helpful tools for evaluating this information. By comprehending these statistical ideas, students can augment their analytical abilities, cultivate a data-driven perspective, and eventually boost their athletic performance. Incorporating these mathematical principles into physical education enhances the educational experience, illustrating the applicability of mathematics in practical situations.

Geometry and Measurement

Geometry and measurement are essential mathematical principles with widespread applications in sports. Comprehending these principles not only improves athletes' performance but also equips them with the means to assess and refine many facets of their sport (Exel & Dabnichki, 2024). This section examines the application of geometric principles to sports fields and equipment, as well as the measurement techniques essential for physical activities.

Geometry is essential in the design and configuration of sports playing fields (Ward et al. 2023). The proportions of a soccer field, basketball court, or tennis court are delineated using geometric shapes and measurements. A soccer pitch is often rectangular, conforming to particular length and width ratios as stipulated by international standards (Borges et al. 2024). Comprehending these elements enables players to devise strategies for their movements and positions on the field. For instance, identifying the angles for passing the ball or the ideal trajectory for a shot can profoundly affect the game's outcome. Geometry facilitates the design of apparatus, such as the curve of a basketball hoop or the aerodynamic contour of a bicycle frame, which can improve performance.

Measurement is a vital component of sports that is fundamentally dependent on mathematical principles (Ostojic et al., 2023). Precise measuring methodologies are crucial for monitoring performance and guaranteeing safety. In track and field competitions, distances must be calculated accurately to ascertain victors and establish records. Athletes frequently utilize measuring tapes, laser instruments, or digital measuring gadgets to guarantee precision. Furthermore, comprehending units of measurement—such as meters, feet, and seconds—is essential for athletes to accurately analyze their performance data.

In physical education, students may participate in several measurement activities that enhance their comprehension of geometry and measurement (Cao et al., 2022). For instance, they can quantify the perimeter and area of various sports grounds, enabling them to ascertain the available space for play. This experiential learning reinforces their comprehension of geometric principles while highlighting the practical uses of mathematics in real-world contexts.

Additionally, students can investigate the concept of angles through activities like basketball shooting or soccer ball kicking. By examining the angles of their approach to the target or their body positioning, they can modify their method for enhancement (Bellido et al. 2023). The application of geometry in athletics boosts performance and cultivates critical thinking and problem-solving abilities.

In conclusion, geometry and measurement are essential to sports, affecting aspects such as field design and equipment performance. By utilizing these mathematical principles, athletes can enhance their performance and make informed judgments during competition. Incorporating geometry and measurement into physical education enhances students' learning experiences, illustrating the significance of mathematics in sports and cultivating a greater appreciation for both fields. This combination enhances students' mathematics abilities and provides understanding of the science behind movement and athletic performance.

Probability and Game Theory

Probability and game theory are influential mathematical principles that significantly impact the realm of sports (Kampakis, 2023). These concepts assist athletes and coaches in making educated judgments, analyzing game results, and formulating plans that can result in success. Comprehending probability in sports results and implementing game theory ideas can improve athletes' performance and augment their strategic reasoning.

Probability quantifies the likelihood of a specific occurrence occurring. In sports, probabilities are utilized to evaluate the likelihood of winning a game, scoring a goal, or attaining a particular performance criterion (Baumer & Matthews, 2023). For example, by examining a basketball player's free throw %, one can ascertain the likelihood of successfully making a free shot based on prior performance data. If a player has successfully completed 80 out of 100 free throws, the chance of making the subsequent free throw is P=80/100=0.8 or 80%. This comprehension of probability enables players to cultivate confidence in their skills and make smart decisions during games.

Additionally, probability can be utilized to forecast game results. Sports analysts frequently employ statistical models to predict a team's probability of victory, considering elements like as player performance, historical data, and opponent strengths (Sarlis & Tjortjis, 2024). For instance, if a football team had a 70% probability of triumphing over a weaker adversary, coaches might create methods that leverage this advantage, so optimizing their game plan accordingly.

Conversely, game theory concentrates on strategic interactions among players or teams (Fang et al., 2021). It entails examining scenarios where the result is contingent not solely on one's actions but also on the actions of others. Game theory can be used to diverse events in sports, including penalty kicks in soccer and strategic plays in basketball. During a penalty shootout, the kicker must determine whether to direct the ball left, right, or center, while the goalie must predict the kicker's decision. Both players base their judgments on the odds of success linked to each alternative, resulting in a dynamic interaction of strategies.

Comprehending game theory can also improve collaboration and communication among participants. Through the analysis of adversaries' methods and the anticipation of their actions, teams can formulate coordinated plays that enhance their likelihood of success (Plakias et al. 2024). In a basketball game, players can apply game theory to decide when to pass, shoot, or set screens according to the defensive techniques utilized by their adversaries.

In summary, probability and game theory are fundamental mathematical principles that profoundly influence sports. By comprehending probability associated with game results and utilizing game theory principles, athletes can make educated decisions, devise effective tactics, and improve their overall performance. Incorporating these concepts into physical education enhances students' quantitative understanding while cultivating critical thinking and strategic planning abilities, equipping them for success in both athletics and life. Through this multidisciplinary approach, students get an appreciation for the significance of mathematics in comprehending and succeeding in the competitive realm of sports.

PHYSICAL EDUCATION AS A LABORATORY FOR MATHEMATICAL APPLICATION

Designing Fitness Programs

Physical education functions as a crucial platform for the application of mathematical principles in practical contexts, especially in the formulation of efficient fitness programs (Osaba et al., 2021). Integrating mathematics into training regimens enables educators and students to maximize workouts, improve performance, and foster general wellness. This chapter examines the application of mathematical principles in developing customized fitness regimens, emphasizing the calculation of goal heart rates and the assessment of training intensities.

A crucial element in developing a fitness program is comprehending the notion of target heart rate (THR). The target heart rate represents the optimal heart rate range that individuals should strive for during exercise to enhance cardiovascular advantages while reducing health concerns (Herbert, 2022). To compute this, one must first ascertain the maximal heart rate (MHR), which can be approximated using the formula MHR=220−age. A 30-year-old individual would have an estimated maximum heart rate (MHR) of 220 minus 30, equating to 190 beats per minute (bpm).

After establishing the MHR, the target heart rate can be computed by assessing the desired workout intensity, generally represented as a percentage of the MHR (Mendelson et al., 2025). The target heart rate for moderate-intensity exercise is typically established at 50-70% of the maximum heart rate, whereas vigorous-intensity exercise aims for 70-85%. In the case of our 30-year-old subject, the moderate-intensity range would be:

Lower limit $= 190 \times 0.50 = 95$ bpm Maximum threshold $= 190 \times 0.70 = 133$ bpm

The recommended heart rate for moderate-intensity exercise ranges from 95 to 133 bpm. This mathematical method allows individuals to customize their workouts according to their fitness levels and objectives, ensuring they operate within a safe and effective heart rate zone.

Mathematical methods can be utilized to ascertain workout intensities, in addition to establishing target heart rates. Individuals can quantify their exercise intensity using the Rating of Perceived Exertion (RPE) scale based on personal perception. The RPE scale generally spans from 1 to 10, where 1 indicates minimal exertion and 10 signifies extreme effort. Educators can instruct students to associate their heart rates with their Rate of Perceived Exertion (RPE), enabling them to modify their workouts according to their perceived effort.

Additionally, students may participate in mathematical activities that require monitoring their advancement over time. By documenting workout durations, distances, and intensities, they may evaluate trends and make educated judgments about their training programs (Taub et al., 2022). For example, they can compute the mean workout intensity throughout a week or discern patterns in their performance enhancements.

In conclusion, the design of fitness programs utilizing mathematical principles enables students to assume responsibility for their health and fitness endeavors. By determining target heart rates and exercise intensities, individuals acquire critical insights into their training, allowing them to optimize their efforts and attain their objectives. Incorporating these mathematical principles into physical education not only improves students' comprehension of fitness but also underscores the significance of mathematics in daily life, promoting a comprehensive approach to health and well-being.

Analyzing Movement and Performance

Examining movement and performance in sports offers a distinctive chance to implement mathematical principles, especially via the perspective of biomechanics (Yeadon & Pain, 2023). Biomechanics examines the mechanical principles governing the movement and structure of living creatures, integrating physics, engineering, and mathematics to improve athletic performance. By comprehending the mathematics of motion, athletes may optimize their approaches, increase efficiency, and eventually elevate their performance.

A fundamental mathematical idea in biomechanics is the examination of forces exerted on the body during motion (Furlong et al.). For instance, when a sprinter sprints off the starting blocks, multiple forces are involved, including gravitational force, friction, and the force generated by the athlete's legs. Athletes can utilize Newton's principles of motion to determine the requisite force needed for a specific acceleration. The relationship can be articulated by the equation:

$$F=ma$$

When F represents the force, m denotes the mass of the athlete, and a signifies the acceleration. Comprehending this link enables athletes to refine their starting method, facilitating the attainment of quicker timings.

An additional significant facet of movement analysis is the examination of angles and trajectories. For example, when a basketball player executes a free throw, the angle of ball release profoundly affects its trajectory and the probability of scoring. Athletes can determine the ideal shooting angle by utilizing concepts of projectile motion (Pakdemirli, 2025). The optimal angle for achieving maximum distance in projectile motion is generally approximately 45 degrees; however, in basketball, the ideal angle may fluctuate depending on the player's position and stature. Athletes can employ quantitative modeling to simulate various shooting angles and ascertain which one maximizes the probability of success.

Furthermore, biomechanics employs metrics of velocity, distance, and duration to evaluate performance. Athletes can monitor their sprinting velocity utilizing the formula:

Speed = Distance/Time

Through the assessment of their performance across diverse distances, athletes can discern their strengths and limitations, enabling them to concentrate on particular areas for enhancement (Torres-Ronda et al. 2022). A runner may evaluate their velocity in short sprints compared to long distances and customize their training program accordingly.

Moreover, video analysis technologies can be utilized to record an athlete's motions in real-time. Through the analysis of these recordings, athletes can examine their form and technique, employing mathematical computations to quantify angles, distances, and velocities (Qiu et al., 2023). This quantitative input is essential for implementing modifications that can enhance performance.

In conclusion, the examination of movement and performance via biomechanics reveals the significant relationship between mathematics and physical education. By utilizing mathematical principles to comprehend forces, angles, and motion, athletes can refine their tactics and maximize their performance. The incorporation of mathematics into physical education enhances students' learning experiences and enables them to use these concepts practically, so cultivating a greater appreciation for both fields. This multidisciplinary approach equips students with the information and skills essential for success in sports and other fields.

Sports Technology and Innovation

The convergence of technology and sports has transformed the methods by which athletes train, compete, and assess performance (Qi et al., 2024). Sports technology includes many methods and systems aimed at improving athletic performance via data gathering, analysis, and feedback. This chapter examines the crucial function of technology in sports analytics and provides case studies that demonstrate how mathematical applications foster innovation in the domain.

Sports analytics entails the methodical examination of data to guide decision-making and enhance performance. Technology is essential in this procedure, facilitating the real-time capture of extensive performance data (Allioui & Mourdi, 2023). Wearable gadgets, including heart rate monitors, GPS trackers, and accelerometers, furnish athletes and coaches with essential insights into training loads, movement patterns, and physiological reactions. Through quantitative analysis of this data, teams can make informed judgments about training protocols, injury mitigation, and tactical strategy.

A significant case study is the application of GPS technology in professional soccer. Teams employ GPS trackers to observe players' movements during training sessions and competitions (Pons et al. 2021). The acquired data encompasses parameters including distance traveled, velocity, and acceleration. Coaches evaluate this data to gauge players' fitness levels and discern patterns that may signify weariness or injury risk. For example, if a player routinely surpasses a specific threshold of high-intensity running, coaches might modify training loads to avert overexertion, so improving player longevity and performance.

An further instance of technology-driven mathematics applications is the utilization of video analysis in basketball. Coaches utilize video recording equipment to document gaming, facilitating comprehensive analyses of player actions and team dynamics. Through the analysis of angles, trajectories, and player positioning, coaches can formulate plans that capitalize on opponents' vulnerabilities (Sheehan et al. 2022). The implementation of shot-tracking technology allows teams to evaluate shooting percentages from diverse positions on the court. This data assists players in identifying their most efficient shooting locations, resulting in enhanced decision-making during matches.

Besides performance monitoring, technology significantly influences fan engagement and sports marketing. Data analytics solutions examine audience behavior and preferences, allowing teams to customize their marketing efforts and improve the entire fan experience. Organizations can utilize statistical models to forecast ticket sales, refine pricing strategies, and enhance consumer satisfaction (Guerrini et al. 2023).

In conclusion, technology's role in sports analytics is revolutionary, equipping athletes and coaches with the means to analyze performance data efficiently. Case examples, such GPS tracking in soccer and video analysis in basketball, illustrate how mathematical applications propel innovation in sports. Integrating technology and mathematics into physical education provides pupils with essential understanding of the scientific principles that govern sports performance. This multidisciplinary approach not only deepens their comprehension of sports but also equips students for future professions in sectors that increasingly depend on data-driven decision-making. As technology advances, the potential for mathematical applications in sports will increase, presenting promising chances for innovation and enhancement.

ENGAGING STUDENTS THROUGH ACTIVE LEARNING

Hands-On Activities and Projects

Involving students in experiential activities and projects effectively connects mathematics with physical education. Educators can cultivate an engaged learning environment that promotes collaboration, critical thinking, and a profound comprehension of mathematics and physical exercise by designing projects that integrate both disciplines (MacKnight, 2021). This chapter examines many projects and classroom activities that enhance participation and underscore the significance of mathematics in physical education.

An effective initiative entails organizing a "Fitness Olympics" event, when students devise their own sports tournaments (Hughes & Gallus). Students may collaborate in teams to create a sequence of physical challenges, such relay races, obstacle courses, or timed sprints. Each team must compute the distances for their events and devise scoring systems based on performance measures. For instance, they might employ mathematical equations to ascertain average velocities or compute points allocated for task completion within designated time intervals. This project promotes physical activity while enabling students to utilize mathematical principles, like measurement, averages, and scoring systems, in a practical setting.

The "Math in Motion" challenge involves students utilizing pedometers or fitness trackers to quantify their physical activity over the course of a week. Students may document their daily steps, distances, and active minutes, thereafter analyzing the data to compute averages and discern trends (Casado-Robles et al. 2022). They can generate graphs or charts to visually depict their findings, enabling them to observe the correlation between physical activity and health. This practice highlights the significance of data analysis and motivates students to establish personal fitness objectives informed by their mathematical understanding.

Furthermore, instructors may integrate geometry into physical education by having pupils conceptualize a novel sports field or gymnasium plan. Students may collaborate in groups to produce scaled representations of their designs, calculating areas for distinct zones (e.g., playing fields, spectator areas) and ascertaining the best size for particular sports (Papastergiou & Mastrogiannis, 2021). This project reinforces geometric fundamentals while promoting teamwork and creativity as students collaborate to produce functional and aesthetically appealing designs.

A supplementary practical project may entail examining the physics behind sports. Students may examine the mechanics of a particular sport, such as basketball or soccer, and perform experiments to quantify variables such as angles, trajectories, and forces (Iuliano et al. 2021). For example, they could utilize protractors to analyze shooting angles and determine the best angle for scoring in basketball. Students get a profound comprehension of the science underlying athletic performance by applying mathematical ideas to real-world sports situations.

In conclusion, experiential activities and projects that integrate mathematics and physical exercise are crucial for captivating kids in the educational process. Through the design of interactive and collaborative projects, educators can illustrate the practical applications of mathematics within physical education, cultivating a greater understanding for both disciplines. These activities enhance physical health while fostering critical thinking, collaboration, and creativity, equipping kids for success in academic and athletic endeavors. This integration of mathematics and physical education enables students to recognize the interconnections across disciplines, so enhancing their educational experience.

Collaborative Learning Environments

Establishing collaborative learning spaces in mathematics and physical education is crucial for cultivating teamwork, improving communication skills, and advancing comprehension of both subjects (Bassachs et al. 2022). By promoting collaborative projects and activities that merge mathematical principles with physical education, educators may foster a feeling of community and collective accountability for learning. This chapter examines techniques to promote collaboration among students and emphasizes the advantages of teamwork within STEAM education.

An excellent technique for fostering collaboration is to develop group tasks that necessitate the integration of mathematical knowledge with physical activity. For instance, in a "Sports Statistics" project, students may collaborate in small teams to collect data on their preferred sports or athletes (Chang-Tik, 2023). They can evaluate statistics such as points scored, miles traversed, or recorded times, and thereafter report their results to the class. This collaborative initiative promotes student engagement with mathematical ideas while facilitating debates on data interpretation and the ramifications of performance measures in sports.

An alternative method involves structuring team-oriented fitness tasks that necessitate the application of mathematical skills in real-time. For example, students could engage in a relay race in which each team is required to compute their cumulative time and average speed based on individual accomplishments. Post-race, students may deliberate on their techniques, evaluate their outcomes, and pinpoint opportunities for enhancement (Chaudhry et al. 2023). This practical experience underscores the significance of collaboration and motivates students to assist each other in attaining shared objectives.

Integrating peer teaching is an effective method for promoting teamwork. Students may be partnered or grouped to instruct one another on particular mathematical ideas pertinent to physical education (Rivadeneira & Inga, 2023). For instance, one student might elucidate the method for calculating goal heart rates, while another illustrates a suitable workout. This approach not only enhances students' comprehension of the subject matter but also cultivates their confidence and communication abilities as they assume teaching responsibilities.

Furthermore, educators may develop interdisciplinary units that integrate mathematics and physical education, enabling students to collaboratively engage in projects that encompass both disciplines (Schmidthaler et al. 2023). A subject on "Biomechanics and Motion" may require students to analyze the angles and forces associated with different sports movements. They could collaborate to devise experiments, gather data, and report their results, therefore deepening their comprehension of mathematical concepts and physical performance.

Ultimately, cultivating a constructive classroom environment that prioritizes cooperation is essential. Educators can cultivate standards that promote respect, active listening, and constructive criticism among students. Commemorating collective accomplishments and acknowledging individual efforts within a team can enhance the collaborative ethos (Richards et al. 2025).

In conclusion, establishing collaborative learning spaces in mathematics and physical education is essential for improving student engagement and comprehension. Through the implementation of group projects, team-based challenges, peer instruction, and interdisciplinary units, educators can cultivate a collaborative culture that enhances teamwork and enriches the educational experience. Through these collaborative endeavors, students enhance their mathematical and physical competencies while also fostering crucial interpersonal skills that will benefit them in their academic and professional pursuits. Integrating collaboration into the educational process equips students to excel in a progressively interconnected society.

Assessing Learning Outcomes

Evaluating learning outcomes in a program that integrates mathematics and physical education is crucial for comprehending student advancement and improving educational efficacy (Mavilidi & Vazou, 2021). Assessing student comprehension and abilities necessitates a comprehensive strategy that takes into account both intellectual and physical skills. This chapter examines diverse methodologies for evaluating learning outcomes and underscores the significance of integrating feedback mechanisms for ongoing enhancement.

A proficient approach for assessing student comprehension is via performance-based evaluations. In a physical education environment, this may entail monitoring kids throughout activities like fitness challenges or team sports. Educators can evaluate students based on certain criteria, including collaboration, strategic implementation, and skill execution (Thornhill-Miller et al. 2023). For example, in a basketball lesson, educators may assess students on their shooting techniques, passing precision, and comprehension of game principles. This practical method enables instructors to assess both physical competencies and students' capacity to implement mathematical ideas, including angles and trajectories, in real-world contexts.

Alongside performance evaluations, educators may employ formative assessments to gauge student comprehension during the learning process. These evaluations may manifest in several formats, such as tests, reflective journals, and group discussions (Stanja et al. 2023). For instance, following the completion of a course on sports statistics, students may undertake a quiz assessing their proficiency in data interpretation and application of statistical principles. Reflective journals facilitate students in expressing their learning experiences, enabling educators to discern areas of student difficulty or proficiency.

Peer assessments are essential for assessing learning outcomes. Through peer assessments, students can offer feedback on each other's performance, promoting a collaborative learning atmosphere (Yin et al., 2022). For example, in a fitness initiative, students might evaluate their classmates' proficiency in calculating goal heart rates and formulating successful workout regimens. This technique enhances their comprehension while promoting critical thinking and constructive feedback.

Integrating feedback loops is essential for ongoing enhancement in student learning. Educators must deliver prompt and detailed feedback to students post-assessment, emphasizing strengths and opportunities for improvement (Wang et al. 2025). For instance, following the observation of a group exercise, a teacher may offer comments regarding the pupils' use of mathematical principles to improve their performance. This feedback must be actionable, providing students with guidance on enhancing their performance in subsequent tasks.

Furthermore, facilitating self-assessment opportunities enables students to assume responsibility for their learning. Through self-reflection on their performance and the establishment of personal objectives, students can discern their strengths and areas for enhancement (Yadav, 2024). Subsequent to a fitness evaluation, students may measure their advancement in attaining particular fitness objectives, thereby cultivating a growth mentality.

In conclusion, evaluating learning outcomes in an integrated mathematics and physical education program necessitates varied approaches that assess both comprehension and proficiency. Through the utilization of performance-based assessments, formative assessments, peer evaluations, and feedback mechanisms, educators can establish a holistic assessment framework that fosters ongoing enhancement. This method not only improves student learning but also equips them to utilize mathematical concepts in practical physical scenarios, thereby cultivating a greater appreciation for the interrelation of these fields. Through efficient assessment strategies, educators can guarantee that students possess the requisite knowledge and skills for success in both academic and athletic pursuits.

FUTURE DIRECTIONS AND BEST PRACTICES

Trends in STEAM Education

As education evolves, STEAM (Science, Technology, Engineering, Arts, Mathematics) education is increasingly recognized as a framework that promotes interdisciplinary learning and critical thinking (Deák & Kumar, 2024). Emerging trends and technology in STEAM are transforming educators' methodologies in teaching and learning, especially regarding the combination of mathematics and physical education. This chapter examines these changes and underscores the changing role of educators in promoting multidisciplinary instruction.

A notable trend in STEAM education is the growing integration of technology to enrich learning experiences. Incorporating tools like virtual reality (VR) and augmented reality (AR) in educational settings is increasingly common, offering immersive experiences that captivate pupils in mathematical ideas and physical activities (Al-Ansi et al. 2023). For example, VR simulations enable students to investigate intricate geometric forms or participate in virtual athletics, facilitating their comprehension of mathematical concepts within a dynamic framework. These tools enhance interactivity in learning and accommodate various learning styles, ensuring meaningful participation for all students.

A notable developing trend is the focus on project-based learning (PBL) within the STEAM framework. Project-Based Learning promotes collaborative engagement among students to address real-world issues, synthesizing knowledge across various disciplines. In physical education, students may develop a fitness program that integrates statistical analysis of performance data, enabling them to utilize mathematical concepts while participating in physical activity (Chang & Zhang, 2022). This practical method cultivates critical thinking, problem-solving, and creativity, competencies vital for success in today's swiftly evolving environment.

The function of educators is likewise transforming in reaction to these trends. Educators are progressively assuming the role of facilitators of learning instead of conventional lecturers. This transition necessitates that educators embrace a more interdisciplinary methodology, prompting students to establish links among disciplines and utilize their knowledge in practical contexts (Harrison & Laco, 2022). Physical education instructors may partner with mathematics educators to provide integrated classes that examine the mathematical principles in sports, such as computing angles for shooting or evaluating statistics related to player performance. This partnership enhances the educational experience and illustrates the significance of both courses in daily life.

Moreover, possibilities for professional development for educators are broadening to encompass training in interdisciplinary teaching methodologies. Educators are urged to pursue continuous education regarding current trends in STEAM education and to exchange best practices with colleagues (Mohamad Hasim et al. 2022). This cooperative professional environment promotes creativity and provides educators with the necessary resources to proficiently incorporate mathematics and physical education.

The future of STEAM education is defined by rising trends and technology that improve transdisciplinary learning. As instructors adopt these modifications, they are crucial in fostering significant links between mathematics and physical education. Through the use of project-based learning, the utilization of technology, and interdisciplinary collaboration, educators can cultivate stimulating learning environments that equip students for success in a progressively interconnected world. Through these initiatives, students will enhance their academic abilities while fostering a lasting passion for learning and discovery.

Best Practices for Integration

The integration of mathematics and physical education under the STEAM framework has demonstrated favorable outcomes in improving student engagement and comprehension (Chen et al., 2023). Successful case studies from diverse educational institutions and programs yield significant insights into optimal integration strategies, presenting advice for educators and curriculum creators aiming to adopt analogous methodologies.

A significant case study originates from a California middle school that established a curriculum named "Mathletics." This effort involved collaboration between mathematics educators and physical education instructors to develop classes that integrated mathematical concepts into physical activities (Armstrong, 2022). Students assessed their heart rates during various exercises and computed their target heart rates via mathematical methods. They moreover examined data regarding their fitness advancement over time, hence reinforcing statistical principles. This approach enhanced kids' mathematics abilities while cultivating a heightened awareness for physical fitness, leading to increased engagement in sports and other activities.

A notable instance is a New York high school that used a project-based learning methodology to investigate the physics and mathematics of sports (Makkonen et al. 2021). Students collaborated in teams to design and execute experiments pertaining to numerous sports, including the analysis of a basketball shot's trajectory and the calculation of the best angle for a soccer kick. They exhibited their findings to their colleagues, illustrating the application of mathematical principles to real-world athletic contexts. This practical experience not only enhanced students comprehension of mathematical topics but also fostered teamwork and collaboration.

Based on these successful case studies, some proposals can be made for educators and curriculum developers seeking to effectively integrate mathematics and physical education.

1. Collaborative Planning: Promote cooperation between mathematics and physical education instructors to develop interdisciplinary lessons that integrate principles from both disciplines. Collaborative planning sessions can generate novel concepts and facilitate resource sharing
2. Practical uses: Emphasize the practical uses of mathematical ideas in physical education. Utilize data from sports and fitness activities to facilitate meaningful analysis among students, including the calculation of averages, percentages, and statistical trends.
3. Project-Based Learning: Establish project-based learning initiatives that necessitate collaborative student efforts to address problems or perform experiments pertinent to sports and fitness. This methodology fosters critical thinking and enables students to utilize their knowledge in practical situations.
4. Utilization of Technology: Employ technology to augment educational experiences. Utilize instruments such as fitness trackers, data analysis applications, and interactive simulations to engage students and enhance data collecting.
5. Continuous Assessment and Feedback: Employ formative assessments that deliver continuous feedback to pupils. Promote self-assessment and peer evaluations to cultivate a reflective learning experience.
6. Professional Development: Offer professional development opportunities for educators to acquire knowledge of interdisciplinary teaching methodologies and optimal practices for combining mathematics and physical education.

In summary, effective case studies demonstrate the efficacy of merging mathematics and physical education via collaborative planning, practical applications, project-based learning, and technology. By adhering to these best practices, instructors can develop engaging and significant learning experiences that promote a deeper comprehension of both subjects. This integration boosts kids' academic abilities while fostering a lifetime appreciation for fitness and healthy living, ultimately equipping them for success in a connected world.

Call to Action

In concluding this examination of the integration of mathematics and physical education within the STEAM framework, it is crucial to contemplate the principal insights articulated throughout the book. The amalgamation of these disciplines not only augments students' comprehension of mathematical topics but also cultivates a comprehensive approach to learning that prioritizes creativity, critical thinking, and practical applications. By integrating mathematics with physical education, educators may cultivate stimulating learning environments that equip students for success in a progressively networked society (Singh et al. 2025).

A key revelation from this work is the substantial significance of mathematics in physical education. Mathematical principles are intricately woven into athletic performance, encompassing the analysis of performance data, the calculation of target heart rates, the comprehension of sports field geometry, and the mechanics of movement (Albantakis et al. 2023). By acknowledging this relationship, educators can assist students in valuing the significance of mathematics in their daily lives, therefore cultivating a favorable disposition towards both disciplines.

The significance of collaborative learning settings is paramount. Educators can foster a feeling of community in the classroom by promoting teamwork and communication through experiential projects and interdisciplinary teaching (Johler, 2022). This collaborative ethos not only boosts student involvement but also fosters critical abilities such as problem-solving, leadership, and adaptability—attributes required for success in the 21st century.

It is imperative for educators to use STEAM integration in their pedagogical approaches as we progress into the future. By implementing innovative tactics like project-based learning, utilizing technology, and integrating real-world applications, educators can cultivate engaging learning experiences that resonate with students (Smeplass, 2023). The case studies in this book illustrate that successful integration is not only feasible but also transformative, resulting in enhanced academic performance and a heightened appreciation for physical health.

We urge educators to pursue professional development opportunities centered on interdisciplinary teaching methodologies. Interdisciplinary collaboration among colleagues can facilitate the creation of stimulating classes that motivate students to investigate the links between mathematics and physical education (Bassachs et al. 2022). Moreover, educators must to promote curriculum modifications that emphasize STEAM integration, guaranteeing that future generations of students receive a comprehensive education.

In conclusion, the amalgamation of mathematics and physical education within the STEAM framework offers a distinctive chance to enhance the educational experience for kids. By adopting this methodology, educators can enable students to become lifelong learners who recognize the interrelation of knowledge and the significance of physical well-being. Let us collectively dedicate ourselves to cultivating a culture of creativity and collaboration inside our schools, thereby facilitating a more promising future for all kids.

CONCLUSION

Integrating mathematics and physical education within the STEAM framework offers a dynamic opportunity to transform student learning, engagement, and application of knowledge in real-world scenarios. This multidisciplinary method transitions from separate subject learning to a comprehensive educational experience that promotes critical thinking, creativity, and physical literacy. By integrating mathematical ideas like measurement, geometry, statistics, and probability into physical activities, educators may render abstract principles more concrete and significant for students.

The research and case studies demonstrate that this integration improves student motivation, engagement, and academic success, while also fostering physical well-being. Initiatives such as fitness data analysis, sports geometry challenges, and game strategy simulations exemplify the practical significance of mathematics and enable students to assume responsibility for their education. Collaborative learning spaces enhance the experience by fostering communication, teamwork, and peer instruction.

Furthermore, STEAM integration accommodates various learning styles and promotes inclusive education by providing many avenues for comprehending knowledge. It facilitates the integration of cognitive abilities with kinesthetic experiences, resulting in enhanced learning and prolonged retention. Educators serve a vital function as facilitators in the creation of interdisciplinary lessons and the promotion of inquiry-based learning.

In conclusion, integrating mathematics and physical education through STEAM is both innovative and crucial for equipping kids for a complex, linked world. By adopting this paradigm, schools can develop comprehensive learners who possess mathematical proficiency, engage in physical activity, and are equipped with the requisite 21st-century abilities to address future academic, personal, and professional problems.

REFERENCES

Al-Ansi, A. M., Jaboob, M., Garad, A., & Al-Ansi, A. (2023). Analyzing augmented reality (AR) and virtual reality (VR) recent development in education. [science-direct.com]. *Social Sciences & Humanities Open*, *8*(1), 100532. DOI: 10.1016/j.ssaho.2023.100532

Albantakis, L., Barbosa, L., Findlay, G., Grasso, M., Haun, A. M., Marshall, W., Mayner, W. G. P., Zaeemzadeh, A., Boly, M., Juel, B. E., Sasai, S., Fujii, K., David, I., Hendren, J., Lang, J. P., & Tononi, G. (2023). Integrated information theory (IIT) 4.0: Formulating the properties of phenomenal existence in physical terms. [plos.org]. *PLoS Computational Biology*, *19*(10), e1011465. DOI: 10.1371/journal.pcbi.1011465 PMID: 37847724

Allioui, H. & Mourdi, Y. (2023). Exploring the full potentials of IoT for better financial growth and stability: A comprehensive survey. Sensors. mdpi.com

Alvarez-Vargas, D., Lopez Perez, J. P., Bermudez, V. N., Beltrán-Grimm, S., Santana, E., Begolli, K., & Bustamante, A. S. (2023). Evidence-based designs for physically active and playful math learning. [HTML]. *Theory into Practice*, *62*(2), 166–180. DOI: 10.1080/00405841.2023.2202131

Armstrong, A. (2022). Technological practices of middle years students with mathematics learning disabilities. [HTML]. *Canadian Journal of Science, Mathematics and Technology Education = Revue Canadienne de l'Enseignement des Sciences, des Mathématiques et de la Technologie*, *22*(2), 376–391. DOI: 10.1007/s42330-022-00208-3

Ashford, M., Abraham, A., & Poolton, J. (2021). Understanding a player's decision-making process in team sports: a systematic review of empirical evidence. Sports. mdpi.com

Bass, M., Dompierre, K. A. B., & McAlister, M. (2023). Creating transformative interdisciplinary learning opportunities for college students. [sagepub.com]. *Journal of Transformative Education*, *21*(1), 118–137. DOI: 10.1177/15413446211066934

Bassachs, M., Serra, T., Bubnys, R., Cañabate, D., & Colomer, J. (2022). Multimodal approaches to math and physical education within cooperative learning to enhance social attitudes. [mdpi.com]. *Sustainability (Basel)*, *14*(24), 16961. DOI: 10.3390/su142416961

Baumer, B. S. & Matthews, G. J. (2023). Big ideas in sports analytics and statistical tools for their investigation. Wiley Interdisciplinary .... [PDF]

Bellido, D., García-García, C., Talluri, A., Lukaski, H. C., & García-Almeida, J. M. (2023). Future lines of research on phase angle: Strengths and limitations. [springer.com]. *Reviews in Endocrine & Metabolic Disorders*, *24*(3), 563–583. DOI: 10.1007/s11154-023-09803-7 PMID: 37043140

Borges, P. H., Ueda, L. S. C., de Souza, P. V., Binda, M. E. V., da Silva, J. F., Ribeiro, J., & Guilherme, J. (2024). Original actions performed by a beginner attacker modify defensive dispersion in small-sided soccer games. [nature.com]. *Scientific Reports*, *14*(1), 28489. DOI: 10.1038/s41598-024-79741-0 PMID: 39558083

Cao, F., Xiang, M., Chen, K., & Lei, M. (2022). Intelligent physical education teaching tracking system based on multimedia data analysis and artificial intelligence. Mobile Information Systems. wiley.com

Casado-Robles, C., Viciana, J., Guijarro-Romero, S., & Mayorga-Vega, D. (2022). Effects of consumer-wearable activity tracker-based programs on objectively measured daily physical activity and sedentary behavior among school-aged children: A systematic review and meta-analysis. [springer.com]. *Sports Medicine - Open*, *8*(1), 18. DOI: 10.1186/s40798-021-00407-6 PMID: 35099630

Chang, L. & Zhang, X. (2022). A Method of Improving College Students' Physical Fitness Test Based on Fuzzy Comprehensive Evaluation of Information Fusion. Advances in Multimedia. wiley.com

Chang-Tik, C. (2023). Collaborative spaces: Investigating the relationships between students' group-based learning and lecturers' approaches. [HTML]. *Educational Research*, *65*(4), 409–427. DOI: 10.1080/00131881.2023.2256747

Chaudhry, I. S., Sarwary, S. A. M., El Refae, G. A., & Chabchoub, H. (2023). Time to revisit existing student's performance evaluation approach in higher education sector in a new era of ChatGPT—A case study. [tandfonline.com]. *Cogent Education*, *10*(1), 2210461. DOI: 10.1080/2331186X.2023.2210461

Chen, H., Rao, F., Chen, R., & Lin, Z. (2023). Teaching STEAM in the shaolin staff program: ways to stimulate student engagement in learning. Frontiers in Psychology. frontiersin.org

Christensen, J., Ekelund, N., Melin, M., & Widén, P. (2021). The beautiful risk of collaborative and interdisciplinary research. A challenging collaborative and critical approach toward sustainable learning processes in academic .... Sustainability. mdpi.com

Damaševičius, R., & Zailskaitė-Jakštė, L. (2023, November). From STEAM to STREAM: Integrating Research as a Part of STEAM Education. In International Conference on New Media Pedagogy (pp. 318-335). Cham: Springer Nature Switzerland. [HTML]

Deák, C. & Kumar, B. (2024). A systematic review of STEAM education's role in nurturing digital competencies for sustainable innovations. Education Sciences. mdpi.com

Du, M., & Yuan, X. (2021). A survey of competitive sports data visualization and visual analysis. [HTML]. *Journal of Visualization / the Visualization Society of Japan*, *24*(1), 47–67. DOI: 10.1007/s12650-020-00687-2

Exel, J. & Dabnichki, P. (2024). Precision sports science: what is next for data analytics for athlete performance and well-being optimization?. Applied Sciences. mdpi.com

Fang, F., Liu, S., Basak, A., Zhu, Q., Kiekintveld, C. D., & Kamhoua, C. A. (2021). Introduction to game theory. Game theory and machine learning for cyber security, 21-46. [HTML]

Furlong, L. A., Girginov, V., & McErlain-Naylor, S. (). Key Concepts in Sports Biomechanics. api.taylorfrancis.com. [HTML]

Gredin, N. V., Bishop, D. T., Williams, A. M., & Broadbent, D. P. (2023). The use of contextual priors and kinematic information during anticipation in sport: Toward a Bayesian integration framework. [tandfonline.com]. *International Review of Sport and Exercise Psychology*, *16*(1), 286–310. DOI: 10.1080/1750984X.2020.1855667

Guerrini, A., Ferri, G., Rocchi, S., Cirelli, M., Piña, V., & Grieszmann, A. (2023). Personalization@ scale in airlines: Combining the power of rich customer data, experiential learning, and revenue management. [springer.com]. *Journal of Revenue and Pricing Management*, *22*(2), 171–180. DOI: 10.1057/s41272-022-00404-8

Harrison, T. & Laco, D. (2022). Where's the character education in online higher education? Constructivism, virtue ethics and roles of online educators. E-Learning and Digital Media. sagepub.com

Herbert, C. (2022). Enhancing mental health, well-being and active lifestyles of university students by means of physical activity and exercise research programs. Frontiers in public health. frontiersin.org

Hughes, J., & Gallus, S. (). Inciting incident causes student concerns over safety on campus. nsuworks.nova.edu. nova.edu

Iuliano, E., Mazzilli, M., Zambelli, S., Macaluso, F., Raviolo, P., & Picerno, P. (2021). Satisfaction levels of sport sciences university students in online workshops for substituting practice-oriented activities during the COVID-19 lockdown. [mdpi.com]. *Education Sciences, 11*(10), 600. DOI: 10.3390/educsci11100600

Johler, M. (2022). Collaboration and communication in blended learning environments. Frontiers in Education. frontiersin.org

Juškevičienė, A., Stupurienė, G., & Jevsikova, T. (2021). Computational thinking development through physical computing activities in STEAM education. [HTML]. *Computer Applications in Engineering Education, 29*(1), 175–190. DOI: 10.1002/cae.22365

Kampakis, S. (2023). The limits of prediction (part b): Game theory, agent-based modeling and complexity (actions and reactions). In Predicting the Unknown: The History and Future of Data Science and Artificial Intelligence (pp. 183-208). Berkeley, CA: Apress. [HTML]

Khorana, A., Pareek, A., Ollivier, M., Madjarova, S. J., Kunze, K. N., Nwachukwu, B. U., Karlsson, J., Marigi, E. M., & Williams, R. J.III. (2023). Choosing the appropriate measure of central tendency: Mean, median, or mode? [HTML]. *Knee Surgery, Sports Traumatology, Arthroscopy : Official Journal of the ESSKA, 31*(1), 12–15. DOI: 10.1007/s00167-022-07204-y PMID: 36322179

Lee, H. S. & Lee, J. (2021). Applying artificial intelligence in physical education and future perspectives. Sustainability. mdpi.com

Li, M. (2024). Adapting legal education for the changing landscape of regional emerging economies: A dynamic framework for law majors. [HTML]. *Journal of the Knowledge Economy.*

MacKnight, C. (2021). Supporting critical thinking in interactive learning environments. The web in higher education. [HTML]

Makkonen, T., Tirri, K., & Lavonen, J. (2021). Engagement in learning physics through project-based learning: A case study of gifted Finnish upper-secondary-level students. [sagepub.com]. *Journal of Advanced Academics, 32*(4), 501–532. DOI: 10.1177/1932202X211018644

Mavilidi, M. F. & Vazou, S. (2021). Classroom-based physical activity and math performance: Integrated physical activity or not?. Acta paediatrica. wiley.com

Mendelson, B. J., Ebersole, K. T., Brau, S. D., & Ebersole, N. T. (2025). Exploration of Heart Rate Recovery After Maximal Treadmill and Three-Minute All-Out Shuttle Tests in Firefighters. Fire. mdpi.com

Mohamad Hasim, S., Rosli, R., Halim, L., Capraro, M. M., & Capraro, R. M. (2022). STEM professional development activities and their impact on teacher knowledge and instructional practices. [mdpi.com]. *Mathematics*, *10*(7), 1109. DOI: 10.3390/math10071109

Osaba, E., Villar-Rodriguez, E., Del Ser, J., Nebro, A. J., Molina, D., LaTorre, A., Suganthan, P. N., Coello Coello, C. A., & Herrera, F. (2021). A tutorial on the design, experimentation and application of metaheuristic algorithms to real-world optimization problems. [PDF]. *Swarm and Evolutionary Computation*, *64*, 100888. DOI: 10.1016/j.swevo.2021.100888

Ostojic, M., Winkler, P. W., Karlsson, J., Becker, R., & Prill, R. (2023). Minimal Clinically Important Difference: Don't just look at the "p-value". [springer.com]. *Knee Surgery, Sports Traumatology, Arthroscopy : Official Journal of the ESSKA*, *31*(10), 4077–4079. DOI: 10.1007/s00167-023-07512-x PMID: 37460662

Pakdemirli, M. (2025). Calculation of the number of players in a defence wall for free kick in football. [HTML]. *International Journal of Mathematical Education in Science and Technology*, •••, 1–10. DOI: 10.1080/0020739X.2025.2464555

Papastergiou, M., & Mastrogiannis, I. (2021). Design, development and evaluation of open interactive learning objects for secondary school physical education. [HTML]. *Education and Information Technologies*, *26*(3), 2981–3007. DOI: 10.1007/s10639-020-10390-2

Pashaie, S., Mohammadi, S., & Golmohammadi, H. (2024). Unlocking athlete potential: The evolution of coaching strategies through artificial intelligence. Proceedings of the Institution of Mechanical Engineers, Part P: Journal of Sports Engineering and Technology, 17543371241300889. [HTML]

Plakias, S., Tsatalas, T., Armatas, V., Tsaopoulos, D., & Giakas, G. (2024). Tactical situations and playing styles as key performance indicators in soccer. [mdpi.com]. *Journal of Functional Morphology and Kinesiology*, *9*(2), 88. DOI: 10.3390/jfmk9020088 PMID: 38804454

Pons, E., García-Calvo, T., Cos, F., Resta, R., Blanco, H., López del Campo, R., Díaz-García, J., & Pulido-González, J. J. (2021). Integrating video tracking and GPS to quantify accelerations and decelerations in elite soccer. [nature.com]. *Scientific Reports*, *11*(1), 18531. DOI: 10.1038/s41598-021-97903-2 PMID: 34535734

Qi, Y., Sajadi, S. M., Baghaei, S., Rezaei, R., & Li, W. (2024). Digital technologies in sports: Opportunities, challenges, and strategies for safeguarding athlete wellbeing and competitive integrity in the digital era. [HTML]. *Technology in Society*, *77*, 102496. DOI: 10.1016/j.techsoc.2024.102496

Qiu, Y., Guan, Y., & Liu, S. (2023). The analysis of infrared high-speed motion capture system on motion aesthetics of aerobics athletes under biomechanics analysis. Plos one. plos.org

Rainio, O., Teuho, J., & Klén, R. (2024). Evaluation metrics and statistical tests for machine learning. Scientific Reports. nature.com

Richards, K. A., Dauenhauer, B., Gaudreault, K., Jones, E. M., McMullen, J., Shiver, V. N., Wilson, W. J., & Wright, P. M. (2025). Intra-Institutional Collaborations to Promote Research and Scholarship: Examples from the Field. [HTML]. *International Journal of Kinesiology in Higher Education*, *9*(1), 58–74. DOI: 10.1080/24711616.2024.2430027

Rivadeneira, J. & Inga, E. (2023). Interactive peer instruction method applied to classroom environments considering a learning engineering approach to innovate the Teaching–Learning process. Education Sciences. mdpi.com

Sarlis, V. & Tjortjis, C. (2024). Sports analytics: data mining to uncover NBA player position, age, and injury impact on performance and economics. Information. mdpi.com

Schmidthaler, E., Schalk, M., Schmollmüller, M., Hinterplattner, S., Hörmann, C., Anđić, B., Rottenhofer, M., Lavicza, Z., & Sabitzer, B. (2023). The interdisciplinary implementation of poly-universe to promote computational thinking: Teaching examples from biological, physical, and digital education in Austrian secondary schools. [frontiersin.org]. *Frontiers in Psychology*, *14*, 1139884. DOI: 10.3389/fpsyg.2023.1139884 PMID: 37008848

Sheehan, W. B., Tribolet, R., Watsford, M. L., Novak, A. R., Rennie, M., & Fransen, J. (2022). Tactical analysis of individual and team behaviour in professional Australian football: Original investigation. [HTML]. *Science & Medicine in Football*, *6*(2), 172–180. DOI: 10.1080/24733938.2021.1923792 PMID: 35475736

Singh, T. M., Reddy, C. K. K., Murthy, B. R., Nag, A., & Doss, S. (2025). Ai and education: Bridging the gap to personalized, efficient, and accessible learning. In *Internet of Behavior-Based Computational Intelligence for Smart Education Systems* (pp. 131–160). IGI Global. [HTML]

Smeplass, E. (2023). Investigating adult learners' experiences from using slow reading as a pedagogical approach. International Journal of Educational Research. sciencedirect.com

Stanja, J., Gritz, W., Krugel, J., Hoppe, A., & Dannemann, S. (2023). Formative assessment strategies for students' conceptions—The potential of learning analytics. [wiley.com]. *British Journal of Educational Technology*, *54*(1), 58–75. DOI: 10.1111/bjet.13288

Taub, M., Banzon, A. M., Zhang, T., & Chen, Z. (2022). Tracking changes in students' online self-regulated learning behaviors and achievement goals using trace clustering and process mining. Frontiers in psychology. frontiersin.org

Thornhill-Miller, B., Camarda, A., Mercier, M., Burkhardt, J. M., Morisseau, T., Bourgeois-Bougrine, S., Vinchon, F., El Hayek, S., Augereau-Landais, M., Mourey, F., Feybesse, C., Sundquist, D., & Lubart, T. (2023). Creativity, critical thinking, communication, and collaboration: Assessment, certification, and promotion of 21st century skills for the future of work and education. [mdpi.com]. *Journal of Intelligence*, *11*(3), 54. DOI: 10.3390/jintelligence11030054 PMID: 36976147

Torres-Ronda, L., Beanland, E., Whitehead, S., Sweeting, A., & Clubb, J. (2022). Tracking systems in team sports: A narrative review of applications of the data and sport specific analysis. [springer.com]. *Sports Medicine - Open*, *8*(1), 15. DOI: 10.1186/s40798-022-00408-z PMID: 35076796

Uwamahoro, J., Ndihokubwayo, K., Ralph, M., & Ndayambaje, I. (2021). Physics students' conceptual understanding of geometric optics: Revisited analysis. [HTML]. *Journal of Science Education and Technology*, *30*(5), 706–718. DOI: 10.1007/s10956-021-09913-4

Wang, W. S., Lin, C. J., Lee, H. Y., Huang, Y. M., & Wu, T. T. (2025). Integrating feedback mechanisms and ChatGPT for VR-based experiential learning: Impacts on reflective thinking and Aiot physical hands-on tasks. [HTML]. *Interactive Learning Environments*, *33*(2), 1770–1787.

Ward, M., Passmore, M. A., Spencer, A., Hanson, H., & Lucas, T. (2023). The effect of surface geometry on the aerodynamic behaviour of a football. [springer.com]. *Sports Engineering*, *26*(1), 33. DOI: 10.1007/s12283-023-00409-5

Yadav, S. (2024). *Designing Effective E-Portfolios for Authentic Assessment: Encouraging Reflection and Promoting Student Ownership*. Cases on Authentic Assessment in Higher Education. [HTML] DOI: 10.4018/979-8-3693-1001-4.ch011

Yeadon, M. R. & Pain, M. T. G. (2023). Fifty years of performance-related sports biomechanics research. Journal of Biomechanics. sciencedirect.com

Yin, S., Chen, F., & Chang, H. (2022). Assessment as Learning: How Does Peer Assessment Function in Students' Learning?. Frontiers in psychology. frontiersin.org

Chapter 4

Designing for People:

Integrating Human-Centric Approaches in Technology Management

Meimoon Ibrahim
https://orcid.org/0000-0002-3549-6646
Universitas Gorontalo, Indonesia

Idrus Usu
Universitas Gorontalo, Kabupaten Gorontalo, Indonesia

Roydah Gani
Universitas Gorontalo, Indonesia

ABSTRACT

This chapter examines the incorporation of human-centric design concepts in technology management to improve user experience and foster creativity. It analyzes empathy, usability, and accessibility as fundamental components, underpinned by historical contexts, psychological insights, and user research. The chapter delineates a complete paradigm for technology design that prioritizes iterative prototyping, interdisciplinary collaboration, and ethical responsibility in alignment with user demands. It also addresses accessibility, data ethics, and AI bias, emphasizing the significance of inclusive and responsible design. Case studies and developing technologies, like AI, AR/VR, and IoT, demonstrate the operationalization of human-centric approaches. The chapter delineates techniques for cultivating a human-centered culture within enterprises, encompassing leadership involvement, training, and key performance indicators (KPIs). The chapter promotes sustainable and inclusive design principles in technological development by integrating innovation with usability and ethical norms.

DOI: 10.4018/979-8-3373-5786-7.ch004

UNDERSTANDING HUMAN-CENTRIC DESIGN

Definition and Principles of Human-Centric Design

Human-centric design prioritizes users' demands, preferences, and behaviors in the design process (Ystgaard et al., 2023). This methodology underscores the significance of developing products, services, and systems that are both functional and personally resonant with users. By emphasizing user experience (UX), designers may guarantee that their solutions are intuitive, engaging, and efficacious in addressing users' actual needs.

The significance of user experience is paramount. In a technologically saturated environment, the success of every product depends on its capacity to deliver a seamless and gratifying experience. An affirmative user experience cultivates client loyalty, improves brand reputation, and eventually propels corporate success (Shahid et al., 2024). In contrast, subpar user experiences may result in dissatisfaction, diminished usage, and adverse opinions of a brand. Consequently, the incorporation of human-centric design concepts is vital for developing technology that genuinely meets the needs of its users.

The fundamental concepts of human-centric design encompass empathy, usability, and accessibility (Ystgaard et al. 2023; Akhtar et al., 2024).

a. Empathy is fundamental to human-centered design. It entails comprehending the emotions, motivations, and obstacles encountered by consumers. Designers must engage deeply with users' settings, watching interactions and collecting insights to guide their design choices. Through the cultivation of empathy, designers can develop solutions that align with users and fulfill their particular requirements.
b. Usability denotes the simplicity with which users can engage with a product or service. An effective design reduces the learning curve and enables users to complete their duties easily. This principle underscores the significance of intuitive interfaces, unambiguous navigation, and responsive feedback. By prioritizing usability, designers can improve user pleasure and diminish the probability of errors or annoyance during interactions.
c. Accessibility guarantees that products and services are operable by those with diverse abilities and limitations. This principle promotes inclusive design methods that accommodate varied user groups, including individuals with visual, auditory, or cognitive disabilities. By emphasizing accessibility, designers develop solutions that are equitable and can be appreciated by a wider audience, so enhancing the user experience for everybody.

In conclusion, comprehending and implementing the tenets of human-centric design—empathy, usability, and accessibility—are essential for developing technology that adequately addresses user demands. By incorporating these concepts into the design process, organizations can stimulate innovation and improve the overall user experience, facilitating effective technology management.

Historical Context

The progression of design thinking has profoundly influenced the realm of human-centric design (Sreenivasan & Suresh, 2024). Originating in the mid-20th century, design thinking arose as a reaction to the increasing intricacy of technical systems and the necessity for a more user-centered methodology. Initially, design techniques predominantly focused on aesthetics and functionality, frequently overlooking the user experience. As technology progressed and customer expectations transformed, designers acknowledged the significance of comprehending consumers' demands, emotions, and behaviors.

During the 1960s, innovators like Herbert Simon and Donald Norman starting promoting a more methodical approach to design (Isaksson et al. 2023). Simon's notion of "design as a problem-solving process" established the foundation for incorporating user input into design methodologies. Norman further underscored the importance of usability, introducing the term "user-centered design" in the 1980s. This transition represented a crucial juncture in design thinking, as practitioners began to integrate user feedback and iterative testing into their methodologies.

The emergence of the digital era in the 1990s expedited the embrace of human-centric design concepts (Ystgaard et al. 2023). As technology became increasingly ubiquitous in daily life, firms acknowledged that customer pleasure directly influenced their performance. This insight resulted in the formation of design firms such as IDEO, which advocated for design thinking as a collaborative and iterative methodology. IDEO's contributions to the inaugural Apple computer and the creation of the Palm V smartphone illustrate the potential of human-centric design to yield new and user-friendly products.

Numerous case studies demonstrate the efficacy of human-centric design. A prominent instance is the reconfiguration of the OXO Good Grips culinary implements. Sam Farber, the creator, acknowledged that conventional culinary utensils frequently caused discomfort for individuals with arthritis (Patrick & Hollenbeck, 2021). Through user research and the inclusion of individuals with impairments in the design process, OXO developed a range of ergonomic equipment that addressed a wider demographic. This strategy enhanced usability and elevated OXO to a market leader, demonstrating the commercial potential of human-centric design.

The creation of the Nest Learning Thermostat presents another convincing point. The design team emphasized user experience by developing a gadget that adapted to user preferences over time, facilitating effortless temperature adjustments. Through user testing and feedback, Nest refined its product, yielding a device that was both useful and aesthetically appealing (Virvou, 2023). This achievement illustrated how comprehending customer requirements may yield unique solutions that appeal to consumers.

The historical backdrop of human-centric design illustrates a notable transition from conventional design methodologies to a more user-oriented paradigm. An analysis of the evolution of design thinking and exemplary case studies reveals that emphasizing user insights is crucial for devising effective and significant technological solutions. This foundation establishes the framework for using human-centric methodologies in technology management.

The Role of Psychology in Design

Psychology is essential in human-centric design, offering critical insights into user behavior and decision-making processes (Hong et al., 2024). By comprehending the psychological principles that dictate user interaction with technology, designers may develop more efficient and captivating experiences. Two primary areas of emphasis in this context are cognitive biases and user behavior, along with human factors and ergonomics.

Cognitive Biases and User Behavior

Cognitive biases are systematic deviations from normative or logical judgment that can profoundly affect user behavior (Korteling et al. 2023). Designers must recognize these biases to predict user interactions with their products. The anchoring effect transpires when individuals excessively depend on the initial piece of information they receive. In a digital interface, customers may be disproportionately swayed by the initial price presented for a product, so impacting their valuation of it.

A prevalent cognitive bias is confirmation bias, in which individuals preferentially accept information that corroborates their previous ideas. In design, this may result in difficulties in introducing novel concepts or functionalities that users could initially oppose (Shih et al. 2023). By comprehending these biases, designers can develop interfaces that direct users towards better informed choices, enhancing a more intuitive experience.

Designers can utilize cognitive biases to improve user engagement (Mele et al. 2021). The scarcity principle posits that individuals are more inclined to covet items viewed as restricted or exclusive. By integrating scarcity into marketing techniques or product availability, designers can generate a sense of urgency that compels user action.

Human Factors and Ergonomics

Human factors and ergonomics is a vital component of design psychology, concentrating on enhancing the connection between users and products (Hasanain, 2024). This domain investigates the impact of physical and cognitive characteristics on user performance and comfort. Utilizing ergonomic principles, designers can develop items that minimize strain and improve usability.

When constructing a computer workstation, factors such as desk height, chair design, and screen positioning are crucial for fostering proper posture and reducing discomfort. Ergonomically designed goods promote user pleasure and productivity by enabling users to work more efficiently without physical impediments.

Moreover, comprehending cognitive load—the mental effort necessary for information processing—is essential in design (Castro-Alonso et al. 2021). Excessively intricate interfaces can inundate users, resulting in dissatisfaction and disconnection. Designers can alleviate cognitive burden and enhance user experience by streamlining navigation, eliminating superfluous information, and offering explicit feedback.

The incorporation of psychology in human-centric design is essential for comprehending user behavior and developing effective solutions. By addressing cognitive biases and implementing human factors and ergonomics, designers can augment usability, elevate user pleasure, and eventually develop technology that resonates with individuals. This psychological basis is crucial for incorporating human-centric methodologies in technology management, guaranteeing that solutions authentically address user wants.

RESEARCH AND USER INSIGHTS

Conducting User Research

User research is a crucial phase in the human-centric design process, offering essential insights into user wants, preferences, and behaviors (Ystgaard et al. 2023). User research can be classified into two main methodologies: qualitative and quantitative. Each strategy fulfills specific functions and provides unique benefits, necessitating that designers comprehend when and how to employ them.

Qualitative vs. Quantitative Methods

Qualitative research emphasizes comprehending the fundamental motives, emotions, and attitudes of users (Song et al., 2023). This method aims to investigate the rationale underlying user behaviors, offering comprehensive, contextual insights that can guide design decisions. Qualitative research frequently utilizes techniques such as interviews, focus groups, and observational studies. Conducting in-depth interviews enables designers to interact with people personally, revealing their experiences, challenges, and aspirations. This methodology cultivates empathy and enables designers to develop solutions that profoundly connect with users.

Conversely, quantitative research prioritizes numerical data and statistical analysis. This strategy aims to address the "how many" and "how often" inquiries, offering quantifiable information that might corroborate theories or guide decision-making. Surveys and experiments are standard instruments employed in quantitative research (Uher, 2022). A designer may administer a survey to collect statistics on customer satisfaction levels or the frequency of feature utilization. This information can facilitate the identification of trends and patterns among a broader user demographic, enabling data-informed design decisions.

Tools for Gathering User Feedback

A variety of technologies and strategies can be utilized to collect user input efficiently. Surveys are a prevalent technique for gathering quantitative data. They may be disseminated online or in person, enabling designers to swiftly engage a broad audience (Kock et al., 2021). Surveys may encompass multiple-choice questions, Likert scales, and open-ended inquiries, offering an extensive perspective on user opinions and experiences.

Interviews are an essential instrument for qualitative research. Through one-on-one dialogues, designers can explore users' thoughts and emotions, acquiring information that surveys may not provide (Matysek, 2023). Interviews facilitate follow-up inquiries, permitting designers to investigate subjects more thoroughly.

Focus groups assemble a limited number of people to deliberate on their experiences and perspectives regarding a certain topic or product (Richard et al. 2021). This approach fosters participant engagement, frequently resulting in the creation of novel ideas and viewpoints. Focus groups offer designers a plenty of qualitative data, since members express their opinions in a collaborative environment.

In summary, performing user research is crucial for incorporating human-centric methodologies in technology management. Utilizing both qualitative and quantitative methodologies, designers can obtain extensive insights that guide their design choices. Employing instruments such as surveys, interviews, and focus groups allows teams to comprehensively grasp user requirements and develop solutions that authentically improve the user experience.

Analyzing User Needs and Pain Points

Assessing user requirements and challenges is an essential phase in the human-centered design methodology (Mirabdolah et al. 2023). It enables designers to get a profound comprehension of their users, guaranteeing that products and services are customized to fulfill actual needs. Two efficacious methodologies for this analysis are the development of user personas and the mapping of user journeys.

Creating User Personas

User personas are fabricated depictions of essential portions of the target audience, derived from authentic data and insights obtained through user research (Huynh et al. 2021). These personas embody the traits, motivations, objectives, and obstacles of various user types, enabling design teams to empathize with their audience and make informed design choices.

Designers initiate the development of effective user personas by gathering qualitative and quantitative data via interviews, surveys, and observations. This information discloses demographic characteristics, behavioral tendencies, and user inclinations (Wallwey & Kajfez, 2023). A persona for a fitness application may encompass characteristics such as age, fitness objectives, technology adeptness, and prevalent grievances with current solutions. Assigning names, backgrounds, and distinct objectives to these personas enables designers to personalize their user demographic, facilitating a more empathetic consideration of user demands during the design process.

User personas act as benchmarks for design choices, assisting teams in prioritizing features and functionalities that correspond with users' requirements (Moustafa, 2023). By considering these personalities, designers may develop solutions that resonate with their target audience, resulting in a more engaging and fulfilling user experience.

Mapping User Journeys

After establishing user personas, mapping user journeys becomes an essential subsequent step. A user journey map illustrates the stages a user undergoes to accomplish a certain objective when engaging with a product or service (Halb and

Seebacher 2021). This process emphasizes the user's experience at each phase, pinpointing critical touchpoints, emotions, and possible pain points throughout.

Designers initially delineate the particular situation or task that the user will engage in to construct a user journey map. They subsequently delineate each phase of the journey, specifying the user's actions, thoughts, and emotions at each level. This encompasses recognizing instances of pleasure, annoyance, or perplexity (Leyer & Schneider, 2021). A user journey for an e-commerce website may commence with product discovery, followed by site navigation, cart addition, and finalizing the purchase.

Through the examination of these touchpoints, design teams can identify opportunities for enhancement, guaranteeing that the product fulfills user requirements while delivering a good and engaging experience (Yin, 2024). User journey mapping facilitates the identification of innovation opportunities, enabling designers to examine enhancements to the user experience at pivotal interaction points.

In conclusion, assessing user requirements and challenges via the development of user personas and the mapping of user journeys is crucial for successful human-centered design. These strategies allow design teams to cultivate a deep comprehension of their users, guaranteeing that the end product is both functional and significant. By emphasizing user insights, firms may stimulate innovation and improve the overall user experience in technology management.

Iterative Design and Prototyping

Iterative design and prototyping are crucial elements of the human-centered design process, enabling designers to enhance their concepts and develop solutions that effectively address user requirements (Ystgaard et al. 2023). This methodology prioritizes ongoing enhancement via feedback and testing, guaranteeing that the ultimate product is both operational and user-centric. Central to this process is the significance of quick prototyping and the diverse methodologies utilized to evaluate and enhance concepts.

Importance of Rapid Prototyping

Rapid prototyping is the swift creation of a functional model of a product or feature to visualize and evaluate concepts prior to comprehensive development (Kulkarni et al. 2022). This approach is essential in human-centric design since it allows designers to investigate many concepts and refine them depending on user input. Through the creation of low-fidelity prototypes—such as sketches, wireframes, or interactive mockups—designers can effectively evaluate their concepts and detect possible flaws early in the design process.

The principal benefit of fast prototyping is its capacity to enhance collaboration and communication among team members and stakeholders Votintseva, 20233). By showcasing actual prototypes, designers may stimulate debates and collect varied viewpoints, ultimately resulting in more informed design choices. Moreover, quick prototyping mitigates the risk of expensive modifications later in the development process by enabling teams to detect and resolve issues prior to allocating substantial resources.

Techniques for Testing and Refining Ideas

Various methodologies can be utilized to evaluate and enhance concepts during the iterative design process. A prevalent technique is usability testing, which entails monitoring actual users as they engage with a prototype (Geszten et al.). This testing may occur in a controlled setting or remotely, yielding useful insights on user navigation, pain point identification, and preference expression. Through the analysis of user interactions and the collection of feedback, designers can implement educated modifications to enhance usability.

A/B testing is another useful strategy that involves presenting users with two or more design modifications to ascertain which performs more effectively (Quin et al., 2024). This approach is very effective for enhancing particular elements, like as call-to-action buttons or layout designs. By assessing user engagement and conversion rates, designers can discern the most effective design components and incorporate them into the final product.

Moreover, design critiques might function as an essential instrument for enhancing concepts. Designers can obtain constructive feedback and varied perspectives by presenting prototypes to peers or stakeholders (Baldassarre et al. 2024). This collaborative method cultivates a culture of ongoing enhancement, prompting teams to question assumptions and investigate alternate solutions.

In summary, iterative design and prototyping are essential for incorporating human-centered methodologies in technology management. The significance of rapid prototyping resides in its capacity to promote collaboration, mitigate risks, and improve user happiness. Utilizing methodologies such as usability testing, A/B testing, and design critiques, designers can proficiently evaluate and enhance their concepts, guaranteeing that the end product satisfies user requirements while providing an engaging and significant experience.

INTEGRATING TECHNOLOGY AND DESIGN

The Intersection of Technology and Human-Centric Design

The convergence of technology and human-centered design is a vibrant domain where innovation aligns with functionality. The rapid evolution of technology significantly impacts user experiences across many platforms and devices (Shanmugasundaram & Tamilarasu, 2023). For designers, comprehending this relationship is essential for developing solutions that both utilize technical improvements and emphasize human wants and preferences.

How Technology Influences User Experience

Technology influences user experience in various aspects, including interface design and product functionality (Jeon, 2021). Technological advancements empower designers to develop more intuitive and interactive experiences. Touchscreens, voice recognition, and gesture controls have revolutionized user-device interactions, rendering them more intuitive and entertaining. The use of artificial intelligence (AI) and machine learning is crucial, as these technologies personalize user experiences by studying behaviors and preferences to provide customized content and recommendations.

Nonetheless, whereas technology can improve user experience, it may also increase complication. As functionalities advance, there exists a potential to inundate users with choices or to develop interfaces that are challenging to use (Rauschnabel et al. 2022). This highlights the significance of sustaining a user-centric emphasis during the design process. Designers must guarantee that technological breakthroughs augment usability instead of diminishing it, thereby crafting experiences that are both pleasurable and efficient.

Balancing Innovation with Usability

Achieving equilibrium between innovation and usability presents a significant problem in human-centric design. Although embracing new technologies and exploring innovative solutions is crucial, designers must prioritize user experience to prevent alienating their audience (Xin, 2025). This equilibrium can be attained by a deliberate design methodology that integrates user feedback and iterative evaluation.

An effective solution is to implement a minimalist design approach, concentrating on important features and functionalities that directly meet user needs (Elahi et al. 2023). By minimizing clutter and streamlining navigation, designers can develop interfaces that enhance usability while integrating innovative features. A mobile application may employ AI to provide tailored recommendations without inundating users with an overabundance of options.

Collaboration between designers and technologists is essential for attaining this equilibrium. By promoting an interdisciplinary approach, teams can guarantee that technological capabilities correspond with user requirements (Rapanta et al. 2021). Consistent communication and feedback mechanisms between design and development teams can facilitate the early identification of possible usability concerns, enabling prompt modifications.

The convergence of technology and human-centered design offers both prospects and obstacles. By comprehending the impact of technology on user experience and endeavoring to harmonize innovation with usability, designers can develop solutions that resonate with people and elevate their whole experience. This approach is crucial for incorporating human-centric techniques into technology management, resulting in products that are both innovative and user-friendly.

Designing for Accessibility

Accessibility design is a crucial component of human-centric design, guaranteeing that products and services are useable by individuals with varying skills and disabilities (Avsec et al. 2024). By adopting universal design principles and utilizing tools and technology for inclusive design, companies may develop solutions that address a broad user base, promoting equality and improving user experience.

Universal Design Principles

Universal design pertains to the development of products and places that are intrinsically accessible to all individuals, irrespective of age, aptitude, or status (Thunberg et al. 2022). The tenets of universal design underscore adaptability, clarity, and inclusiveness. A fundamental principle is equitable usage, which guarantees that design is accessible to all individuals, offering uniform ways of use for every user. This philosophy urges designers to account for diverse user needs from the beginning, rather than incorporating accessibility features subsequently.

A crucial principle is simplicity and simple usability. Designs must be comprehensible and user-friendly, reducing complexity for all individuals. This encompasses unambiguous navigation, direct directions, and uniform interface components (Macenski et al. 2022). The notion of error tolerance urges designers to mitigate hazards and negative outcomes of unintended acts, for as by offering undo choices or confirmation prompts.

Facilitating flexibility in usage is crucial, enabling people to select their preferred method of interaction with a product. For instance, offering various input methods—such as keyboard shortcuts, voice commands, or touch gestures—can cater to users with diverse preferences and capabilities.

Tools and Technologies for Inclusive Design

Designers can employ many tools and technologies to effectively execute universal design principles that foster diversity. Accessibility evaluation tools, such screen readers and color contrast analyzers, assist in identifying potential obstacles in digital interfaces (Kulal et al. 2024). These tools allow designers to evaluate the accessibility of their products for individuals with visual impairments or color blindness, ensuring that information is conveyed in a manner comprehensible to all.

Moreover, design software frequently incorporates elements that enhance accessibility. Adobe XD and Figma have accessibility plugins that automatically verify adherence to standards like the Web Content Accessibility Guidelines (WCAG). These tools assist designers in developing interfaces that adhere to legal standards and optimal accessibility practices.

Assistive technology are essential for improving accessibility. Assistive technologies, including voice recognition software, alternate input devices, and adaptable hardware, enable users with disabilities to engage with technology efficiently (Fernández-Batanero et al. 2022). Incorporating these technologies in the design process enables designers to produce products that are both accessible and improve the overall user experience.

In conclusion, accessible design is essential for incorporating human-centric methodologies in technology management. By using universal design principles and utilizing tools and technology for inclusive design, companies can develop solutions that are accessible to all individuals. This dedication to accessibility fosters equality and enhances the user experience, resulting in more successful and impactful products.

Ethical Considerations in Technology Management

As technology progressively infiltrates daily life, ethical questions have gained paramount significance in technology management (Kaddoura & Al Husseiny, 2023). Two essential domains necessitating focus are data privacy and user permission, with the mitigation of biases in artificial intelligence (AI) and algorithms. By emphasizing ethical standards, firms may guarantee that their human-centric design methodologies correspond with social norms and cultivate trust among users.

Data Privacy and User Consent

Data privacy constitutes a paramount ethical issue in technology management, especially as firms gather and scrutinize extensive volumes of user data (Renuka et al. 2025). Users anticipate that their personal information will be managed with responsibility and transparency. Companies must employ stringent data protection procedures to secure user information from unwanted access and breaches.

Securing informed user permission is essential for data privacy. Organizations must explicitly convey the data being gathered, its intended use, and the parties with whom it will be shared. This transparency enables consumers to make educated decisions regarding their data and cultivates confidence in the company (Mills, 2022). Establishing intuitive consent procedures, including explicit opt-in and opt-out alternatives, can augment user autonomy and guarantee that users feel at ease disclosing their information.

Furthermore, enterprises ought to implement a privacy-by-design strategy, embedding data protection measures into the development process from the beginning. This proactive method not only mitigates hazards but also complies with legislative obligations, such as the General Data Protection Regulation (GDPR) in Europe (Babu et al. 2021). By emphasizing data privacy and user consent, enterprises can cultivate a more ethical technological environment that honors user rights and improves user experience.

Addressing Biases in AI and Algorithms

A crucial ethical consideration in technology management is the existence of biases in artificial intelligence and algorithms. Machine learning systems are educated on historical data, which may unintentionally mirror societal prejudices and sustain inequities (Hanna et al. 2024). This may result in biased outcomes in domains such as recruitment, credit assessments, and policing.

Organizations must promote fairness and inclusion in their AI development processes to mitigate these biases (Hanna et al. 2024). This entails broadening training datasets to guarantee representation of a broad spectrum of populations and experiences. Furthermore, conducting regular audits of AI systems can assist in identifying and alleviating biases, ensuring that algorithms function fairly across diverse user groups.

Engagement with ethicists, social scientists, and impacted groups can significantly improve the ethical advancement of AI systems (Runcan et al. 2025). By incorporating multiple viewpoints, organizations can enhance their comprehension of the ramifications of their algorithms and devise solutions that foster equity and justice.

In conclusion, ethical issues in technology management are essential for the efficient integration of human-centric approaches. By emphasizing data protection and user consent, along with mitigating biases in AI and algorithms, firms may cultivate trust and establish a more equal technological environment. This dedication to ethical standards not only improves user experience but also corresponds with the overarching societal principles that support responsible technology development.

IMPLEMENTATION STRATEGIES

Building a Human-Centric Culture in Organizations

Establishing a human-centric culture inside enterprises is crucial for the effective implementation of human-centric methodologies in technology management (Balaji2025). This culture transformation necessitates dedication from leadership, efficient team dynamics, and continuous training and development in design thinking. By cultivating an environment that emphasizes user demands, firms can augment invention, promote cooperation, and ultimately provide more effective solutions.

Leadership and Team Dynamics

Leadership is essential in cultivating a human-centric culture. Leaders must promote the significance of user experience and endorse design thinking principles across the organization (Beagan, 2021). This entails not just conveying the significance of human-centric design but also exemplifying behaviors that emphasize user insights in decision-making processes. When executives actively participate in user research and exhibit a dedication to comprehending customer demands, they establish a standard for the entire organization.

Moreover, cultivating successful team relationships is crucial for establishing a human-centric culture. Interdisciplinary collaboration among design, development, marketing, and customer support teams fosters varied views and enhances a comprehensive grasp of user requirements (Sarkar, 2024). By dismantling silos and promoting transparent communication, firms can cultivate an environment where all team members participate in the design process, thereby augmenting creativity and problem-solving capabilities.

Establishing a secure environment for testing and feedback is essential. Teams ought to be permitted to express ideas, contest assumptions, and derive lessons from failures without the apprehension of penalties (Hunt et al. 2021). This psychological safety fosters innovation and enables teams to refine their designs according to authentic customer feedback.

Training and Development for Design Thinking

Integrating human-centric principles into the organizational framework necessitates continuous training and development in design thinking. Organizations ought to allocate resources towards workshops, seminars, and courses that furnish personnel with the requisite abilities and information to implement design thinking techniques proficiently (Todd & Stewart, 2023). The training sessions must encompass essential concepts including empathy mapping, user journey mapping, and fast prototyping, empowering employees to integrate user insights into their regular tasks.

Furthermore, firms might gain advantages by implementing mentorship programs that link seasoned design thinkers with novices in the field. This peer-to-peer learning cultivates a culture of perpetual enhancement and promotes the exchange of optimal practices among teams.

Integrating real-world case studies and practical projects into training programs can significantly augment learning (May et al. 2023). Enabling employees to confront real user difficulties facilitates the application of design thinking principles in a practical setting, thereby strengthening their comprehension and dedication to human-centric design.

In summary, cultivating a human-centric culture inside enterprises necessitates robust leadership, efficient team dynamics, and continuous training in design thinking. By emphasizing customer requirements and cultivating a collaborative atmosphere, organizations can augment their innovative capabilities and develop solutions that align with user preferences. This cultural transformation is crucial for effectively incorporating human-centric methodologies in technology management, resulting in enhanced user experiences and organizational success.

Collaborating Across Disciplines

Interdisciplinary collaboration is fundamental to effective human-centered design. In the current intricate technological environment, cross-functional teams that integrate various knowledge are crucial for developing creative solutions that effectively address customer needs (Harison, 2024). By promoting collaboration among diverse departments—such as design, engineering, marketing, and customer support—organizations may utilize a wide array of perspectives and expertise, thereby improving the user experience.

Importance of Cross-Functional Teams

Cross-functional teams are essential for numerous reasons. Initially, they promote a comprehensive grasp of customer requirements by synthesizing views from several fields of expertise. Designers can gain a deeper comprehension of technical limitations through close collaboration with engineers, while marketers can offer significant insights into consumer behavior and market dynamics (van et al. 2023). This collaborative method guarantees that all facets of a product—functionality, usability, and marketability—are addressed from the beginning.

Furthermore, interdisciplinary teamwork promotes innovation. Diverse team members contribute distinct perspectives and methodologies for problem-solving. This diversity of opinion can generate innovative ideas that might not have arisen in an isolated setting (Ungureanu et al. 2021). Moreover, collaborative teams may iterate swiftly, as they can promptly respond to feedback from many stakeholders, enhancing designs based on a thorough comprehension of user requirements.

Case Studies of Successful Collaboration

Numerous case studies demonstrate the efficacy of cross-functional collaboration in human-centric design. A prominent instance is the creation of the Airbnb platform. The company's success is attributable to its focus on collaboration among design, engineering, and customer support teams (Kopp et al. 2021). Airbnb consistently improves its platform to elevate user experience by incorporating feedback from consumers and customer care staff. This collaborative method has enabled the organization to swiftly discover pain points and execute solutions that align with user needs, hence enhancing customer satisfaction and loyalty.

The makeover of the Nike website presents another convincing case. Nike established cross-functional teams of web designers, developers, and marketing specialists to enhance the user-friendly nature of their online purchasing experience (De Silva & Taherdoost, 2025). Through user research and usability testing in partnership with several teams, Nike successfully improved navigation, optimized product presentations, and enhanced personalization features. The outcome was a notable rise in user engagement and sales, illustrating the efficacy of collaborative design initiatives.

In conclusion, interdisciplinary collaboration is crucial for incorporating human-centric methodologies in technology management. Cross-functional teams use varied knowledge, promoting creativity and assuring comprehensive attention to all facets of user experience. Case studies such as Airbnb and Nike illustrate the concrete advantages of collaboration, demonstrating how firms may develop solutions that authentically address user requirements. By emphasizing cross-functional collaboration, firms can augment their innovative capabilities and provide significant user experiences.

Measuring Success and Impact

Evaluating the efficacy and influence of human-centric design is crucial for enterprises seeking to confirm that their products and services authentically address customer requirements (Ystgaard et al. 2023). By defining key performance indicators (KPIs) and implementing continuous feedback mechanisms, companies can evaluate the efficacy of their design strategies and make informed enhancements over time.

Key Performance Indicators for Human-Centric Design

Key performance indicators (KPIs) are quantifiable metrics that illustrate the extent to which a company is fulfilling its goals. In human-centric design, key performance indicators should emphasize user pleasure, engagement, and overall experience (Atoum, 2023). Typical Key Performance Indicators (KPIs) encompass:

a. User Satisfaction Metrics: Surveys and feedback systems can be utilized to assess user satisfaction with a product or service. Metrics like Net Promoter Score (NPS) and Customer Satisfaction Score (CSAT) offer insights into consumer perceptions of their experience and their likelihood of recommending the product to others.
b. Usability Metrics: These metrics evaluate the ease with which people can engage with a product. Prevalent usability metrics encompass task success rate, time spent on task, and error rate. Through the analysis of these indicators, companies can pinpoint areas of user difficulty and implement requisite modifications to enhance usability.
c. Engagement Metrics: Monitoring user engagement enables firms to assess the efficacy of their products in resonating with users. Metrics including daily active users (DAU), session duration, and frequency of feature usage can yield insights into user behavior and preferences.
d. Conversion Rates: For products with defined objectives, like as e-commerce platforms, assessing conversion rates can reveal the efficacy of the design in directing users toward intended behaviors, such as finalizing a purchase or subscribing to a newsletter.

Continuous Feedback Loops and Improvement Strategies

Establishing ongoing feedback loops is essential for enhancing human-centric design. These loops allow businesses to collect continuous customer feedback and implement incremental enhancements based on practical usage (Dehbozorgi et al. 2024). Techniques for creating feedback loops encompass:

a. User Testing: Consistent usability testing sessions yield significant insights into user interactions with a product. Monitoring users as they interact with the interface facilitates the identification of challenges and opportunities for enhancement.
b. Surveys and Polls: Regular surveys can gather user feedback on particular features or general satisfaction levels. Organizations can utilize this feedback to prioritize improvements and resolve issues.
c. Analytics Tools: Employing analytics tools enables firms to monitor user behavior and engagement metrics in real time. This data can guide design decisions and underscore tendencies that may necessitate attention.
d. Stakeholder Feedback: Soliciting contributions from cross-functional teams and stakeholders can yield varied insights regarding user experience and design efficacy. Frequent design evaluations and cooperative ideation sessions can cultivate a culture of ongoing enhancement.

In conclusion, evaluating success and impact in human-centric design is crucial for firms aiming to improve user experience. Organizations can evaluate the efficacy of their design methods and adopt informed enhancements by identifying key performance indicators and instituting ongoing feedback loops. This iterative method promotes innovation and guarantees that products and services fit with customer requirements, ultimately resulting in enhanced happiness and success in technology management.

FUTURE TRENDS IN HUMAN-CENTRIC DESIGN

Emerging Technologies and Their Impact on Design

As technology advances, emerging advancements like artificial intelligence (AI), virtual reality (VR), augmented reality (AR), and the Internet of Things (IoT) are profoundly impacting human-centric design (Carayannis et al. 2022). These technologies not only improve user experience but also offer new potential for developing more intuitive and engaging interactions.

AI, VR, and AR in User Experience

Artificial intelligence is transforming user experience through personalized interactions and process automation. AI algorithms assess user behavior and preferences, facilitating customized content distribution and recommendations (Haleem et al. 2022). Streaming platforms such as Netflix employ artificial intelligence to recommend series and films according to consumers' viewing histories, thereby augmenting engagement and happiness. Moreover, AI-driven chatbots and virtual assistants offer immediate assistance, enhancing accessibility and responsiveness in customer service.

Virtual reality (VR) and augmented reality (AR) are revolutionizing user engagement with digital content (Ye & Li, 2022). Virtual reality immerses users in a completely replicated environment, offering a distinctive platform for activities including training simulations, virtual tours, and immersive gaming. This technology enables users to interact with knowledge in a very engaging way, cultivating profound emotional connections and improving educational results.

Augmented Reality (AR) superimposes digital information onto the physical world, thereby integrating physical and digital experiences. Applications like IKEA Place enable users to imagine the appearance of furniture in their homes prior to purchase (Nair et al. 2024). This talent not only improves decision-making but also diminishes the probability of buyer's remorse. By incorporating VR and AR into design, firms can develop more captivating, interactive, and tailored user experiences.

The Role of IoT in Creating Connected Experiences

The Internet of Things (IoT) is a disruptive technology that is redefining human-centric design. The Internet of Things (IoT) denotes a network of interconnected devices that communicate and exchange data with one another (Ystgaard et al., 2023). This connectedness facilitates effortless interactions between people and their surroundings, resulting in a more cohesive experience.

For instance, smart home gadgets like thermostats, lighting systems, and security apparatus can be managed remotely using mobile applications. This interconnectivity allows users to tailor their surroundings to their preferences, so improving convenience and comfort. Moreover, IoT devices can gather data on user behavior, yielding insights that guide subsequent design enhancements.

In healthcare, IoT devices facilitate real-time monitoring of patient conditions, allowing for proactive treatments and tailored care. Wearable gadgets, like fitness trackers, furnish consumers with essential feedback regarding their health, enabling them to make informed decisions about their well-being (Krizea et al. 2022).

In conclusion, developing technologies such as artificial intelligence, virtual reality, augmented reality, and the Internet of Things are profoundly influencing human-centric design by improving user experiences and fostering more interconnected interactions. As these technologies advance, designers must harness their potential to stimulate innovation while addressing user requirements. By incorporating these innovations into the design process, companies may develop solutions that are both functional and highly engaging, effectively addressing the varied needs of users. This progressive strategy is crucial for effective technology management in a progressively digital environment.

Sustainability and Ethical Design

Amidst global environmental difficulties, the significance of sustainability and ethical design has become more pronounced in human-centric design processes (Balaji, 2025). Designers and organizations are now tasked with developing solutions that improve user experience while also promoting a sustainable future. This chapter examines the principles of sustainable design and the essential importance of social responsibility in technology.

Designing for a Sustainable Future

Designing for sustainability entails the development of products, services, and systems that reduce environmental impact across their entire lifecycle (Valdivia et al. 2021). This methodology incorporates several tactics, such as utilizing sustainable resources, minimizing waste, and enhancing energy efficiency. For example, companies such as Patagonia have adopted sustainable practices by including recycled materials in their apparel and advocating for repair and reuse instead of fast fashion.

A proficient approach to sustainable design is the principle of circular design, which emphasizes the development of goods that are readily reusable, repairable, or recyclable (Aguiar et al. 2022). By prioritizing durability and flexibility in design, businesses can save waste and prolong the lifespan of their goods. Furniture businesses are progressively providing modular designs that enable buyers to modify or substitute components instead of disposing of full items. This not only advantages the environment but also improves consumer pleasure by offering customisable alternatives.

Furthermore, digital design can enhance sustainability by diminishing the necessity for tangible items (Mondejar et al. 2021). E-books and online courses offer alternatives to conventional printed materials, reducing resource use. By utilizing technology to develop virtual experiences, designers may minimize their ecological impact while providing important content to consumers.

The Importance of Social Responsibility in Technology

Social responsibility in technology highlights the ethical consequences of design decisions and their effects on society. As technology increasingly permeates daily life, designers must evaluate the impact of their products on diverse stakeholders, including consumers, communities, and the environment (McCampbell et al., 2022). This obligation transcends mere regulatory adherence; it encompasses the proactive advancement of equity, accessibility, and inclusivity.

Organizations that emphasize ethical design methods guarantee that their goods are accessible to those with impairments. This dedication not only satisfies regulatory requirements but also improves the overall user experience by making technology accessible to a wider audience. Corporations like as Microsoft have achieved considerable advancements in this domain by integrating accessibility elements into their offerings and proactively soliciting feedback from varied user demographics.

Furthermore, social responsibility in technology includes data ethics, especially in relation to user privacy and security. Organizations must emphasize transparency and user permission in their data gathering activities to cultivate trust and accountability (Cheng et al., 2024). By implementing ethical data practices, firms can exhibit their dedication to user rights and responsible technology governance.

In summary, sustainability and ethical design are essential factors for the future of human-centered design. By prioritizing sustainable solutions and adopting social responsibility, corporations may enhance planetary health and promote societal equity. This comprehensive approach not only improves user experience but also corresponds with the increasing demand for responsible practices in technology management, ensuring that design benefits both individuals and the environment.

Preparing for the Next Generation of Users

As the technology landscape evolves, designers must plan for the upcoming generation of consumers, especially Generation Z (Gen Z) and future cohorts (Pichler et al., 2021). Comprehending the distinct traits and inclinations of these people is crucial for formulating effective design methods that address their changing expectations and behaviors.

Understanding Gen Z and Beyond

Generation Z, generally characterized as individuals born between the mid-1990s to the early 2010s, is the inaugural generation to have the internet and digital technology as a ubiquitous aspect of their existence (Zaka & Al Juboori, 2023). This group is defined by their technological proficiency, heightened social awareness, and expectation of authenticity. They prioritize experiences over tangible goods and are more inclined to interact with brands that reflect their values.

Furthermore, Generation Z is significantly swayed by social media and peer endorsements. Users anticipate flawless digital experiences and promptly forsake sites that fail to satisfy their requirements or deliver captivating interactions (Sun & Xing, 2022). This generation stresses inclusivity and diversity, seeking products and services that align with their ideals and the surrounding world.

Adapting Design Strategies for Evolving User Expectations

Organizations must modify their design strategies to meet the expectations of Gen Z and future users for effective engagement. A fundamental strategy is to emphasize mobile-first design (Evanick, 2024). Given that Gen Z primarily engages with content via smartphones, it is imperative to optimize user interfaces for mobile devices. This entails guaranteeing rapid load times, user-friendly navigation, and aesthetically pleasing designs that appeal to younger demographics.

Integrating interactive and immersive experiences constitutes an additional effective method. Generation Z users are attracted to gamified features and interactive material that promote engagement (Sinha & Srivastava, 2022). By employing technologies like augmented reality (AR) and virtual reality (VR), designers may craft engaging experiences that captivate consumers and promote exploration.

Moreover, firms ought to prioritize authenticity and openness in their branding and communication efforts. Generation Z prioritizes products that demonstrate authenticity and social responsibility. By demonstrating their dedication to ethical standards, sustainability, and social issues, corporations can cultivate trust and loyalty among younger consumers (Walters, 2021). This may entail disseminating behind-the-scenes material, showcasing user-generated content, and participating in substantive dialogues on social media channels.

Furthermore, personalization is essential in fulfilling the demands of the next generation of users. By utilizing data analytics and artificial intelligence, firms can develop customized experiences that align with individual preferences (Theodorakopoulos and Theodoropoulou 2024). This include tailored recommendations, content, and user interfaces that adjust to the user's behavior and preferences.

In conclusion, preparing for the forthcoming generation of users necessitates a profound comprehension of their distinctive traits and anticipations. By modifying design techniques to emphasize mobile usability, interactivity, authenticity, and personalization, firms can successfully engage Generation Z and subsequent cohorts. This proactive strategy not only improves user experience but also enables enterprises to succeed in a constantly changing technological environment, assuring their relevance and responsiveness to future users' needs.

CONCLUSION

This chapter has shown the essential significance of incorporating human-centric design concepts into technology management. By prioritizing empathy, usability, and accessibility, designers may guarantee that technologies are not just effective but also significant, inclusive, and intuitive for various user demographics. Historical progress, from the initial promotion of design thinking to modern methodologies influenced by cognitive psychology and ergonomics, demonstrates a continual shift towards more user-centered strategies. The integration of comprehensive user research—both qualitative and quantitative—empowers design teams to acquire profound insights into user requirements and challenges, hence fostering the creation of adaptive and pertinent solutions.

Additionally, iterative prototyping and interdisciplinary cooperation are emphasized as essential ways to promote innovation and guarantee alignment between technical capabilities and human requirements. Addressing ethical factors, including data privacy and algorithmic bias, enhances the integrity of human-centric technology development, promoting trust and sustained involvement.

The discourse encompasses forward-looking viewpoints, particularly the influence of emerging technologies (AI, AR/VR, IoT) and sustainability in cultivating more flexible, fair, and responsible design ecosystems. Practical implementation strategies—such as fostering a human-centric organizational culture, promoting cross-functional collaboration, and utilizing KPI-driven assessments—ensure that these ideas are not only theoretical but executable.

In conclusion, human-centric design in technology management is not merely a process but a philosophy that prioritizes individuals at the heart of technical innovation. This strategy allows firms to develop technologies that are compassionate, ethical, and sustainably impactful in a swiftly changing digital environment.

REFERENCES

Aguiar, M. F., Mesa, J. A., Jugend, D., Pinheiro, M. A. P., & Fiorini, P. D. C. (2022). Circular product design: Strategies, challenges and relationships with new product development. [HTML]. *Management of Environmental Quality*, *33*(2), 300–329. DOI: 10.1108/MEQ-06-2021-0125

Akhtar, M. A. K., Kumar, M., & Nayyar, A. (2024). The Role of Human-Centered Design in Developing Explainable AI. In Towards Ethical and Socially Responsible Explainable AI: Challenges and Opportunities (pp. 99-126). Cham: Springer Nature Switzerland. [HTML] DOI: 10.1007/978-3-031-66489-2_4

Atoum, I. (2023). Measurement of key performance indicators of user experience based on software requirements. [HTML]. *Science of Computer Programming*, *226*, 102929. DOI: 10.1016/j.scico.2023.102929

Avsec, S., Jagiełło-Kowalczyk, M., Żabicka, A., Gil-Mastalerczyk, J., & Gawlak, A. (2024). Human-Centered Systems Thinking in Technology-Enhanced Sustainable and Inclusive Architectural Design. [mdpi.com]. *Sustainability (Basel)*, *16*(22), 9802. DOI: 10.3390/su16229802

Babu, M. S., Raj, K. B., & Devi, D. A. (2021). Data security and sensitive data protection using privacy by design technique. In *2nd EAI International Conference on Big Data Innovation for Sustainable Cognitive Computing: BDCC 2019* (pp. 177-189). Springer International Publishing. [HTML] DOI: 10.1007/978-3-030-47560-4_14

Balaji, K. (2025). Human-Centric Innovation: Building Sustainable Organizations for Industry 5.0. In Human-Centric, Sustainable, and Resilient Organizations in the Digital Age (pp. 101-124). IGI Global Scientific Publishing. [HTML]

Baldassarre, B., Calabretta, G., Karpen, I. O., Bocken, N., & Hultink, E. J. (2024). Responsible Design Thinking for Sustainable Development: Critical Literature Review, New Conceptual Framework, and Research Agenda. [springer.com]. *Journal of Business Ethics*, *195*(1), 25–46. DOI: 10.1007/s10551-023-05600-z PMID: 39507515

Beagan, J. R. (2021). A Phenomenological Study of How Transformational Leadership Is Influenced by the Human-Centered Design Approach in Developing Organizational Synergy. [HTML]

Carayannis, E. G., Dezi, L., Gregori, G., & Calo, E. (2022). Smart environments and techno-centric and human-centric innovations for Industry and Society 5.0: A quintuple helix innovation system view towards smart, sustainable, and inclusive solutions. [springer.com]. *Journal of the Knowledge Economy*, *13*(2), 926–955. DOI: 10.1007/s13132-021-00763-4 PMID: 40477337

Castro-Alonso, J. C., de Koning, B. B., Fiorella, L., & Paas, F. (2021). Five strategies for optimizing instructional materials: Instructor-and learner-managed cognitive load. [springer.com]. *Educational Psychology Review, 33*(4), 1379–1407. DOI: 10.1007/s10648-021-09606-9 PMID: 33716467

Cheng, L., Han, J., & Nasirov, J. (2024). Ethical considerations related to personal data collection and reuse: trust and transparency in language and speech technologies. International Journal of Legal Discourse. [HTML]

De Silva, C. S. B., & Taherdoost, H. (2025). *E-Business: Strategic Approaches to E-Business Transformation*. Mastering Innovation in Business. [HTML]

Dehbozorgi, M. H., Postell, J., Ward, D., Leardi, C., Sullivan, B. P., & Rossi, M. (2024). Human in the loop: Revolutionizing industry 5.0 with design thinking and systems thinking. [cambridge.org]. *Proceedings of the Design Society, 4*, 245–254. DOI: 10.1017/pds.2024.27

Elahi, M., Afolaranmi, S. O., Martinez Lastra, J. L., & Perez Garcia, J. A. (2023). A comprehensive literature review of the applications of AI techniques through the lifecycle of industrial equipment. [springer.com]. *Discover Artificial Intelligence, 3*(1), 43. DOI: 10.1007/s44163-023-00089-x

Evanick, D. J. (2024). Implementing Mobile-First Strategies in Online Education. *The Learning Ideas Conference*. [HTML]

Fernández-Batanero, J. M., Montenegro-Rueda, M., Fernández-Cerero, J., & García-Martínez, I. (2022). Assistive technology for the inclusion of students with disabilities: A systematic review. [springer.com]. *Educational Technology Research and Development, 70*(5), 1911–1930. DOI: 10.1007/s11423-022-10127-7

Geszten, D., Hámornik, B. P., & Hercegfi, K. (). Empirical study of Team Usability Testing: a laboratory experiment. Cognition. springer.com

Halb, F., & Seebacher, U. G. (2021). User experience and touchpoint management: A touchpoint performance management toolkit for the buyer journey. In *B2B Marketing: A Guidebook for the Classroom to the Boardroom* (pp. 285–315). Springer International Publishing. [HTML] DOI: 10.1007/978-3-030-54292-4_12

Haleem, A., Javaid, M., Qadri, M. A., Singh, R. P., & Suman, R. (2022). Artificial intelligence (AI) applications for marketing: A literature-based study. [sciencedirect.com]. *International Journal of Intelligent Networks, 3*, 119–132. DOI: 10.1016/j.ijin.2022.08.005

Hanna, M., Pantanowitz, L., Jackson, B., Palmer, O., Visweswaran, S., Pantanowitz, J., & Rashidi, H. (2024). Ethical and Bias considerations in artificial intelligence (AI)/machine learning. [sciencedirect.com]. *Modern Pathology*, •••, 100686. PMID: 39694331

Harison, E. (2024). Educating to Innovate: Fostering Innovation Through Interdisciplinary Collaboration Between Design and Engineering Students. In Preconceptions of Policies, Strategies, and Challenges in Education 5.0 (pp. 51-62). IGI Global. [HTML]

Hasanain, B. (2024). The role of ergonomic and human factors in sustainable manufacturing: A review. Machines. mdpi.com

Hong, S. W., Lee, J., & Lee, J. K. (2024). Human behaviour simulation for promoting usefulness and user-centric values in parametric design. [HTML]. *Automation in Construction*, *162*, 105386. DOI: 10.1016/j.autcon.2024.105386

Hunt, D. F., Bailey, J., Lennox, B. R., Crofts, M., & Vincent, C. (2021). Enhancing psychological safety in mental health services. [springer.com]. *International Journal of Mental Health Systems*, *15*(1), 1–18. DOI: 10.1186/s13033-021-00439-1 PMID: 33853658

Huynh, T., Madsen, A., McKagan, S., & Sayre, E. (2021). Building personas from phenomenography: A method for user-centered design in education. [emerald.com]. *Information and Learning Science*, *122*(11/12), 689–708. DOI: 10.1108/ILS-12-2020-0256

Isaksson, O., Wynn, D. C., & Eckert, C. (2023). Design perspectives, theories, and processes for engineering systems design. In *Handbook of engineering systems design* (pp. 1–47). Springer International Publishing. [HTML]

Jeon, J. E. (2021). The effects of user experience-based design innovativeness on user-metaverse platform channel relationships in South Korea. Journal of distribution science. koreascience.kr

Kaddoura, S. & Al Husseiny, F. (2023). The rising trend of Metaverse in education: Challenges, opportunities, and ethical considerations. PeerJ Computer Science. peerj.com

Kock, F., Berbekova, A., & Assaf, A. G. (2021). Understanding and managing the threat of common method bias: Detection, prevention and control. [HTML]. *Tourism Management*, *86*, 104330. DOI: 10.1016/j.tourman.2021.104330

Kopp, T., Baumgartner, M., & Kinkel, S. (2021). Success factors for introducing industrial human-robot interaction in practice: An empirically driven framework. [springer.com]. *International Journal of Advanced Manufacturing Technology, 112*(3-4), 685–704. DOI: 10.1007/s00170-020-06398-0

Korteling, J. E., Paradies, G. L., & Sassen-van Meer, J. P. (2023). Cognitive bias and how to improve sustainable decision making. [frontiersin.org]. *Frontiers in Psychology, 14*, 1129835. DOI: 10.3389/fpsyg.2023.1129835 PMID: 37026083

Krizea, M., Gialelis, J., Protopsaltis, G., Mountzouris, C., & Theodorou, G. (2022). Empowering people with a user-friendly wearable platform for unobtrusive monitoring of vital physiological parameters. [mdpi.com]. *Sensors (Basel), 22*(14), 5226. DOI: 10.3390/s22145226 PMID: 35890907

Kulal, A., Dinesh, S., Abhishek, N., & Anchan, A. (2024). Digital access and learning outcomes: A study of equity and inclusivity in distance education. [HTML]. *International Journal of Educational Management, 38*(5), 1391–1423. DOI: 10.1108/IJEM-03-2024-0166

Kulkarni, A. R., La Rocca, G., Veldhuis, L. L. M., & Eitelberg, G. (2022). Subscale flight test model design: Developments, challenges and opportunities. [sciencedirect.com]. *Progress in Aerospace Sciences, 130*, 100798. DOI: 10.1016/j.paerosci.2021.100798

Leyer, M., & Schneider, S. (2021). Decision augmentation and automation with artificial intelligence: Threat or opportunity for managers? [HTML]. *Business Horizons, 64*(5), 711–724. DOI: 10.1016/j.bushor.2021.02.026

Macenski, S., Foote, T., Gerkey, B., Lalancette, C., & Woodall, W. (2022). Robot operating system 2: Design, architecture, and uses in the wild. [science.org]. *Science Robotics, 7*(66), eabm6074. DOI: 10.1126/scirobotics.abm6074 PMID: 35544605

Matysek, A. (2023). The use of one-on-one interviews in library and information science: A scoping review. [HTML]. *Journal of Information Science*, 01655515231171088. DOI: 10.1177/01655515231171088

May, D., Terkowsky, C., Varney, V., & Boehringer, D. (2023). Between hands-on experiments and Cross Reality learning environments–contemporary educational approaches in instructional laboratories. [tandfonline.com]. *European Journal of Engineering Education, 48*(5), 783–801. DOI: 10.1080/03043797.2023.2248819

McCampbell, M., Schumann, C., & Klerkx, L. (2022). Good intentions in complex realities: Challenges for designing responsibly in digital agriculture in low-income countries. Sociologia Ruralis. wiley.com

Mele, C., Spena, T. R., Kaartemo, V., & Marzullo, M. L. (2021). Smart nudging: How cognitive technologies enable choice architectures for value co-creation. [sciencedirect.com]. *Journal of Business Research, 129*, 949–960. DOI: 10.1016/j.jbusres.2020.09.004

Mills, K. (2022). Consent and the Right to Privacy. Journal of Applied Philosophy. wiley.com

Mirabdolah, A., Alaeifard, M., & Marandi, A. (2023). User-Centered Design in HCl: Enhancing Usability and Interaction in Complex Systems. [ijahci.com]. *International Journal of Advanced Human Computer Interaction, 1*(1), 16–33.

Mondejar, M. E., Avtar, R., Diaz, H. L. B., Dubey, R. K., Esteban, J., Gómez-Morales, A., Hallam, B., Mbungu, N. T., Okolo, C. C., Prasad, K. A., She, Q., & Garcia-Segura, S. (2021). Digitalization to achieve sustainable development goals: Steps towards a Smart Green Planet. [sciencedirect.com]. *The Science of the Total Environment, 794*, 148539. DOI: 10.1016/j.scitotenv.2021.148539 PMID: 34323742

Moustafa, A. W. (2023). Integrating User Experience in Practices of Human-Centered Design Process in Product Design. International Design Journal. ekb.eg

Nair, A. J., Manohar, S., Mittal, A., & Chaudhry, R. (2024). Unleashing Digital Frontiers: Bridging Realities of Augmented Reality, Virtual Reality, and the Metaverse. In The Metaverse Dilemma: Challenges and Opportunities for Business and Society (pp. 85-112). Emerald Publishing Limited. [HTML]

Patrick, V. M., & Hollenbeck, C. R. (2021). Designing for all: Consumer response to inclusive design. [HTML]. *Journal of Consumer Psychology, 31*(2), 360–381. DOI: 10.1002/jcpy.1225

Pichler, S., Kohli, C., & Granitz, N. (2021). DITTO for Gen Z: A framework for leveraging the uniqueness of the new generation. Business horizons. sciencedirect.com

Quin, F., Weyns, D., Galster, M., & Silva, C. C. (2024). A/B testing: A systematic literature review. Journal of Systems and Software. sciencedirect.com

Rapanta, C., Botturi, L., Goodyear, P., Guàrdia, L., & Koole, M. (2021). Balancing technology, pedagogy and the new normal: Post-pandemic challenges for higher education. [springer.com]. *Postdigital Science and Education, 3*(3), 715–742. DOI: 10.1007/s42438-021-00249-1 PMID: 40477266

Rauschnabel, P. A., Babin, B. J., tom Dieck, M. C., Krey, N., & Jung, T. (2022). What is augmented reality marketing? Its definition, complexity, and future. [HTML]. *Journal of Business Research, 142*, 1140–1150. DOI: 10.1016/j.jbusres.2021.12.084

Renuka, O., RadhaKrishnan, N., Priya, B. S., Jhansy, A., & Ezekiel, S. (2025). Data Privacy and Protection: Legal and Ethical Challenges. Emerging Threats and Countermeasures in Cybersecurity, 433-465. [HTML]

Richard, B., Sivo, S. A., Orlowski, M., Ford, R. C., Murphy, J., Boote, D. N., & Witta, E. L. (2021). Qualitative research via focus groups: Will going online affect the diversity of your findings? [HTML]. *Cornell Hospitality Quarterly*, *62*(1), 32–45. DOI: 10.1177/1938965520967769

Runcan, R., Ha egan, V., Toderici, O., Croitoru, G., Gavrila-Ardelean, M., Cuc, L. D., Rad, D., Costin, A., & Dughi, T. (2025). Ethical AI in Social Sciences Research: Are We Gatekeepers or Revolutionaries? [mdpi.com]. *Societies (Basel, Switzerland)*, *15*(3), 62. DOI: 10.3390/soc15030062

Sarkar, S. B. (2024). *The Role of Leaders in Implementing Cross-Functional Business Processes: From Silos to Synergy*. BVIMSR Journal of Management Research. [HTML]

Shahid, R., Mozumder, M. A. S., Sweet, M. M. R., Hasan, M., Alam, M., Rahman, M. A., Prabha, M., Arif, M., Ahmed, M. P., & Islam, M. R. (2024). Predicting Customer Loyalty in the Airline Industry: A Machine Learning Approach Integrating Sentiment Analysis and User Experience. [comien.org]. *International Journal on Computational Engineering*, *1*(2), 50–54. DOI: 10.62527/comien.1.2.12

Shanmugasundaram, M. & Tamilarasu, A. (2023). The impact of digital technology, social media, and artificial intelligence on cognitive functions: a review. Frontiers in Cognition. frontiersin.org

Shih, H. P., Lai, K. H., & Cheng, T. C. E. (2023). Complied by belief consistency: The cognitive-information lens of user-generated persuasion. [mdpi.com]. *Journal of Theoretical and Applied Electronic Commerce Research*, *18*(1), 372–393. DOI: 10.3390/jtaer18010020

Sinha, M., & Srivastava, M. (2022). Augmented reality-enabled Instagram game filters: Key to engaging customers. [HTML]. *Journal of Promotion Management*, *28*(4), 467–486. DOI: 10.1080/10496491.2021.2008577

Song, H. G., Kim, Y. S., & Hwang, E. (2023). How attitude and para-social interaction influence purchase intentions of Mukbang users: A mixed-method study. Behavioral Sciences. mdpi.com

Sreenivasan, A. & Suresh, M. (2024). Design thinking and artificial intelligence: A systematic literature review exploring synergies. International Journal of Innovation Studies. sciencedirect.com

Sun, Y. & Xing, J. (2022). The impact of social media information sharing on the green purchase intention among generation Z. Sustainability. mdpi.com

Theodorakopoulos, L., & Theodoropoulou, A. (2024). Leveraging big data analytics for understanding consumer behavior in digital marketing: A systematic review. [wiley.com]. *Human Behavior and Emerging Technologies*, *2024*(1), 3641502. DOI: 10.1155/2024/3641502

Thunberg, G., Johnson, E., Bornman, J., Öhlén, J., & Nilsson, S. (2022). Being heard–Supporting person-centred communication in paediatric care using augmentative and alternative communication as universal design: A position paper. [wiley.com]. *Nursing Inquiry*, *29*(2), e12426. DOI: 10.1111/nin.12426 PMID: 34076320

Todd, E. M., & Stewart, P. (2023). Guidelines for training design thinking in organizations. [HTML]. *Industrial and Commercial Training*, *55*(3), 364–374. DOI: 10.1108/ICT-10-2022-0076

Uher, J. (2022). Functions of units, scales and quantitative data: Fundamental differences in numerical traceability between sciences. Quality & Quantity. springer.com

Ungureanu, P., Cochis, C., Bertolotti, F., Mattarelli, E., & Scapolan, A. C. (2021). Multiplex boundary work in innovation projects: The role of collaborative spaces for cross-functional and open innovation. [emerald.com]. *European Journal of Innovation Management*, *24*(3), 984–1010. DOI: 10.1108/EJIM-11-2019-0338

Valdivia, S., Backes, J. G., Traverso, M., Sonnemann, G., Cucurachi, S., Guinée, J. B., Schaubroeck, T., Finkbeiner, M., Leroy-Parmentier, N., Ugaya, C., Peña, C., Zamagni, A., Inaba, A., Amaral, M., Berger, M., Dvarioniene, J., Vakhitova, T., Benoit-Norris, C., Prox, M., & Goedkoop, M. (2021). Principles for the application of life cycle sustainability assessment. [springer.com]. *The International Journal of Life Cycle Assessment*, *26*(9), 1900–1905. DOI: 10.1007/s11367-021-01958-2

van den Adel, M. J., de Vries, T. A., & van Donk, D. P. (2023). Improving cross-functional teams' effectiveness during supply chain disruptions: The importance of information scouting and internal integration. [rug.nl]. *Supply Chain Management*, *28*(4), 773–786. DOI: 10.1108/SCM-06-2022-0243

Virvou, M. (2023). Artificial Intelligence and User Experience in reciprocity: Contributions and state of the art. Intelligent Decision Technologies. sagepub.com

Votintseva, A. (2023, July). Rapid Prototyping Platform for Multi-stakeholder Involvement in the Design of User Interaction. In International Conference on Human-Computer Interaction (pp. 302-313). Cham: Springer Nature Switzerland. [HTML] DOI: 10.1007/978-3-031-35596-7_19

Wallwey, C. & Kajfez, R. L. (2023). Quantitative research artifacts as qualitative data collection techniques in a mixed methods research study. Methods in Psychology. sciencedirect.com

Walters, P. (2021). Are generation Z ethical consumers? In *Generation Z Marketing and Management in Tourism and Hospitality: The Future of the Industry* (pp. 303–325). Springer International Publishing. [HTML] DOI: 10.1007/978-3-030-70695-1_12

Xin, P. (2025). Ethical and Philosophical Perspectives on Human-Computer Interaction in the Design of Intelligent Products: A Comprehensive Analysis. Cultura: International Journal of Philosophy of Culture and Axiology, 22(1). culturajournal.com

Ye, W. & Li, Y. (2022). Design and research of digital media art display based on virtual reality and augmented reality. Mobile Information Systems. wiley.com

Yin, C. C. (2024). Integrating or tailoring? Optimizing touchpoints for enhanced omnichannel customer experience. [HTML]. *Journal of Research in Interactive Marketing*. Advance online publication. DOI: 10.1108/JRIM-11-2023-0418

Ystgaard, K. F., Atzori, L., Palma, D., Heegaard, P. E., Bertheussen, L. E., Jensen, M. R., & De Moor, K. (2023). Review of the theory, principles, and design requirements of human-centric Internet of Things (IoT). [springer.com]. *Journal of Ambient Intelligence and Humanized Computing*, *14*(3), 2827–2859. DOI: 10.1007/s12652-023-04539-3

Zaka, K. & Al Juboori, M. M. S. (2023). The Impact of Generation-Z on International Branding Strategy: An Analysis of Startup Fashion Brands: What are the possible challenges and advantages faced by .... diva-portal.org

Chapter 5
Integrating Artificial Intelligence and Design Thinking:
Enhancing Students' Practical Skills

Stacy Grau
https://orcid.org/0000-0002-7150-3583
Texas Christian University, USA

Tracey Rockett
https://orcid.org/0000-0003-1035-9693
Texas Christian University, USA

ABSTRACT

Design thinking is a creative problem framework that has been instrumental in fostering innovation in a variety of contexts. Made popular by Stanford's D School and design consultancy IDEO, it is used and taught in K-12 as well as higher education. It is an experiential framework that is useful in the workplace. But it can be time consuming. AI tools and generative AI like Chat GPT and Gemini have started to transform the way that design thinking is practiced. Offering efficiency and deeper insights, is no doubt useful to aspects of the framework. But can technology augment such a uniquely human activity?

DOI: 10.4018/979-8-3373-5786-7.ch005

INTRODUCTION

Design thinking (DT), or human-centered design, is a creative problem-solving framework that emphasizes a deep understanding of people and their needs, followed by the development of human-centered solutions to those problems. While it has gained popularity in business over the past few decades, it has also found traction in other fields such as healthcare, social innovation, entrepreneurship, engineering, and education. Social innovators combine design thinking with additional frameworks to tackle wicked problems. Healthcare leaders employ design thinking to focus on patients when creating health interventions. Entrepreneurs utilize it to grasp customer needs and pain points, seeking opportunities to establish a business. Educators have embraced the principles of design thinking to foster more engaging learning environments. In recent years, courses, minors, and degrees in design thinking and/or human-centered design have emerged, highlighting the importance of the mindsets, frameworks, methods, and tools associated with design thinking (University of Texas, Stanford University, Northwestern University). This chapter examines the application of design thinking frameworks in undergraduate courses, where they play a significant role. These courses exist across various departments.

Artificial intelligence (AI) refers to machines designed to think and learn like humans. Although AI has existed for decades, the 2022 release of Chat GPT 3.5 accelerated its application across various contexts. Key technologies include machine learning (ML) for pattern recognition, natural language processing (NLP) for interpreting human language, and computer vision for data visualization. Early adopters of AI and design thinking have reported significant benefits, such as faster iteration cycles, more data-informed decision-making, and the ability to generate and test more solutions (IDEO.com). Integrating AI into design thinking frameworks enables teams to combine two complementary catalysts to enhance creativity and innovation.

Using design thinking and AI together has its pros and cons. Utilizing AI technology accelerates certain processes, which at times can be a significant constraint on innovation. AI can quickly analyze qualitative and quantitative data, uncovering patterns that humans may overlook. It enables efficient and effective testing of solutions. However, there exists a paradox in using technology to understand humans, which raises issues of data bias and ethics. Practitioners advocate for employing AI with humans rather than instead of humans.

As AI has transformed the education world, there is a growing tendency to revert to non-tech solutions for educating some students. Concerns about plagiarism and shortcutting learning are valid. However, AI has changed the way we approach education, making it crucial to teach students how to use AI responsibly, as it is an essential skill set for the workplace. That said, employers emphasize the need for more critical thinking, adaptability, and problem-solving skills from graduates

(Van Laar et al, 2020). Coupled with the rapid expansion of knowledge, especially in AI, educators (K-12 and higher education) must discover ways to cultivate these skills in students.

This chapter highlights the value of design thinking as a creative problem-solving framework and explores where and how AI can be effectively integrated into this framework to maintain a focus on humans while leveraging its technological advantages. Given that this is a new topic, there is currently limited academic literature published on it. Therefore, this chapter aims to guide faculty seeking ways to teach students how to use AI responsibly. Administrators can utilize this chapter to incorporate essential skills for students, particularly technology and creativity. Policymakers can begin to identify the necessary guardrails to ensure that AI augmentation in educational settings is feasible, ethical, and safe. Employers will recognize that students will become professionals in various organizations and contexts, inevitably using AI technology in the workplace. This is especially true in business, law, and creative fields. The chapter will outline the benefits and challenges of AI in design thinking specifically and include considerations for educators teaching design thinking to higher education students and professionals.

The chapter begins with a discussion of what students will need to be successful in future workplaces and how artificial intelligence and design thinking can be useful frameworks and tools. There is a section on design thinking, including the framework, mindsets, advantages, and disadvantages as well as educational use cases. The next section follows a similar format by introducing artificial intelligence, its advantages and disadvantages in general, and educational use cases. Next, current research examines the integration of AI and design thinking that includes a deeper dive into the key areas – research and discovery, insight development, ideation, and prototyping and testing – with a focus on how AI complements the framework. This includes use cases. And the chapter wraps up with a focus on student learning as well as best practices for faculty, administrators, and policymakers in education.

STUDENTS AND THE FUTURE

To succeed in today's competitive landscape, students must develop critical thinking along with technological mindsets and skill sets. Design thinking and AI are two areas with which students need to familiarize themselves and become skilled in utilizing to thrive in future jobs. Mindsets are often considered attitudes that guide an individual's thinking and behaviors. A design thinking mindset will be highly desirable for students as they enter the workforce since competitive organizations recognize that this mindset is essential for success (Martin, 2009). Characteristics of a design thinking mindset include a human-centered focus, an affinity for teamwork, the ability to use language as a tool, and a bias for adaptability (Owen, 2007). While these characteristics pertain to design thinking, it is evident that they possess broader utility for other crucial business skills such as leadership, innovation, teamwork, negotiations, and conflict management. More on this later.

A design thinking mindset and skills using design thinking tools can be taught in schools (Razzouk & Shute, 2012). For instance, schools use design thinking to foster creative confidence (Rauth et al., 2010) and enhance critical thinking along with problem-solving skills (Matthee & Turpin, 2019). Li and Zhan (2022) reviewed research on design thinking education in K-12 schools. They found that design thinking education has gained popularity over the last ten years. However, much of the incorporation of design thinking methods in K-12 has been within STEM classes and curricula. There is room for expansion into other disciplines. Additionally, universities and graduate schools, such as Stanford, MIT, and Northwestern University, are teaching design thinking not only to STEM students but also more broadly to those in the arts and business (Kurokawa, 2013). The teaching methods are varied, but the outcomes are consistent in that they train students to collaborate in teams to solve challenging problems using "designerly" ways of thinking (Kolko 2010, 2015).

In addition to the rise in design thinking education over the last decade, there has been a steep increase in the use of AI in education in recent years (especially since 2022 with the launch of ChatGPT). Educators use AI to help develop curricula, conduct assessments, and serve as personal learning assistants for students (Ejjami, 2024; Ng et al., 2025). Students utilize AI for studying, developing outlines, and assisting with both math and writing. However, more recently, there has been a shift towards teaching students how to use AI effectively, as it will likely become a core skill for work in the near future.

Teaching students to approach difficult problems with a human-centered focus and the power of AI will yield many benefits for all students. K-12 teachers are eager to expose kids to AI tools and let them experiment with these tools, quite literally, using things like Lego Robotics and gaming programs while introducing more complexity in understanding as they progress through the grades. The Association for the Advancement of Artificial Intelligence (AAAI) and the Computer Science Teachers Association (CSTA) partnered in 2018 to provide guidelines for teaching K-12 students about AI (Touretzky, 2019). They generated five key ideas that all kids should learn in school, starting with basic concepts about how AI works in K-2 grades and progressing to societal impacts and ethical issues in 9-12 grades (AI4K12). Higher education faculty are using AI and Design thinking in a variety of ways to provide this cultivation to students (Krebs & Rosenbaum, 2023).

While there has been some agreement on standards for K-12 students, at the university and adult education levels, there has been less consensus. The discussion continues regarding what should be included in teaching AI literacy (Laupichler et al., 2022). However, examples of AI education at the college level exist. For instance, educators teach college students how to use AI Agents and platforms for software development to solve problems collaboratively (Ng et al., 2023). Professional education institutions, such as medical schools, can train students to use AI to analyze large datasets to improve decision-making and treatment options (Paranjape et al., 2019). It remains to be seen if and how universities will organize and agree on principles for AI education. Some (like the University of Florida) have doubled down, while others are more cautious. Regardless, there seems to be little consensus on the role of AI and education to date.

Three competencies have been identified as particularly important for students to develop when using AI: AI knowledge, AI skills, and AI attitudes (Kim et al., 2021). The first two competencies focus on understanding the tools and how to use them, while the last, AI attitudes, intersects with the design thinking mindset. This is because the AI attitude is human-centered and posits that students should be taught about the social impact of AI and how to collaborate with AI (Kim et al., 2021). Adopting a human-centered approach to problem-solving while utilizing AI to assist with the steps of design thinking can unleash an entirely new way of addressing "wicked problems" and big data in organizations. As technology changes rapidly and as the world is faced with more problems, it is important to consider what and how to teach students – the future professionals of the world.

DESIGNING FOR HUMANS: USING A DESIGN THINKING FRAMEWORK

Design thinking is a framework that illustrates how to solve problems creatively. It is also referred to as human-centered design due to its focus on the human elements of problem-solving and has enjoyed increased attention for its flexibility across a broad spectrum of contexts. Design thinking is a human-centered approach to innovation that puts people at the heart of the design process (IDEO). It emerged in the mid-20th century when researchers like Herbert Simon argued that design is a distinct form of problem-solving (Johansson-Skoldberg et al., 2013). Other researchers contended that it aids in addressing ill-defined, complex problems. Early academic perspectives—known as designerly thinking—established design as a mode of thinking (Johansson-Skoldberg et al., 2013). In the 2000s, design thinking was popularized by IDEO and Stanford's d.school, characterizing the framework as a "human-centered approach to innovation" (Brown 2009).

There are various perspectives on design thinking, ranging from a set of methods and tools for innovation to a general theory of design to a cognitive style of innovators. First, some definitions center on the structure of the framework and the tools related to design thinking. Gruber et al. (2015) define it as "a human centered approach to innovation that puts the observation and discovery of often highly nuanced, even tacit, human needs right at the forefront of the innovation process," (pg. 2). Liedtka (2011, 2018) argues that design thinking includes a "series of iterative activities: an initial exploratory set of activities focused on data gathering to identify user needs, design criteria and problem definition, followed by a generation of ideas, which are then prototyped and tested" (pg. 3). Auernhammer and Roth (2021) found that throughout the evolution of the literature, design thinking had evolved as a process.

Second, design thinking can be defined by considering its impact. Tim Brown, former CEO of design consultancy IDEO, emphasizes that innovation exists at the intersection of technology (is this feasible to do?), business (is this a viable proposition?), and human value (is this usable and desirable by people?). He defines design thinking as "a human-centered approach to innovation that draws from the designers' toolkits to integrate the needs of people, the possibilities of technology, and the requirements for business success" (Brown 2009).

Third, definitions focus on the types of thinking needed for design thinking to be effective. Kolko (2010) states that "the designer's task is to produce an appropriate solution by organizing complexity and finding clarity in chaos through a process of patterned synthesis of aesthetic, cultural, technology trends and consumer and business needs" (p. 15). He extends this definition by stating that the process of synthesis was described as abductive thinking aimed at collecting, organizing, pruning, and filtering data in order to produce a potential solution. Abductive thinking is different from deductive and inductive reasoning, where the focus is on finding an effective solution (Kolko 2010; Kolko 2015; Elsbach & Stigliani 2018). Abductive thinking uses inferences to help designers see potential solutions to problems.

The common elements of design thinking include understanding user needs, ideation, prototyping, and testing those ideas (Auernhammer & Roth, 2021). Design thinking is acknowledged for its problem-framing and solving approach through an interdisciplinary lens (Micheli et al., 2019; Verganti et al., 2021). Taking all of this into consideration, design thinking can be defined as *a framework that translates creativity into innovation by focusing on human elements to understand users in a meaningful way through primarily ethnographic research, synthesizing that data, and identifying key insights that provide the foundation for understanding the right problem to solve. The framework includes tools to generate and select ideas, as well as to prototype and test those ideas to maximize success. Design thinkers should approach problem-solving with an open design mindset* (Grau, 2021). This section will discuss the elements of a design thinking framework, the mindsets important to design thinking, the pros and cons of using design thinking, and how design thinking is being used in education generally.

Design Thinking Frameworks

For design thinking, there are frameworks, methods, tools, and mindsets. While various frameworks exist (e.g., Stanford's D School, IDEO, IBM, Double Diamond), each one tends to encompass four common elements: research or discovery, insight development, ideation, and prototypes/tests. This chapter will focus on these elements to facilitate adaptation to many popular frameworks (such as the Double Diamond framework). Methods refer to the approaches that designers use (e.g., observational research), while tools are the specific instruments. Additionally, it is important to note that these frameworks are not meant to be linear – rather, they are intended to be flexible and adaptable to the challenge at hand. Design thinking is a people-first framework (Brown 2009).

The first element involves discovery or inquiry and problem framing. This marks the research phase of the framework, which consists of both primary and secondary research, emphasizing qualitative and quantitative methods. Primary data is gathered for a specific purpose and can be qualitative (for example, interviews, observations, focus groups) or quantitative (surveys). Secondary data is collected for a different purpose and assists in understanding the overall issues and contexts related to the design challenge or problem to be solved. This type of data includes reports, articles, and literature reviews, as well as internal documents from organizations that may be using design thinking to address a problem. Overall, the objective is to cast a wide net (e.g., use divergent thinking) to comprehend the problem at hand and the stakeholders involved.

Once data is collected, it is important to ensure clarity. The define phase aims to frame a problem statement by breaking down the findings and insights from the research (Liedtka 2015). This is where insight development occurs and typically involves a set of tools such as affinity mapping, personas, and journey maps. Teams use these tools to understand the problem that needs solving and the key user. This approach also helps to narrow or focus on the problem, sometimes leading to a reframe of the issue. The goal is to converge—to determine the key insights from the data that will provide a foundation for solution development.

Ideation moves from problems to solutions (Brown 2009). It plays a crucial role in design thinking, likely representing what most people envision when they think of it. Numerous approaches exist, and countless books and toolkits have been created on ideation, creativity, and brainstorming. Therefore, there is no singular method; the choice of technique should be customized to fit the design challenge. One key objective of ideation is to think broadly, focusing on both quantity and creativity. Generating hundreds of ideas to choose from often results in more effective solutions. Typically, the initial ideas are not the best ones. Additionally, embracing "crazy ideas" can be beneficial, as it is easier to refine wild concepts and potentially achieve a breakthrough. This process also involves selecting the best ideas to develop further. Again, many methods exist for this, but the aim is to generate multiple ideas for prototyping and testing.

A key value of design thinking is the prototype—a physical representation of ideas. This is important for ensuring that the team is aligned on the concepts and for providing something to share with others. The goal is to present this to users and gather feedback, which is then integrated into the concept. This process may involve several rounds of prototyping and iteration, but ultimately, it should lead to stronger ideas. Prototyping should be done quickly and efficiently. The mantra here is "iterate, iterate, iterate." Testing includes obtaining specific user feedback on the prototypes (and there are several strategies for doing this work). The aim is to understand whether new needs or insights emerge, which can sometimes send the teams back to earlier phases of the framework. Ultimately, testing should lead to stronger ideas that can be launched successfully. From there, it is important to consider how to implement and scale those ideas.

Design Thinking Mindsets

Beyond frameworks, methods, and tools, designer mindsets and guiding principles form important foundations for design thinking. Mindsets represent the attitudes with which designers approach problem-solving, and advocates argue that this is the most crucial aspect of practicing design thinking effectively. It serves as an essential precursor to design thinking frameworks. IDEO and Stanford's d.school have articulated several mindsets.

Given its foundation on human values, there is a focus on empathy and human-centeredness. Stanford calls this a "focus on human values." Empathy involves going beyond the surface to understand users more deeply, allowing them to perceive the world from multiple perspectives and keeping users at the center of the work. This is where the discovery work becomes particularly important—especially qualitative work with real people in an intentional manner (Stanford dschool).

Another guiding principle involves curiosity and embracing ambiguity. Many challenges are ill-defined problems, so accepting the ambiguity inherent in such issues is crucial. This requires patience and trust in the process. It also entails resisting the urge to rush toward solutions (a very human trait) and instead "fall in love with the problem." Designers should maintain open-mindedness and continue to ask questions throughout the design thinking process.

Designers need to have a bias toward action and embrace experimentation. A mantra is "prototype early and often," meaning there is no room for endless debates and over-analysis of ideas. Instead, create a prototype and bring it to the users for feedback. With a bias toward action, ideas can be discarded or developed quickly.

By embracing experimentation, failure is destigmatized as it is seen as useful for iteration.

Collaboration and diversity of thinking are also important foundational principles. Stanford's d.school espouses "radical collaboration," meaning this is about working with others who have different backgrounds, experiences, and points of view. Ideas can come from everywhere, and having a cross-disciplinary team increases the odds of success. Indeed, design thinking is often thought of as a common language to bridge the backgrounds of business, science, education, policy, engineering, and others. The team culture is important as it fosters psychological safety for all.

Having a growth mindset—one based on iterative improvement—is also helpful. Designers understand that the first ideas are rarely the right ones and that succeeding on the first try is also uncommon. Therefore, it often takes several iterations to make progress, which makes resilience an important trait. Designers recognize that the goal is to reach a solution.

Tom and David Kelley argue for the importance of "creative confidence," which is the freedom and courage to fail, take creative risks, and recognize that all ideas have some value (Kelley & Kelley 2013). These mindsets are crucial because design thinking frameworks are typically only as effective as the design thinkers and their approach to the problem. Design thinking is as much about how you think as it is about the steps, methods, or tools.

Design Thinking: The Pros and Cons

Design thinking has several advantages. First, as it starts with empathy for the user, design thinking addresses pain points, user needs, and contexts. Teams can then develop products, services, and experiences that meet these needs. Second, the framework and related methods and tools encourage "wild ideas," allowing teams to explore solutions and prototype ideas. Ideally, this helps unearth creative solutions. Third, design thinking relies on cognitive diversity and collaboration, enabling teams to frame and reframe challenges in unique ways. Lastly, because design thinking focuses on iterative learning, it allows teams to "fail faster to succeed sooner," meaning they can arrive at solutions more quickly and reliably.

Design thinking is not without its detractors. While it has a robust history in design literature, some believe it is undertheorized in management (Johansson-Skoldberg et al., 2013), touting design thinking as a cure-all for innovation. Others believe that it is "hype" - just a repackaging of old ideas into something new (Verganti et al., 2021). Critics feel that it also does not consider the difficulty of embedding innovation into organizational culture (Kimbell, 2011) and that design thinking is not universally applicable, especially for highly complex systems (Ackerman, 2023). Additionally, design thinking is challenging to measure, leading to difficulties in justifying the time and cost associated with it. It requires buy in from the top in order to be effective.

Design Thinking in Education

Design thinking has gained significant momentum in educational contexts. In K-12, schools both teach these skills to students and apply them to areas such as curriculum development and student support services. Design thinking skills are particularly useful for problem-based learning. The framework encourages students to deeply understand the problem before generating solutions. Faculty are also weaving design thinking into existing subjects like history, English, science, and math, transforming these subjects into more application-based exercises. Moreover, the emphasis on developing empathy is a particularly beneficial skill for younger students. In higher education contexts, there are courses and workshops dedicated to design thinking. Grau and Rockett (2022) identified several ways design thinking is used in classes, allowing students to solve complex problems. Design thinking can also serve as a helpful "bridge" between majors, allowing for a common language. Additionally, design thinking can be used to reimagine aspects of the student experience – from application to orientation to student support.

ARTIFICIAL INTELLIGENCE: AN OVERVIEW

Artificial Intelligence (AI) refers to the development of computer systems that can perform tasks typically requiring human intelligence, such as learning, problem-solving, pattern recognition, and decision-making. It is defined as the "ability of a system to identify, interpret, make inferences, and learn from data to achieve pre-determined organizational and societal goals" (Mikalef & Krogstie, 2020, p. 3). AI is broadly classified into two categories: narrow AI, which is designed for specific tasks (e.g., recommendation algorithms, chatbots, and image recognition), and general AI, a more theoretical form of AI that could perform any intellectual task a human can. Most AI applications today fall under narrow AI, driven by techniques like machine learning (ML), deep learning (DL), natural language processing (NLP), and computer vision. Machine learning enables systems to learn from experience and improve over time without explicit programming. Deep learning is a specialized approach to machine learning that uses artificial neural networks with several layers to process and learn from vast data sources. Natural language processing is a subfield of AI that allows computers to comprehend human language. Computer vision enables machines to interpret and understand visual data (Sreenivasan & Suresh 2024).

Generative AI, a subfield of AI, focuses on creating new content rather than merely analyzing existing data. Unlike traditional AI models that classify or predict based on given inputs, generative AI models, such as OpenAI's GPT, Google's Gemini, and Meta's LLaMA, generate human-like text, code, or even images from learned patterns. These models are trained on vast datasets using deep learning, particularly transformer architectures for text generation and diffusion models for image synthesis. Consequently, generative AI can create realistic artwork, compose music, generate human-like conversations, and assist with coding tasks. By leveraging deep learning models such as LLMs and diffusion models, generative AI aids in creative processes by generating design concepts, brainstorming solutions, and rapidly prototyping ideas. AI has already permeated various sectors and contexts, demonstrating its versatility and power in augmenting human insight. AI's ability to process immense amounts of data quickly and efficiently has made design thinking more effective and impactful in several cases. It equips people with powerful tools to extract insights, frame problems, and make decisions (Sreenivasa & Suresh 2024).

Artificial Intelligence: The Pros and Cons

Generative Artificial Intelligence, capable of creating new content such as text, images, audio, and code, presents a double-edged sword with numerous potential benefits and significant risks. Understanding these aspects is crucial as this technology becomes increasingly integrated into various industries and daily life. Generative AI is both exciting and terrifying; it can be a transformational partner as well as a perilous one for humans. Table 1 includes advantages and disadvantages inherent in generative AI at this point.

Table 1. advantages and disadvantages for generative AI

Advantages	Disadvantages
AI enhances creativity and innovation, serving as a powerful tool to inspire creativity and assist in generating novel ideas, designs, and content across various domains. AI increases efficiency by automating content generation and completing repetitive tasks; generative AI significantly boosts productivity and efficiency. This applies to areas such as writing reports, drafting emails, creating marketing materials, and generating code snippets, freeing up human efforts for more complex and strategic work. AI enables personalization at scale based on user data in various fields. AI accelerates research and development, particularly in medicine and material sciences. AI improves accessibility and understanding by summarizing and reframing complex documents and content, which is especially beneficial for individuals with language barriers and learning differences	there is a potential for misinformation and malicious use through deepfakes, misleading content, and the risks of spreading misinformation. There are ethical concerns and biases, given that AI models are trained on vast datasets that may contain biases which perpetuate stereotypes. AI still hallucinates, meaning it generates false information. There are issues with intellectual property and copyright, as determining who owns the output of a generative AI model trained on existing works presents a complex legal challenge. Generative AI can be exploited by malicious actors for various cyberattacks, including generating sophisticated phishing attempts, creating malicious code, and developing more advanced hacking tools. There is a lack of transparency and explainability in how Generative AI arrives at its outputs. In education, there are issues surrounding plagiarism, as students may shortcut critical thinking and writing skills. Developing, training, and running large-scale generative AI models require significant computational resources and energy consumption, raising concerns about environmental impact and accessibility for smaller organizations or individuals.

Several frameworks are being created and tested to mitigate some of the downsides. Most of these intentionally emphasize the role of humans first and AI second. Human-centered AI, for example, emphasizes that AI should not be developed solely based on technical capabilities but should be aligned with human and societal goals as well (Mhalanga 2022). This framework centers on ethics, fairness, accountability, beneficence, and justice. Efforts to increase explainability—ensuring the transparency and interpretability of AI—are also important. This focuses on understanding how and why an AI system arrives at a particular decision in order to build trust with humans (Kim et al, 2024).

AI in Education

Generative AI shows promise in a variety of educational contexts. Increasingly, AI is being used for personalized learning through adaptive learning platforms that meet students where they are in terms of their individualized learning needs. Students can access AI tutors like Khan Academy, which simulates one-on-one tutoring in any subject. Faculty have used AI to automate some grading and assessments, particularly for objective assessments as well as help generating lessons plans, student materials, and exercises. Administrators are using AI to streamline tasks like scheduling, communication, and managing student records. Administrators can also use AI's predictive analytics to identify students at risk which helps mitigate retention issues.

INTEGRATION: AI + DESIGN THINKING

AI, including generative AI and advanced analytics, is increasingly integrated into design thinking methodologies. Although it is relatively new and has little published research, there appears to be a growing incorporation of AI tools into innovation management. Design thinking emphasizes empathy, creativity, and iterative problem-solving—qualities that are considered inherently human. AI provides methods to enhance efficiency and effectiveness by offering more data-driven insights, pattern recognition, and rapid generative capabilities for ideation and prototyping, thereby augmenting the human team.

There is a great deal of hype among companies of all sizes regarding how to apply AI for innovation. Brem et al. (2021) found that companies are utilizing AI for innovation as well as for revising and renewing corporate processes. Kakatkar et al. (2020) highlight how companies from various industries incorporate AI into the four phases of the double diamond for need identification and idea generation. Integrating AI into design thinking can significantly enhance the innovation process. User research and sentiment analysis, data-driven problem recognition and prioritization, rapid and diverse idea generation, and rapid prototyping and testing are all areas where AI makes an impact. AI's analytical strength complements human creativity and insight, fostering more innovative solutions (Sreenivasan & Suresh, 2024). AI tools can analyze extensive datasets and transcripts, predict user behaviors, and uncover patterns, providing deeper user insights than manual research alone. Additionally, AI tools can automate routine or labor-intensive tasks, increasing data analysis efficiency and reducing the time required while also improving quality in many cases (Bouschery et al., 2023).

Using AI can enhance the human aspects of design thinking by reducing cognitive load. It helps eliminate routine, data-heavy, and time-consuming tasks, thereby freeing designers to concentrate on creative problem-solving. Some AI-assisted tools, such as voice assistants and adaptive interfaces, may provide greater accessibility and inclusion for certain users. AI also supports designers by facilitating ethical reflections that help identify and mitigate bias. Furthermore, some of these tools encourage greater real-time collaboration among stakeholders, ensuring broader participation in the design process (Tschepe 2024).

AI can be a powerful creative partner. It can maximize the quantity of ideas by generating numerous concepts and sketches, expanding the solution space beyond human imagination. Grilli and Pedota (2024) found that AI has a profound impact on creativity, particularly emphasizing convergent and divergent thinking. AI can contemplate "crazy" ideas more easily than humans in many cases. It can also facilitate faster and better prototyping and iteration, allowing for quicker access to final solutions. AI enables designers to generate a multitude of options to explore, including those that might not have been previously considered. All things considered, its ability to analyze data and eliminate routine tasks, along with its capacity to maximize iterative learning loops, makes AI powerful.

However, utilizing AI and design thinking presents challenges. One significant risk is data bias, which can lead to ethical concerns. AI systems learn from human-generated data and may inadvertently perpetuate human biases; if not addressed, they can reinforce stereotypes or overlook certain viewpoints. It is especially important to consider specific user types, such as patients or students, since incorporating their data into AI can be problematic (and possibly illegal). Strong data governance is essential.

Another challenge is the transparency of the data and the repeatability of the output. Given that it is generative, understanding the reasoning behind the analysis can be difficult, as well as whether it would yield consistent results if executed again or if a different tool is used. This may improve over time; for example, Open AI's Deep Research does have a running "conversation" about its analysis. Additionally, while hallucinations have improved, questions remain regarding the quality of the analysis—specifically, how much of it is accurate and how much is fabricated.

Even though AI has already been integrated into several research tools (e.g., Miro, Mural, NVivo, Google Optimize, MS Co-pilot, and Google Gemini), designers need to develop new skills to utilize AI tools and create effective prompts as the technology evolves. While AI can generate large volumes of ideas, there is a risk that it may lead to safe, predictable solutions since its ideas are based on past data. This lack of originality and "sameness" poses a threat. Additionally, there is concern that AI may diminish the importance of human knowledge and intuition, causing individuals to prioritize quantitative data over qualitative data and overlook cultural nuance. AI struggles with emotional intelligence and can misinterpret slang and sarcasm, which may lead to misaligned insights. Designers should not rely so heavily on automation and AI that they lose direct contact with users.

Designers may become overly reliant on AI while engaging in design thinking work. In an exploratory study, Polster et al (2024) found that designers experienced a decrease in social interaction with team members during their work. This limited human collaboration and diminished communication. They also found that designers exhibited a decline in creative energy and critical thinking, along with a reduced willingness to challenge AI-generated suggestions. Furthermore, designers felt a weaker connection to ideas generated by AI compared to those created solely by humans.

Context is important, and since AI is not human, there is a question of whether it can analyze human experiences without actually experiencing them. AI struggles with emotional intelligence, which is essential for design thinking. Ultimately, the question remains: can you create human-centered solutions without a human?

GUIDING PRINCIPLES FOR INTEGRATING AI AND DESIGN THINKING

As AI becomes more integrated into design thinking, it is important to establish ethical, practical, and human-first guidelines to ensure that AI augments rather than replaces human creativity and empathy. HPI d-school (Tschepe 2024) outlined several principles to consider as humans collaborate with machines on another level.

- *Data-driven support, human decision-making.* One of the benefits of using AI with design thinking is its ability to analyze large datasets to uncover insights. That said, it is important that humans collaborate to examine contexts and ethics. The ultimate decision-making should be in the hands of human designers who can interpret AI-driven results as part of a larger context. In other words, AI should not replace humans as analysts but rather partner with them, especially given the importance of intuition and ethical considerations.
- *Dynamic iteration through AI.* AI can assist human designers by generating, refining, testing, and iterating solutions more efficiently than ever. This enables rapid processing of information and inputs. This ability to iterate dynamically is essential for understanding user needs and contextual trends. AI should not be a one-time tool but rather provide continuous assistance in the iteration process. It will help teams refine their solutions.
- *Finding the right balance between AI and human skills is crucial.* While AI makes design more efficient, it may not be beneficial in all cases— in other

words, it might not be effective. AI should support human creativity, judgment, and decision-making without encouraging an over-reliance on technology. We should capitalize on the strengths of both humans and technology.

- *Continuous learning for both AI and humans is essential.* Human teams and AI systems evolve and adapt over time. For AI, this involves learning from new data to enhance performance. For humans, it entails staying updated on the evolving capabilities of AI.
- *Upholding ethical standards.* Integrating AI into design thinking must be guided by a robust ethical framework. AI should be developed to protect rights, promote fairness and identity, and mitigate bias while building trust in the system.
- *Transparency and trust in AI systems are essential.* This necessitates openness regarding how AI systems analyze data, generate suggestions, and integrate into broader processes. Ideally, designers should understand the reasoning behind the AI systems' analyses and solutions. There should be a clear explanation of the data.

Additionally, there should be a guiding principle ensuring that AI does not replace "humanity" and empathy in the process. AI should help facilitate empathy-driven design, not diminish human connection. AI should adapt to human context, not the other way around. Ideas should suggest divergent concepts instead of playing it safe. AI should challenge cognitive biases and introduce unexpected but valuable solutions. AI accelerates research and analysis, expands ideation, enhances personalization, while humans provide the heart, creativity, empathy, and humanity of design (Tschepe 2024).

PUTTING IT TOGETHER - DISCOVERY, INQUIRY, AND PROBLEM FRAMING

Discovery, inquiry, and problem framing constitute the research phase and can include both secondary and primary data that is qualitative and quantitative. Generally, teams delve deeply into discovery, accumulating pages of reports and transcripts, along with databases and surveys. The objective in most discovery efforts is to cast a wide net by utilizing divergent thinking skills. Therefore, in many challenges, it is difficult to manage this process without losing sight of the core issues and ensuring that the team focuses on the most relevant information. Tschepe (2024) argues that AI can assist teams in broadening perspectives by analyzing data, refining focus, facilitating user access and insights, and enhancing interview skills. By employing quantitative analysis and qualitative insights, organizations can develop more user-centered problems and solutions. AI has numerous applications in discovery, inquiry, and problem framing. This section outlines the ways that AI augments early elements of design thinking.

Using AI to Manage Research

Often, launching design thinking projects requires extensive research. This can be challenging to manage and organize. Consequently, several AI-powered tools are available to help manage and structure research effectively. For instance, tools like Open AI's Deep Research provide an in-depth exploration of a topic, drawing from various online sources including academic references. AI tools can summarize notes and transcriptions, edit research summaries, generate research reports and literature reviews, and lay a strong foundation to kickstart projects.

Data Mining and Analysis

One of the key advantages of AI is its analytical capability, enabling it to process vast amounts of data. AI accelerates the research phase by gathering, analyzing, and synthesizing extensive data more efficiently than humans alone. Specifically, AI can identify patterns in data available online. Data sources include social media, customer feedback, and behavioral data. AI-enabled tools can mine social media accounts to gain insights and analyze patterns of emotions and sentiments. It can examine online reviews from rating sites and assess customer feedback both internally and externally to gain deep insights into user needs. AI tools essentially scrape user-generated content, using natural language processing to identify patterns. These tools can also analyze text, images, videos, and audio to recognize patterns in user behavior across different environments. AI chatbots can even be used to collect primary data, offering a less expensive and, in many cases, more authentic way to gather direct information from people.

AI and Trend Forecast

AI tools can be used to forecast trends. They can identify historical data to predict emerging behavior using predictive analytics and machine learning. Using tools like Google Trends and Foresight AI is an easy way to do this. This provides a robust understanding of the overall context. This ability to forecast also helps determine the potential success of a design, reducing risk and guiding the development of ideas.

Preparing for Interviews and Ethnography

The objective is to understand user needs through interviews, observations, and immersion. AI can help create, revise, and test interview questions, as well as assist with interview practice. AI can be used to analyze successful interview strategies and suggest optimized questions. Prompts in ChatGPT and other tools (Gemini, Claude) can prove helpful, especially since interviewing is an area where students need more practice and confidence. AI aids in gathering data and taking notes (using AI tools on Zoom, for example), allowing a focus on the interviewee. It can also simulate interviews, offering teams the chance to practice their interviewing skills, especially when considering very specific user groups (such as vulnerable consumers or children).

Behavioral Analysis

There are several advanced AI applications that involve AI observing human behavior and interpreting facial expressions, voice tone, or even biometrics to infer emotional states during discovery and user testing. AI-driven computer vision detects human interactions in videos and images, providing a means to observe behavior (think Amazon Go stores). Other tools analyze text and categorize qualitative research.

Simulated User Research

There are situations where it is difficult to access users for discovery work. In these cases, AI can simulate user interactions and create detailed personas (more later) based on available data. This provides an alternative path to user insights—and should not be the norm—but can be useful in the early stages and when the team needs to understand a global or diverse user base (Tschepe 2024).

Pedagogical Needs

This is an area where good, solid research principles are important, as they will lay the foundation for students to gauge whether AI is making good suggestions. Educators should ensure that students create meaningful questions and conduct effective interviews while using tools to augment their data collection through note-taking and recording. This includes asking good questions and focusing on conducting productive interviews with humans. It also involves instruction on performing good observational studies. Other skills, such as active listening and empathy as they relate to qualitative research, are important skill sets. Students should also learn data literacy; they should be taught to recognize what constitutes good data and what does not. It all goes back to the old adage: junk in, junk out. Educators should also ensure that students are able to hone their critical thinking skills and bias awareness so they can challenge preconceptions and recognize assumptions.

PUTTING IT TOGETHER: INSIGHT DEVELOPMENT

Insight development, also known as define or synthesis, creates clarity from the collected data. The goal of insight development is to understand the key themes from research, unveiling needs, connections, and problems, and then generating inferences and insights. Organizing, processing, and analyzing data is crucial, and detecting underlying connections and patterns within the data is important and often takes time. This may involve refining or reframing the problem based on various evidence. This phase is significant as it is when problems are articulated, and the project's scope is defined. AI is beneficial in many ways during this phase. This section highlights how AI enhances clarity for insight discovery and problem reframing.

Making Sense of Data

Processing and structuring data sets, particularly large ones, is an area where AI excels. It can efficiently manage vast volumes of data, including interpreting unstructured or raw data and converting it into usable formats. Designers can achieve this more effectively by using AI tools. This analysis encompasses the detection of patterns, relationships, and themes that humans often overlook. AI employs data analytics to quantify user experiences, prioritizing needs and design challenges based on data-driven insights and assessments of market trends (www.sorenkaplan.com).

AI clustering algorithms can discover patterns in qualitative research, reducing the time needed for manual synthesis. These are similar to affinity maps and concept maps. For example, AI is integrated into robust platforms such as Mural and Miro that create these maps, and NVivo is a qualitative analysis platform that has successfully leveraged AI. Algorithms help uncover hidden needs. Once the data is analyzed, AI also aids designers as they develop actionable problem statements. Teams utilize insights to refine statements and set the stage for more targeted and effective ideation.

Personas, Empathy Maps and User Journey Maps

Personas, empathy maps, and user journey maps are essential tools for designers. Leveraging AI to analyze interview text and user interaction logs can facilitate a quicker production of first drafts of empathy maps, reducing the time spent on this task and allowing designers to focus on other areas. AI tools can also sift through quotes and data to identify pain points and challenges for persona creation and user journey maps. These outputs are potentially less biased since they are not influenced by a single designer's perspective. Designers then refine these tools further, adding human nuance and context. Some personas can be developed quickly using real-time data. Tools like Delve.ai create them from web traffic analytics, while teams at Adobe utilize AI-generated personas to enhance user journeys. Chat GPT is an effective tool for developing personas, generating insights, and refining problems. One of the most valuable aspects of AI is its ability to adapt personas and user journeys with a variety of real-time data (Intonics-innovation.com).

Problem Reframing and Refinement

AI can also support decision-making by predicting or highlighting which user needs are most critical. Some design teams use AI rating systems to prioritize insights. For instance, an algorithm might score user problems based on how frequently they are mentioned or how strongly they correlate with negative sentiment, helping the team focus on the right problem to solve. The result is a more precise and evidence-based insight development stage where the design challenge is clearly framed. The caveat is that designers must critically interpret AI outputs; the team should verify that automatically clustered insights truly make sense and ensure that the final problem statement resonates with the lived reality of users. When done right, AI-powered synthesis can sharpen this phase by combining the best of AI's analytical rigor and human judgment.

Detecting Bias in Research Analysis

Collecting primary data is time-consuming and costly. It can also be biased, depending on the methodology used. AI tools can help detect cognitive bias in problem framing, questions, and user responses. AI can analyze language and identify whether diverse perspectives have been included. AI tools—like IBM Open Fairness 360—can check for inherent bias in datasets and research conclusions. This detection also fosters more reflection on ethics and responsible innovation (Tschepe 2024).

Pedagogical Needs

During this phase, critical thinking and synthesis skills are key. The more experience students gain in practicing these tools, the better. This includes sensemaking, stakeholder analysis, systems thinking, and problem reframing. Educators also need to ensure that students don't rely on tools that could compromise their critical thinking skills. They should help students understand that design thinking and AI are collaborative efforts. While efficiency is important, they must always recognize that collaborating with humans, rather than replacing their work with AI, is the best (and only) approach. Educators should help students validate their findings with human insights, using AI as a supplement rather than a replacement for direct engagement with people. Finally, narrative structure and storytelling are important, as students learn to tell stories about problems and people using insights and data.

PUTTING IT TOGETHER: IDEATION

Ideation (known as brainstorming or develop) generates a wide range of innovative solutions. There are thousands of tools and processes available for ideation. However, this is an area where some people struggle, particularly when it comes to moving beyond the most common ideas. Eapen et al. (2024) identified several problems associated with ideation, including a lack of an efficient method for evaluating ideas, the difficulty domain experts have in accepting new ideas, the constraints of feasibility, and the challenges of synthesizing different ideas. They argued that generative AI could help mitigate these challenges.

The goal during ideation is to generate a wide range of ideas and creative solutions. AI can act as a creative partner by enhancing brainstorming and serving as a creative catalyst. AI helps with 'the blank page" by providing teams with a starting point. Notably, AI can increase both the quantity and quality of ideas. Traditional brainstorming often emphasizes the sheer volume of ideas, which requires time to sort and refine. AI tools, however, can be guided (via prompts or parameters) to focus on ideas that meet certain criteria—for instance, aligning with the needs of a persona or a business goal. Generative AI models encourage divergent thinking and provide more inspiration for visualizing abstract concepts. Tools like ChatGPT can be utilized through innovative prompting, and diffusion models like DALL-E or Midjourney can be employed for visual concepts.

Additionally, during this phase, teams must organize ideas into clusters and determine which ones are the strongest to bring forward as prototypes. AI also assists by creating a foundation for idea selection with clear and relevant criteria (Tschepe 2024).

Generating Ideas

Designers can leverage AI tools to brainstorm concepts, generate alternatives, or provoke inspiration. AI can significantly expand the ideation process by producing many ideas and a wider range of concepts based on data patterns, user behaviors, and trends. AI can suggest unique combinations and perspectives that may not be immediately apparent. By utilizing prompt engineering techniques, AI tools can propose new ideas, concepts, and analogies with tools like ChatGPT, Midjourney, and DALL-E.

Crafting the Prompt

Prompt engineering is the practice of crafting effective inputs (prompts) to obtain the best possible responses from AI models. It essentially involves how a designer directs generative AI tools like Gemini and ChatGPT. This practice includes structuring prompts in a way that maximizes clarity, specificity, and creativity while leveraging AI's capabilities for brainstorming. Generally, the more direction a designer provides, the better the output. This direction can include criteria such as personas, needs, user journeys, key criteria, and other useful information. See Table 2 for prompt structures.

Table 2. Prompt structures for ideation

Structure	Example
Open ended	Generate 10 creative ideas for solving the reading gap for third graders.
Role based	You are a social entrepreneur focused on sustainability. How would you create a zero waste shopping experience?
Divergent Thinking	If budget and technology were unlimited, how could we revolutionize urban transportation?
Analogical thinking	How would an ant colony design a traffic system to reduce congestion?
Constraint based	How can we provide clean drinking water in remote villages with only locally available materials?
Reversal and opposite thinking	What would an anti-customer service company look like? What lessons can we learn from that?
SCAMPER (substitute, combine, adapt, modify, put to another use, eliminate, reverse)	How could we adapt video game mechanics to make a fitness app more engaging?
Iterative and refinement	Rewrite this startup pitch to be more emotionally compelling.
Prompts chains	Using multiple steps for the prompt.

AI and Visual Tools

Visual generative models (like DALL E or Midjourney) can create concept sketches or storyboards from simple text descriptions, enabling teams to visualize ideas that might be difficult to draw by hand. These AI-generated ideas serve as a starting point for human designers to critique and build upon. Additionally, AI can act as a stimulus for further ideation. A generative language model (like ChatGPT) can quickly produce dozens of concept statements or even rough user stories in response to prompts.

Co-Creation with AI

AI-powered tools also assist with co-creation by providing real-time suggestions for ideas. These AI assistants are integrated into several applications like Figma and Canva. Using AI in the ideation process works best as a collaborative loop: designers should iteratively refine AI prompts and merge fragments of AI-generated ideas with their own expertise. AI might propose an unconventional approach that a human team can then recognize as promising and further develop. Likewise, designers can encourage AI to elaborate on a half-formed idea or explore variations, effectively using it as a brainstorming partner. The key benefit is an expanded creative horizon – AI can tap into countless examples and domains, inspiring cross-pollination of ideas. Still, designers must employ their judgment to filter out impractical suggestions (AI can sometimes generate ideas that are too far-fetched or not context-aware). When balanced correctly, generative AI can supercharge the ideation stage, yielding a rich pool of innovative concepts to consider.

Establishing Criteria

AI tools can assist by establishing criteria to help humans determine which ideas to pursue. They can facilitate objective, data-driven evaluations by analyzing past successes and failures, as well as current users. They provide valuable feedback on "must haves" and identify which ideas meet user needs and organizational objectives.

Pedagogical Needs

Creativity is one of the most important "human" aspects of what we do. Therefore, it is imperative that creativity—human creativity—never dies. Students should be introduced to a variety of ideation techniques and understand how and why they are used. AI should be a creative partner, not a creative outsource. Educators must ensure that students challenge and critically evaluate the output by using AI and other techniques. Additionally, educators should introduce students to various methods of selecting meaningful criteria to judge ideas. There are several ways to "vote" for ideas as well, and this should be a robust part of any student's design toolkit. In other words, AI cannot replace humans.

PUTTING IT TOGETHER: PROTOTYPING, TESTING, IMPLEMENTING, AND SCALING

Once teams have generated solutions, it is time to prototype and test them with users. This is commonly called "deliver" or "prototype and test," depending on the design thinking framework. This step includes creating and testing prototypes—tangible representations of solutions—testing them with users, and refining the designs based on feedback. This phase is based on a classic create, test, iterate cycle. This is an area where AI has a significant impact on efficiency and effectiveness. Generally, AI accelerates prototype creation, allowing teams to develop more solutions quickly and efficiently. AI also enables quick analysis of feedback data.

Rapid Prototyping with AI

In the Prototype stage, teams turn ideas into tangible forms—ranging from sketches and physical models to interactive designs—that can be tested. One way AI contributes is through the rapid generation of prototype content. Traditionally, creating an initial mock-up could take days. With AI, it takes minutes. For instance, AI coding assistants (like GitHub Copilot) can help developers generate interface code or algorithm logic more quickly. AI accelerates prototyping by automating parts of the build process and optimizing designs. It compensates for limited prototyping skills by providing intuitive and user-friendly tools for rapidly creating prototypes of solutions. AI can render changes, make suggestions, and predict the results of various prototype versions based on data. Tools like ChatGPT, Midjourney, Krea.ai, and Figma are useful here.

Prototype Refinement

Beyond generating prototypes quickly, AI can also enhance their quality and alignment with user needs through predictive analytics. Machine learning models can simulate how a design might perform. For example, given large datasets of user interactions, an AI could predict which design option may be more intuitive or which layout might lead to faster task completion. This helps teams make informed adjustments to prototypes before presenting them to users. Some AI tools can even conduct simulated usability tests – for instance, by computing visual salience to predict what users will notice first, or by generating synthetic users to navigate a workflow and identify obstacles. While these simulations don't replace real user testing, they serve as an early warning system for obvious usability issues.

Rapid Testing

Testing involves evaluating prototypes with users and gathering feedback to inform improvements. AI can make testing more thorough and insights-driven. One advantage is scalability. AI can automate the collection and analysis of feedback from a much larger group of users than a design team could manage manually. For example, instead of testing with 5-10 users in person, a team might deploy a prototype to hundreds of users online and use AI to analyze the resulting interaction data, survey responses, or behavioral metrics. AI algorithms excel at detecting patterns in this raw data—they can quickly pinpoint common pain points, performance issues, or usage trends by sifting through logs and feedback text. This results in a more comprehensive view of how a design performs under various conditions.

Another contribution is speed and rigor in analysis. Traditional usability testing requires manual note-taking and laborious review of recordings or feedback forms. AI tools (like sentiment analysis or NLP) can instantly categorize open-ended feedback into positive/negative sentiment or into themes (e.g., "navigation issue" or "feature request"), providing designers with an immediate read on what works and what doesn't. Similarly, AI-based analytics can monitor in-app user behavior (clicks, navigation, errors) and flag anomalies. For instance, an AI might detect that a specific step in a process is causing users to drop off more frequently, highlighting a UX problem to fix. These data-driven insights increase the objectivity of the testing phase, ensuring that design tweaks address actual user behavior patterns and not just the test moderator's interpretations.

AI can also facilitate advanced forms of testing that would be difficult to conduct manually. For example, AI-driven simulation can "stress test" a design by simulating thousands of usage scenarios or edge cases. A chatbot-based AI could act as a stand-in user to test conversational interfaces with endless queries. Computer vision AI can observe test session videos to measure participants' facial expressions or eye movements for signs of confusion or delight. By extending testing in these ways, AI helps reveal hidden flaws or usability issues that a small-scale manual test might miss. The net effect is a more rigorous testing stage with greater confidence in the results. Designers can iterate prototypes with clear evidence of what to improve. That said, human involvement remains crucial: interpreting test findings, asking follow-up questions, and understanding why users feel a certain way are tasks for which human empathy and expertise are still irreplaceable. AI provides the data and preliminary analysis, but designers must synthesize that into meaningful design decisions. When human-centered judgment guides the AI-driven testing insights, teams can iterate toward solutions that meet user needs.

Personalization

AI can also tailor solutions to different user segments dynamically based on preferences. Additionally, AI refines design through automated A/B testing, usability testing, and at a larger scale. This approach allows for more comprehensive data collection and analysis than what is possible manually. Furthermore, AI provides significant options to customize user experiences and identify friction points.

Pedagogical Needs

Using AI is highly effective for prototyping and testing; in fact, many current tools are augmented by AI to enhance their efficiency. That said, there is no substitute for some basic training on how to visualize ideas simply. This can involve simple sketching and graphing, as well as some fundamental graphic design experience, depending on the type of prototype. Educators should ensure that students incorporate hands-on prototyping and that they can refine their critical thinking skills by balancing AI-generated insights with human judgment. This includes strategic thinking and decision-making, usability and marketing testing, and iterative improvement. They also need to understand that failure presents an opportunity for learning. Students require information and experience with cross-collaboration, effective communication, and teamwork.

USE CASES

As mentioned earlier, organizations and companies have embraced AI quickly and enthusiastically in most cases. Again, the relationships between AI and design thinking should be considered complementary, where AI amplifies human capabilities rather than diminishing them. Global design consultancy IDEO, a leader in design thinking, is an early adopter of integrating AI. IDEO has been at the forefront of exploring and implementing AI into design thinking frameworks and tools. As a thought leader, IDEO has created a workshop series called AIxDesign Thinking, offered to professionals (www.ideou.org). IDEO has also employed AI in its product designs. IBM, also a leader in design thinking, developed the IBM Essentials Framework course and used it to reinvent its internal IT support systems. This is a solid example of a very large organization using AI and design thinking to innovate internal processes. Nike has utilized AI to analyze customer data to predict emerging trends and inform product design, while General Electric (GE) has extracted data from maintenance logs and customer feedback for product development.

And while AI and design thinking are still new, many universities have created workshops and courses aimed at building capacity. They recognize the value of this combination and understand the need to foster a more nuanced understanding of the ethical implications of AI. Many of the workshops are held in design centers at universities (e.g., Elon University, Carnegie Mellon, University of Illinois-Chicago, Coursera). These courses target executives, professionals, students, and other interested parties.

CONSIDERATIONS FOR STUDENT LEARNING

As AI becomes a valuable tool in design work, today's design, business, and engineering students need to develop new competencies and mindsets to effectively incorporate AI into human-centered design. AI literacy is key – students should understand, at a basic level, how AI algorithms work (especially machine learning and generative models), their capabilities, and where they have limitations. This doesn't mean every designer must become a data scientist, but being able to communicate with AI specialists, interpret AI outputs, and use AI-driven tools is increasingly important. For example, students should practice using tools for AI-based user research or generative brainstorming and learn how to ask the right questions of these tools (a skill often called prompt engineering). Knowing how to craft effective prompts for a text generator or adjust parameters in a data analysis tool will be as important in the AI-integrated design process.

Teams and team development are crucial to successful design thinking. In fact, a deep level of trust and psychological safety is essential. Psychological safety is the belief that a team is safe for interpersonal risk-taking—members can speak up, experiment, and fail without fear of judgment or punishment. AI can also be significant for teams. Utilizing AI enhances efficiency, creativity, decision-making, and collaboration. Teams need to recognize that over-reliance on AI can lead to lazy critical thinking, predictable ideas, misalignment of empathy and human nuance, and reduced in-depth discussions within the team. AI can serve as a team member—a co-collaborator in various phases of design thinking.

Students also need to hone their uniquely human skills, as those will complement AI rather than be replaced by it. Critical thinking is one such skill—when an AI provides an insight or suggestion, a student must critically evaluate its relevance and validity. Instead of accepting AI outputs at face value, students should learn to ask: Does this make sense in our context? Could there be bias here? Similarly, empathy and user advocacy remain essential. No matter how much data or automation is available, design thinking begins and ends with real human experiences. Students must learn to balance data with empathy, ensuring they continue to conduct user observations and interviews to ground truth in what the AI is telling them. Creativity and imagination are other human advantages—while generative AI can produce novel combinations, it's the human who provides vision and judgment to select the best ideas and give them meaning. Educational programs are thus emphasizing "human-AI collaboration" exercises, where students practice co-creating with AI tools while also diverging from AI suggestions when their own inspiration strikes.

Another important consideration is ethical awareness and responsibility. Students should be educated on the ethical implications of using AI in design. This includes understanding algorithmic bias and fairness, and how they can impact design outcomes, as well as issues of privacy, such as knowing when they can or cannot use user data to feed an AI. They should be aware of ethical design principles for AI systems, such as transparency and accountability, especially if they are designing AI-driven user experiences. Coursework might include case studies of AI ethics failures to emphasize why careful consideration is needed. It's also recommended that educators model responsible use of AI in the classroom. For instance, if a class uses ChatGPT to assist in idea generation, the instructor should clarify expectations, indicating that AI is a starting point, not the final answer, and encourage students to critique and improve upon AI outputs rather than copy them verbatim. By doing so, students learn that their role is to guide and supervise the AI's contributions, maintaining ownership of the design's human-centered vision.

Finally, adaptability and continuous learning are crucial attitudes. AI technologies evolve rapidly—the tools popular today might be outdated in a few years, possibly months. Students need to become comfortable with learning new tools on the fly and keeping abreast of technology trends that influence design. This might involve some cross-disciplinary exposure, such as basic coding or data analysis, so they can quickly prototype custom AI solutions or better understand technical constraints. In summary, students preparing to integrate AI into design thinking should focus on developing a blend of skills: technical literacy with AI tools, strong human-centered design fundamentals (empathy, creativity, ethics), and the strategic mindset to know when and how to leverage AI in the design process. Educators can support this by creating project experiences where AI's role is thoughtfully included, ensuring that the next generation of designers is ready to harness AI without losing the human touch (Poleac 2024).

CONCLUSION

Best Practices for Today

As we approach a future where AI and design thinking are integrated, preparation is crucial. The integration of AI is most successful when guided by human-centered design thinking. Despite the advantages of using AI in design thinking, it is not without skeptics. There are concerns about degrading critical thinking and analysis skills, creating an overreliance on technology, diminishing ideation skills, and over-shadowing human intuition. AI can indeed accelerate research, synthesis, creativity, prototyping, and testing in the design thinking process – leading to faster and often more innovative results – but it requires careful curation, ethical consideration, and a clear focus on human needs. By learning from these early integrations of AI and staying grounded in human-centered principles, designers (and students) can confidently embrace AI as a powerful tool in their toolkit, ushering in a new era of augmented creativity and problem-solving in design thinking. Educators should create more hands-on assignments that emphasize multi-modal thinking. They can integrate role-playing, critique sessions, and active debate in class. Additionally, educators can encourage students to iterate by fostering an environment that embraces failure, redesign, and refinement over finding the "one" answer. Table 3 identifies important issues to consider for faculty, administrators and policy makers.

Table 3. Issues for consideration

Faculty	**Emphasize Human-AI Collaboration**: Frame AI tools not as replacements for human intelligence but as partners that can assist with tasks like brainstorming, research, or content generation. Design assignments where students use AI but are required to apply critical thinking, creativity, and their unique human perspectives to the final output. **Design for Personalized Learning with AI**: Utilize AI-powered tools that can adapt to individual student needs and learning styles. Employ design thinking to empathize with diverse learners and define how AI can help create more inclusive and differentiated learning experiences. **Integrate AI Ethically and Transparently**: Be open with students about how AI is used in the course, whether by the instructor or the students. Use design thinking to involve students in discussions about the ethical implications of AI, potential biases, and data privacy, fostering a shared understanding of responsible AI use. **Redesign Assignments for a World with AI**: Shift from assignments easily completed by AI (like basic summaries) to those requiring higher-order thinking, creativity, and problem-solving. **Experiment and Iterate**: Start with small-scale integration of AI tools in specific assignments. Use a design thinking approach to gather feedback from students on their experience, evaluate the effectiveness of the AI tool, and iterate on your teaching strategies based on the outcomes. **Focus on Process, Not Just Product**: In assignments where AI is used, assess the student's process of working *with* the AI, rather than solely the final AI-generated output. This aligns with design thinking's emphasis on the iterative process of problem-solving. **Promote AI Literacy**: Educate students on how AI works, its capabilities, and its limitations. Design activities that help students develop the skills to use AI tools effectively, critically evaluate AI-generated content, and understand the human-centered considerations behind AI design.

continued on following page

Table 3. Continued

Administrators	**Develop a Human-Centered AI Strategy:** Approach AI integration with a design thinking mindset by focusing on the needs and experiences of students, teachers, and staff. Empathize with their challenges and concerns regarding AI and define how AI can genuinely solve problems and enhance the educational environment. **Invest in Professional Development Focused on Human-AI Interaction:** Provide training for educators that goes beyond the technical aspects of AI tools. Offer professional learning opportunities that help teachers understand how to use AI to personalize learning, facilitate critical thinking, and maintain meaningful human connection in the classroom, aligning with design thinking's focus on user needs. **Foster a Culture of Experimentation and Collaboration:** Encourage faculty and staff to experiment with AI tools in low-stakes environments and share their experiences. Create cohorts or communities of practice where educators can collaboratively explore AI and design thinking, iterating on effective strategies. **Implement Transparent and Iterative AI Policies:** Develop clear policies regarding AI use that are created with input from all stakeholders (students, parents, teachers, administrators) using a design thinking approach to understand diverse perspectives. Recognize that AI is evolving rapidly and design policies that can be reviewed and adapted over time based on feedback and new developments. **Prioritize Equity and Access:** Ensure that AI tools and training are accessible to all students and educators, regardless of socioeconomic background or technical proficiency. Use design thinking to understand the unique needs of underserved communities and design AI integration strategies that promote inclusivity and reduce the digital divide. **Align AI with Existing Pedagogical Goals:** Instead of viewing AI as a separate initiative, integrate it as a tool to support existing school goals and initiatives, such as project-based learning, personalized learning, or social-emotional learning. Use design thinking to explore how AI can enhance these established practices.

continued on following page

Table 3. Continued

Policymakers	**Develop Human-Centered AI Governance Frameworks:** Create policies and regulations that prioritize the safety, privacy, and well-being of students and educators. Use a design thinking approach to involve diverse stakeholders in the policy development process, ensuring that regulations are informed by real-world needs and concerns. **Champion AI Literacy and Capacity Building:** Develop policies and allocate resources to ensure that all educators and students have opportunities to develop AI literacy – understanding how AI works, its potential, limitations, and ethical implications. This builds the human capacity needed to effectively integrate AI in a human-centered way. **Promote Equity and Access in AI Rollout:** Design policies that guarantee equitable access to necessary infrastructure, AI tools, and professional development across all schools and regions, paying special attention to underserved populations. Policy should aim to prevent AI from exacerbating existing disparities, reflecting an empathetic approach to systemic change. **Incorporate Flexibility and Continuous Evaluation:** Recognize the rapid evolution of AI and design policies that are adaptable and subject to regular review and updates. Establish mechanisms for continuously monitoring the impact of AI in education, using feedback loops akin to the "test" and "iterate" phases of design thinking to refine policies. **Incentivize Human-Centered AI Innovation:** Encourage the development and adoption of AI tools that are designed with the user (students and educators) at the forefront, focusing on enhancing teaching and learning rather than simply automating existing processes. Policies can support research and pilot programs that explore innovative, human-centered applications of AI in education. **Provide Clear Guidance on Responsible AI Use:** Issue clear guidelines for schools and districts on the ethical and responsible use of AI, addressing issues like data privacy, algorithmic bias, academic integrity, and appropriate levels of AI assistance in student work. These guidelines should be informed by an understanding of the practical challenges faced by educators and administrators.

By embracing these best practices, educational stakeholders can work collaboratively to harness the power of AI within a human-centered design thinking framework, creating more effective, equitable, and engaging learning environments for the future. Balancing human intuition with AI capabilities is key. AI should not replace human critical thinking or human creativity. Humans should always be at the center of experiences, and as such, engaging with humans is particularly important.

REFERENCES

Auernhammer, J., & Roth, B. (2021). The origin and evolution of Stanford University's design thinking: From product design to design thinking in innovation management. *Journal of Product Innovation Management, 38*(6), 623–644. DOI: 10.1111/jpim.12594

Bouschery, S., Blazevic, V., & Pillar, F. (2023). Augmenting human innovation teams with artificial intelligence: Exploring transformer-based language modes. *Journal of Product Innovation Management, 40*(2), 139–153. DOI: 10.1111/jpim.12656

Brem, A., Giones, F., & Werle, M. (2021). The AI digital revolution in innovation: A conceptual framework of artificial intelligence technologies for the management of innovation. *IEEE Transactions on Engineering Management, 70*(2), 770–776. DOI: 10.1109/TEM.2021.3109983

Brown, T. (2009). *Change by Design: How Design Thinking Transforms Organizations and Inspires Innovation.* HarperCollins.

Eapen, T., Finkenstadt, D. J., Folk, H., & Venkataswamy, L. (2024). How Generative AI Can Augment Human Creativity. *SSRN*, (Fall), 25–32. DOI: 10.2139/ssrn.4759930

Ejjami, R. (2024). The future of learning: AI-based curriculum development. *International Journal for Multidisciplinary Research, 6*(4).

Elsbach, K. D., & Stigliani, I. (2018). Design thinking and organizational culture: Aa review and framework for future research. *Journal of Management, 44*(6), 2274–2306. DOI: 10.1177/0149206317744252

Grau, S. (2021). Using design thinking to drive human-centered innovation in marketing. In Pantano, E. (Ed.), *Creativity + Marketing: The Fuel for Success* (pp. 85–99). Emerald Publishing. DOI: 10.1108/978-1-80071-330-720211006

Grau, S., & Rockett, T. (2022). Creating Student Centered Experiences Using Design Thinking to Create Student Engagement. *The Journal of Entrepreneurship, 31*(25), 1355–1395.

Grill, L., & Pedota, M. (2024). Creativity and artificial intelligence: A multilevel perspective. *Creativity and Innovation Management, 33*(2), 234–247. DOI: 10.1111/caim.12580

Gruber, M., De Leon, N., George, G., & Thompson, P. (2015). Managing by Design. *Academy of Management Journal, 58*(1), 1–7. DOI: 10.5465/amj.2015.4001

IDEO The intersection of Design Thinking and AI: Enhancing Innovation, IDEO blog www.ideou.com/blogs/inspiration/ai-and-design-thinking/

Itonics www.intonics-innovation.com

Johansson-Sköldber, U., Woodilla, J., & Çetinkaya, M. (2013). Design Thinking: Past, Present and Possible Futures. *Creativity and Innovation Management*, *22*(2), 121–146. DOI: 10.1111/caim.12023

Kakatkar, C., Bilgram, V., & Fuller, J. (2020). Innovation analytics: Leveraging artificial intelligence in the innovation process. *Business Horizons*, *63*(2), 171–181. DOI: 10.1016/j.bushor.2019.10.006

Kelley, T., & Kelley, D. (2013). *Creative Confidence: Unleashing the Creative Potential Within us all.* Random House.

Kim, J., Mathius, H., & Sent, D. (2024). Human-centered evaluation of explainable AI applications: A systematic review. *Frontiers in Artificial Intelligence*, *7*, 1456486. https://www.frontiersin.org/journals/artificial-intelligence/articles/10.3389/frai.2024.1456486/full. DOI: 10.3389/frai.2024.1456486 PMID: 39484154

Kim, S., Jang, Y., Kim, W., Choi, S., Jung, H., Kim, S., & Kim, H. (2021, May). Why and what to teach: AI curriculum for elementary school. In *proceedings of the AAAI Conference on Artificial Intelligence* (Vol. 35, No. 17, pp. 15569-15576). DOI: 10.1609/aaai.v35i17.17833

Kimbell, L. (2011, November). Rethinking design thinking: Part 1. *Design and Culture*, *3*(3), 285–306. DOI: 10.2752/175470811X13071166525216

Kolko, J. (2010). Abductive thinking and sensemaking: The drivers of design synthesis. *Design Issues*, *26*(1), 15–28. DOI: 10.1162/desi.2010.26.1.15

Kolko, J. (2015, September). Design thinking comes of age. *Harvard Business Review*, *93*(9), 66–69.

Krebs, D., & Rosenbaum, A. (2023). The use of generative AI tools in design thinking academic makeathon. *CERN ideaSquare Journal of Experimental Innovation*, *13*(1), 1470.

Kurokawa, T. (2013). Design thinking education at universities and graduate schools. *Science & Technology Trends Quarterly Review*, *46*, 50–62.

Laupichler, M. C., Aster, A., Schirch, J., & Raupach, T. (2022). Artificial intelligence literacy in higher and adult education: A scoping literature review. *Computers and Education: Artificial Intelligence*, *3*, 100101. DOI: 10.1016/j.caeai.2022.100101

Li, T., & Zhan, Z. (2022). A systematic review on design thinking integrated learning in K-12 education. *Applied Sciences (Basel, Switzerland)*, *12*(16), 8077. DOI: 10.3390/app12168077

Liedtka, J. (2018). Exploring the Impact of Design Thinking in Action. Darden Working paper series.

Liedtka, J. (2020). Putting Technology in its place: Design thinking's social technology at work. *California Management Review*, *62*(2), 53–83. DOI: 10.1177/0008125619897391

Liedtka, J., & Ogilvie, T. (2011). *Design for Growth: A Design thinking toolkit for managers.* Columbia Business School Publishing.

Martin, R. L. (2009). *The design of business: Why design thinking is the next competitive advantage.* Harvard Business Press.

Matthee, M., & Turpin, M. (2019). Teaching critical thinking, problem solving, and design thinking: Preparing IS students for the future. *Journal of Information Systems Education*, *30*(4), 242–252.

Mhalanga, D. (2022). Human-Centered Artificial Intelligence: The Superlative Approach to Achieve Sustainable Development Goals in the Fourth Industrial Revolution. *Sustainability (Basel)*, *14*(13), 7804. DOI: 10.3390/su14137804

Ng, D. T. K., Chan, E. K. C., & Lo, C. K. (2025). Opportunities, Challenges and School Strategies for Integrating Generative AI in Education. *Computers and Education: Artificial Intelligence*, 100373.

Ng, D. T. K., Lee, M., Tan, R. J. Y., Hu, X., Downie, J. S., & Chu, S. K. W. (2023). A review of AI teaching and learning from 2000 to 2020. *Education and Information Technologies*, *28*(7), 8445–8501. DOI: 10.1007/s10639-022-11491-w

Owen, C. (2007). Design thinking: Notes on its nature and use. *Design research quarterly*, *2*(1), 16-27.

Panke, S. (2019). Design thinking in education: Perspectives, opportunities and challenges. *Open Education Studies*, *1*(1), 281–306. DOI: 10.1515/edu-2019-0022

Paranjape, K., Schinkel, M., Panday, R. N., Car, J., & Nanayakkara, P. (2019). Introducing artificial intelligence training in medical education. *JMIR Medical Education*, *5*(2), e16048. DOI: 10.2196/16048 PMID: 31793895

Poleac, D. (2024). Design thinking with AI. *Proceedings of the International Conference on Business Excellence*, 18(1): June.

Polster, L., Bilgram, V., & Gortz, S. (2024). AI-Augmented Design Thinking: Potentials, Challenges, and Mitigation Strategies of Integrating Artificial Intelligence in Human-Centered Innovation Processes. *IEEE Engineering Management Review*, *99*, 1–36. DOI: 10.1109/EMR.2024.3512866

Rauth, I., Köppen, E., Jobst, B., & Meinel, C. (2010). Design thinking: An educational model towards creative confidence. In *DS 66-2: Proceedings of the 1st international conference on design creativity (ICDC 2010).*

Razzouk, R., & Shute, V. (2012). What is design thinking and why is it important? *Review of Educational Research*, *82*(3), 330–348. DOI: 10.3102/0034654312457429

Sreenivasa, A., & Suresh, M. (2024). Design thinking and artificial intelligence: A systematic literature review exploring synergies. *International Journal of Innovation Studies*, *8*(3), 297–312. DOI: 10.1016/j.ijis.2024.05.001

Touretzky, D., Martin, F., Seehorn, D., Breazeal, C., & Posner, T. (2019, February). Special session: AI for K-12 guidelines initiative. In *Proceedings of the 50th ACM technical symposium on computer science education* (pp. 492-493). DOI: 10.1145/3287324.3287525

Tschepe, S. (April 2024). AI-enhanced design thinking. HPI d-school, www.hpi.de

Van Laar, E., Van Duerson, A. J., van Dikk, J. A., & de Haan, J. (2020). Determinants of 21st-Century Skills and 21st-Century Digital Skills for Workers: A Systematic Literature Review. *SAGE Open*, *10*(Jan-Mar), 1–14. DOI: 10.1177/2158244019900176

Vergani, R., Vendraminelli, L., & Swan, K. (2021). Design thinking: Critical analysis and future evolution. *Journal of Product Innovation Management*, *38*(6), 603–622. DOI: 10.1111/jpim.12610

Verganti, R., Vendraminelli, L., & Iansiti, M. (2020). Innovation and Design in the Age of Artificial Intelligence. *Journal of Product Innovation Management*, *37*(3), 212–227. DOI: 10.1111/jpim.12523

Chapter 6
Dimensions of Cognitive Processes:
Integrating Concepts, Decision-Making, Reasoning, and Creativity in Learning

Nurfaida Tasni
https://orcid.org/0000-0003-4256-6849
Universitas Negeri Makassar, Indonesia

Andi Syukriani
Universitas Negeri Makassar, Indonesia

Hamzah Upu
Universitas Negeri Makassar, Indonesia

ABSTRACT

This chapter examines the interconnected dimensions of cognitive processes, emphasizing concept formation, decision-making, reasoning, problem-solving, intelligence, creativity, and emotion. These elements shape human cognition, particularly in learning and problem-solving contexts like mathematics education. Concept formation underpins understanding abstract ideas, enabling effective decision-making, while reasoning supports logical conclusions and innovative problem-solving. Intelligence enhances information processing, and creativity introduces novel solutions. Emotions influence cognition, with positive emotions boosting creativity and problem-solving, while negative emotions like anxiety may hinder them. Using qualitative research and literature reviews, the chapter highlights the integration of these cognitive dimensions in education, offering strategies to enhance cognitive and emotional development for better learning outcomes and personal achievements.

DOI: 10.4018/979-8-3373-5786-7.ch006

INTRODUCTION

Education is a human effort and activity aimed at enhancing personality by nurturing individual potentials, including spiritual (thought, will, reasoning, creativity, and conscience) and physical (senses and skills) aspects (Rahman et al., 2022). Philosophical, historical, psychological, sociological, and juridical foundations form the basis of education (Purwaningsih et al., 2022). From a psychological perspective, education is expected to produce individuals who excel not only cognitively but also in affective and psychomotor aspects (Ekaningtyas, 2022). In psychological studies, one of the fundamental aspects of education is cognition.

Cognition is a general concept encompassing activities such as thinking, understanding, and reasoning (Aminah et al., 2022). Cognition or mental processes in psychology include concept formation, decision-making, reasoning, and problem-solving, all of which play vital roles in various human activities, from daily life to scientific achievements and technological innovations (Ramadanti et al., 2022). Additionally, elements such as intelligence, creativity, and emotion serve as supportive factors for the success of cognitive processes (Sulaiman & Neviyarni, 2021).

Concept formation refers to the ability to classify ideas, objects, or phenomena based on common characteristics, facilitating the recognition of patterns and relationships (Skemp, 2012). This serves as the foundation for effective decision-making, where individuals must choose the most appropriate actions based on previously formed concepts. Effective decision-making requires strong reasoning skills, such as the ability to analyze information and consider various possible outcomes (Eki et al., 2024).

Furthermore, one of the critical cognitive skills required to address complex situations is problem-solving (Patnani, 2013). Through problem-solving, individuals are required to formulate and implement the best solutions to overcome specific obstacles (Wardani, 2020). In this process, intelligence and creativity are essential components that support individuals in finding innovative and effective solutions. Indrawijaya & Siregar (2022) state that intelligence relates to a person's capacity to comprehend information, while creativity involves generating new ideas. Additionally, emotion significantly influences cognitive processes.

Emotions can affect how individuals think and make decisions, either positively or negatively (Pashar & Dwiantoro, 2020). For instance, positive emotions characterized by happiness can enhance creativity and facilitate problem-solving, while negative emotions such as anxiety or fear may hinder these processes. This article explores the interconnected cognitive elements and their interactions, particularly their influence on thinking and learning abilities, especially in mathematics education. Therefore, further exploration is needed to describe concept formation, decision-making, reasoning, problem-solving, intelligence, creativity, emotion, and cognitive processes comprehensively.

The approach used in this study is qualitative descriptive, employing the library research method. Library research refers to theoretical studies, references, and scientific literature, including books, articles, notes, journals, and supporting documentation, without requiring field research (Haryono et al., 2024). The data sources for this research consist of books, journals, and previous research articles selected based on their relevance to the study's topic. The collected data have been thoroughly reviewed and explored to ensure that the references used are pertinent to the subject matter being discussed.

CONCEPT FORMATION

A concept is an abstract idea that allows individuals to connect events or objects and determine whether an object is an example or not. Broadly, a concept is an idea or definition abstracted from a concrete event (Mandasari, 2018). Concept formation in mathematics learning is a mental process in which students internalize and understand abstract concepts related to mathematics. Skemp explains that concepts are not directly formed from symbolic understanding but begin with concrete experiences and gradually develop into abstract understanding. At the initial stage, students tend to require tangible objects or visual representations to grasp fundamental concepts (Skemp, 2012). For instance, in understanding the concept of addition, students may use objects such as marbles or seeds before transitioning to mathematical symbols.

Concept formation is often associated with abstraction in mathematics learning. The abstraction process involves students building their understanding based on prior knowledge and using concrete objects in mathematics learning (Kholiyanti, 2018). For example, when learning geometry, students observe various geometric shapes in their surroundings, which indirectly helps them understand the properties of geometry through touch, sight, or usage.

Skemp (2012) distinguishes between relational understanding and instrumental understanding. Relational understanding involves a student's ability to see connections between various mathematical concepts, such as how addition relates to subtraction. Conversely, instrumental understanding refers to a student's ability to use rules or formulas without comprehending the underlying reasons.

Concept formation rooted in relational understanding enables students to apply concepts flexibly in various contexts. However, instrumental representations are also important as they help students transfer their knowledge to new situations, making them more applicable and robust.

DECISION-MAKING

A decision is an action taken by individuals over time, whether consciously or unconsciously. Even decisions made consciously require careful calculation, thorough consideration, adequate preparation, and a readiness to perform analysis (Maulana & Rizki, 2018). The activity of selecting strategies or actions during the problem-solving process is also referred to as decision-making (Setiawan, 2019). In the context of mathematics learning, decision-making is a crucial aspect. Students must choose the most appropriate strategy or method to solve a problem. At every step of problem-solving, students face various options that demand a deep understanding of the concepts being studied.

Skemp emphasizes that good decisions should be based on relational understanding rather than mere memorization of procedures. With relational understanding, students can connect various concepts or principles relevant to solving mathematical problems and provide explanations regarding why a particular solution works (Sudrajat, 2022). Additionally, Skemp highlights the critical role of reasoning and logic in decision-making. Students who can comprehend the relationships between mathematical concepts are more likely to make better decisions.

Mathematics education equips students with logical thinking skills, which are essential and necessary for learning mathematics (Wahyuddin et al., 2021). Logical thinking enables students to identify errors and correct them, thereby improving the quality of their learning experience. Decision-making errors often present valuable learning opportunities; students can identify the source of their mistakes and use them to strengthen their understanding (Skemp, 2012). For this reason, in the teaching process, teachers should not only teach mathematical procedures but also train students in decision-making.

REASONING

Reasoning is a cognitive process used to draw conclusions in the form of knowledge. Fundamentally, humans are beings who think, feel, act, and behave. Their actions and attitudes are often derived from knowledge acquired through feeling or thinking. Reasoning generates knowledge associated with cognitive activities rather than emotions, though, as Pascal noted, the heart has its own logic. However, it should be recognized that not all cognitive activities rely on reasoning. Thus, reasoning is a thinking process characterized by specific traits aimed at discovering the truth.

For the knowledge derived from reasoning to have a basis in truth, the thinking process must adhere to certain methods. A conclusion is deemed valid if it is drawn according to these methods, which are referred to as logic.

Aristotle outlined three principles of reasoning: the principle of identity, where an entity is identical to itself; the principle of contradiction, where something cannot simultaneously be itself and not itself at the same time; and the principle of the excluded middle, which states there is no third possibility. There are two types of reasoning:

Direct Reasoning

Direct reasoning involves premises consisting of only one proposition, immediately followed by another proposition as its conclusion. This reasoning is derived from a single premise. Drawing a direct conclusion provides complete clarification of the given proposition by explicitly stating what has been implicitly conveyed in the premise.

Example: All football stars use Rejois shampoo (S=P). Therefore, some users of Rejois shampoo are football stars.

The term direct reasoning originates from Aristotle, denoting reasoning where the premise consists of only one proposition. The conclusion is directly drawn by comparing the subject and predicate of that proposition

Indirect Reasoning

Indirect reasoning involves conclusions drawn from more than one proposition. The conclusion is derived from two premises.

Example: All students are diligent individuals. Budi is a student. Therefore, Budi is a diligent individual.

Reasoning is a broad concept referring to a thinking process that leads to a new conclusion derived from known statements. These statements consist of concepts that are clearly defined to avoid ambiguity. Reasoning is a specialized type of thinking in which conclusions are drawn based on premises or prior statements. It is a cognitive process that starts with sensory observation (empirical observation or facts) to generate concepts and understanding. Similar observations lead to similar propositions, and based on these propositions, individuals deduce new conclusions previously unknown. This process is called reasoning.

In reasoning, propositions serving as the basis for conclusions are called premises (antecedents), while the derived conclusions are referred to as consequences. The relationship between premises and conclusions is known as consequence. Reasoning is a thinking process that connects evidence, facts, clues, or other forms of proof to arrive at a conclusion.

PROBLEM-SOLVING

According to Marzano et al. (1988), problem-solving is a cognitive process that involves the ability to address and resolve issues. The term "problem-solving" is extensively used in cognitive psychology to describe all forms of awareness, understanding, or cognition. For instance, Anderson (1983), as cited by Marzano et al. (1988), classified all goal-directed behaviors (whether conscious or unconscious) as problem-solving. Wickelgren (1974) defined problem-solving as an effort to achieve specific goals, while Van Dijk and Kintsch (1983), as cited by Marzano et al. (1988), stated that problem-solving occurs when achieving a specific goal requires particular performance and mental steps.

According to Palumbo (1990), problem-solving functions as a process where specific stimuli are received as input through sensory memory, processed and encoded via working memory (short-term memory), and stored along with associations and related events (histories) in long-term memory.

On the other hand, as Marzano et al. (1988) noted, educators tend to interpret problem-solving more narrowly. They often use the term to refer to specific tasks presented to learners in subjects like mathematics, science, and social studies. Problem-solving involves recalling rules and applying steps that guide learners to the desired solution. For example, a problem in a social studies lesson might require learners to predict the growth of shops in a local shopping center based on projected housing patterns in the surrounding area.

Girl et al. (2002) state that problem-solving is a process involving the application of knowledge and skills to achieve a goal. According to Gagne and Briggs (1979), problem-solving performance entails the creation and application of complex and higher-level rules to arrive at a solution. In problem-solving, learners must recall or retrieve lower-level rules and relevant information assumed to have been learned previously. Once higher-level rules have been acquired, learners are likely to apply them in situations that are physically different but formally similar. In other words, the newly acquired, more complex rules enable the transfer of learning. Thus, the term "problem-solving" can generally be defined as a complex cognitive process involving a series of mental activities to find solutions to problems.

The steps of problem-solving proposed by Polya (as cited in Suherman, 2003:99) are as follows:

a. Understanding the problem.
b. Planning and selecting a problem-solving strategy.
c. Implementing the plan.
d. Reviewing and verifying the obtained results.

INTELLIGENCE

Definition of Intelligence

The term "intelligence" originates from the English word "intelligence" and the Latin words intellectus and intelligentia (Pane et al., 2023). Translated into Indonesian, intelligence means the ability to understand. Alfred Binet, a pioneer in intelligence measurement, defined intelligence as comprising three components: the ability to direct thoughts and actions, the ability to change the direction of actions after they are executed, and the ability for self-criticism (autocriticism) (Uyun et al., 2021).

According to Veriansyah et al. (2018), Edward Lee Thorndike described intelligence as the ability to respond appropriately based on an understanding of truth or facts. Meanwhile, David Wechsler defined intelligence as the capacity or totality of human abilities to act with a specific purpose, think rationally, and effectively deal with the environment.

From the various expert definitions of intelligence, it can be concluded that intelligence is the ability to think rationally, understand, and solve problems, thereby enabling directed responses in the form of purposeful actions.

Measurement of Intelligence

According to Triwulandari and Supardi (2022), each individual possesses varying levels of intelligence. Human intelligence can be measured using various intelligence tests to determine its level. The unit of measurement used to represent intelligence scores is known as IQ (Intelligence Quotient). The reference system for measuring intelligence is developed based on the results of intelligence tests or sample assessments considered representative of the population. The classification of IQ is shown in Table 1 below.

Table 1. IQ classification

IQ	Klasifikasi
30-69	*Mentally Defective*
70-79	*Borderline Defective*
80-89	*Low Average*
90-109	*Normal or Average*
110-119	*High Average*
120-139	*Superior*
140-169	*Very Superior*

Intelligence tests allow us to calculate a person's IQ. IQ is a numerical value that enables us to compare an individual's level of intelligence (Malelak et al., 2022).

Factors Influencing Intelligence

Several factors can influence intelligence (Huwaida et al., 2020). These include:

a. Genetic Factors
b. Environmental Factors
c. Stability of Intelligence and IQ
d. Interest and Personal Disposition
e. Autonomy Factors
f. Nutritional Factors

The Role of Intelligence in Teaching and Learning

As a cognitive element, intelligence is considered to play a vital role. There is sometimes a perception that intelligence has a disproportionately significant influence compared to its actual role (Jufrizal, 2023). It is widely believed that intelligence greatly impacts an individual's academic achievement. Students with higher intelligence levels, or those who excel in their classes, are typically active and engaged in learning (Azizah et al., 2020).

Intelligence influences a student's academic performance because students with high levels of intelligence or IQ tend to learn more easily, quickly grasp lessons, and achieve better academic results. Conversely, students with lower intelligence levels often face difficulties in learning, struggle to understand lessons quickly, and consequently achieve lower academic performance. This highlights that intelligence levels directly correlate with positive academic outcomes for students (Afniola et al., 2020).

Individual differences in intelligence must be recognized and understood by teachers, particularly regarding student grouping. Furthermore, teachers should align their teaching objectives with the students' intelligence capacities. Differences in student intelligence levels should not lead teachers to underestimate less capable students. Instead, teachers should strive to ensure that their teaching accommodates all students, employing diverse methods to meet their needs (Huwaida et al., 2020).

CREATIVITY

The ability to think beyond what others typically conceive, resulting in new and useful ideas or products for oneself or others, is referred to as creativity (Estheriani & Muhid, 2020). James J. Gallagher stated that creativity is a mental process involving ideas or new products, or a combination of both, which ultimately becomes inherent in the individual (Rahayu in Gallagher, 2022). In contrast, Irawan (2022) argued that creativity is part of the human psyche, but it is also a unique talent possessed by individuals with extraordinary creative abilities in specific fields. Creativity is also related to discovering new ideas concerning products and innovations applied simultaneously (Wiyono et al., 2020).

From various expert perspectives, creativity can be summarized as the ability to think outside the norm and produce new, beneficial ideas or products. It involves intelligence, cognitive style, and personality, as well as a mental process that combines new ideas with flexibility and innovation. Creativity is also viewed as a unique state of mind and a special talent in certain fields. Through creativity, students can exhibit a strong sense of curiosity, perseverance, and resilience, as well as confidence and independence. They may feel challenged, take risks, and think divergently (Rindiantika, 2021).

In cognitive terms, creative thinking is a mental activity focused on developing or discovering original, aesthetic, and constructive ideas related to conceptual perspectives, emphasizing intuitive and rational thinking. In the mathematical domain, creative thinking is considered a higher-order skill compared to critical thinking. Individuals with critical thinking abilities must also possess creative thinking skills. Those who excel in creative thinking, often referred to as divergent thinking, exhibit high levels of creativity that are beneficial to many (Nurjan, 2018). Therefore, teaching creative thinking skills is essential in schools.

Individuals who generate creative ideas can effectively address the challenges they face. Creative thinking can be identified through several characteristics: fluency, flexibility, originality, elaboration, and evaluation (Manurung et al., 2020). Fluency in learning processes can be seen in the ability to ask numerous questions; flexibility is marked by applying concepts in varied ways; originality involves choosing unique approaches; elaboration is demonstrated by enriching or expanding on others' ideas; and evaluation is indicated by selecting appropriate solutions.

Encouraging creative characteristics in education is crucial because such traits enable individuals to innovate and progress in various fields, assist students in solving problems, express themselves authentically and uniquely, and help them adapt to continuous changes and challenges (Lestari et al., 2024). Santrock (2018) identifies the creative process as consisting of several stages: preparation, incubation, insight, evaluation, and elaboration.

EMOTION

Emotion is a psychological factor that influences an individual's perception, choices, and judgments in specific situations. This theory suggests that emotions such as anxiety, satisfaction, or anger impact a person's response to choices. For instance, negative emotions marked by anxiety may cause a person to avoid risks, whereas positive emotions, characterized by joy, tend to encourage risk-taking (Sari et al., 2024). Emotional intelligence refers to an individual's ability to understand, manage, and direct their own emotions as well as the emotions of others. Furthermore, emotions stem from internal feelings that are specific, short-lived, and vary in intensity, typically embedded in a particular context (Gutierrez & Boero, 2006).

Based on various expert perspectives, emotions can be concluded as psychological feelings that affect an individual's perception, choices, and judgments. They involve biological and psychological states, along with the ability to recognize, understand, manage, and direct one's own emotions and those of others. Emotions can have both positive and negative effects on a person's decisions and actions, depending on the context and intensity.

Understanding emotions can contribute to the mental well-being of students. Teachers who are sensitive to their students' emotions can assist them in overcoming stress, anxiety, or other negative feelings that may disrupt the learning process. Emotional awareness helps students develop emotional regulation skills, teaching them how to cope with negative emotions and manage stress—essential skills for daily life (Mutyati et al., 2023). Papurungan and Paputungan (2023) state that emotions play a critical role in influencing students' motivation, enhancing their attention to learning materials, particularly in mathematics, affecting decision-making processes, shaping information processing and learning algorithms, and influencing students' comprehension and engagement.

COGNITIVE PROCESSES

Cognitive psychology is an effort to understand various systematic empirical forms of human observation, which are then developed into theories. It is concerned with the processes of information perception, understanding, thinking, and problem-solving (Ramadanti et al., 2022). Cognitive processes refer to a series of thought patterns students use to receive, manage, and apply knowledge (Hasan, 2020). Cognitive structures represent organizational frameworks in an individual's memory that integrate fragmented knowledge elements into coherent concepts (Ekawati, 2019). Ardiana (2022) offers a different perspective, stating that cognitive processes are related to an individual's intelligence level, which is demonstrated through interests, ideas, and learning.

Based on expert perspectives, cognitive processes can be summarized as mental mechanisms involving information perception, understanding, thinking, and problem-solving. These processes include the thought patterns used by students to receive, manage, and interpret their knowledge while involving organizational structures in memory that connect fragmented knowledge into universal concepts. Additionally, cognitive processes are closely tied to an individual's intelligence level, which influences their ideas and other capabilities.

Piaget divided cognitive processes into several aspects based on their stages. These include schemas, characterized by the child's brain constructing an understanding of the developing world and creating mental frameworks; assimilation and accommodation, where children incorporate new information into their schemas and adjust existing schemas to align with new information and experiences; organization, marked by the grouping of isolated thoughts into higher-level systems; and equilibration, characterized by shifts in children's cognitive mechanisms to more advanced stages of thinking (Santrock, 2018). Through cognitive processes, students can integrate new information and make decisions based on the acquired knowledge.

Cognitive processes serve as a foundational framework applied in classifying educational objectives, test designs, and curricula (Dewi et al., 2020). Within the cognitive domain, (Nafiati, 2021) categorized it into several levels: C1 (remembering), C2 (understanding), C3 (applying), C4 (analyzing), C5 (evaluating), and C6 (creating). Overall, cognitive processes are the basis of many higher mental functions, enabling humans to adapt and thrive in complex environments. By understanding the components and interactions within cognitive processes, we can better develop educational strategies and interventions that support cognitive and emotional development, particularly in mathematics learning.

CONCLUSION

Cognitive psychology highlights various critical aspects of understanding the human mind. Concept formation, for example, is a fundamental mental process where we organize information and experiences into meaningful categories. This process enables us to comprehend the world more efficiently. Reasoning, on the other hand, involves the use of logic to draw conclusions from existing information. This ability allows us to solve problems, make decisions, and plan actions.

Intelligence and creativity are two complementary cognitive aspects. Intelligence relates to the ability to think logically, solve problems, and learn from experience. Creativity involves the capacity to generate new, innovative, and original ideas. Both interact closely in addressing complex problem-solving processes. Additionally, emotions play a significant role in human cognition, influencing thinking processes, decision-making, and even memory.

In summary, various cognitive aspects—such as concept formation, reasoning, problem-solving, intelligence, creativity, and emotion—are interconnected and work together to shape how we think, learn, and interact with the world. Understanding these cognitive processes is essential across multiple fields, including education and psychology. By comprehending how the human mind operates, we can develop more effective strategies for learning, problem-solving, and personal development.

REFERENCES

Aminah, S., Ramawani, N., Azura, N., Fronika, S., Hasanah, S. M., & Salsabillah, T. (2022). Pengaruh Metode Belajar Sambil Bermain Terhadap Perkembangan Kognitif Anak Usia Sekolah Dasar. *SICEDU : Science and Education Journal, 1*(2), 465–471. https://doi.org/https://doi.org/10.31004/sicedu.v1i2.66

Ardiana, R. (2022). Strategi Guru dalam Mengembangkan Kemampuan Kognitif Anak Usia 5-6 Tahun di Taman Kanak Kanak. *Murhum: Jurnal Pendidikan Anak Usia Dini*, *3*(2), 1–10. DOI: 10.37985/murhum.v3i2.116

Dewi, A. R. T., Mayasarokh, M., & Gustiana, E. (2020). Perilaku Sosial Emosional Anak Usia Dini. *Jurnal Golden Age*, *4*(1), 181–190.

Ekaningtyas, N. L. D. (2022). Psikologi dalam Dunia Pendidikan. *Padma Sari: Jurnal Ilmu Pendidikan*, *2*(1), 29–38. DOI: 10.53977/ps.v2i01.526

Ekawati, M. (2019). Teori Belajar Menurut Aliran Psikologi Kognitif serta Implikasinya dalam Proses Belajar dan Pembelajaran. *Jurnal E-Tech*, *7*(4), 1–12. DOI: 10.1007/XXXXXX-XX-0000-00

Eki, K. A. O., Sulang, M., Sari, P. N., & Lawalata, M. (2024). Penerapan Logika Dalam Kehidupan Pemuda : Sebuah Refleksi. *Sinar Kasih: Jurnal Pendidikan Agama Dan Filsafat, 2*(2), 209–224. https://doi.org/https://doi.org/10.55606/sinarkasih.v2i2.323

Estheriani, N. G. N., & Muhid, A. (2020). Pengembangan Kreativitas Berpikir Siswa di Era Industri 4.0 melalui Perangkat Pembelajaran dengan Media Augmented Reality. *Insight: Jurnal Ilmiah Psikologi, 22*(2), 118–129. https://doi.org/https://dx.doi.org/10.26486/psikologi.v22i2.1206

Gutierrez, A., & Boero, P. (2006). *Handbook of Research on the Psychology of Mathematics Education*. DOI: 10.1163/9789087901127

Haryono, E., Suprihatiningsih, S., Septian, D., Widodo, J., Ashar, A., & Sariman, S. (2024). New Paradigm Metode Penelitian Kepustakaan (Library Research) di Perguruan Tinggi. An-Nuur, 14(1).

Hasan, B. (2020). Proses Kognitif Siswa Field Independent dan Field Dependent dalam Menyelesaikan Masalah Matematika. [Jurnal Pembelajaran Matematika Inovatif]. *JPMI*, *3*(4), 323–332. DOI: 10.22460/jpmi.v3i4.323-332

Indrawijaya, S., & Siregar, A. P. (2022). Peningkatan Kreativitas melalui Penerapan Pembelajaran Team Based Project pada Mata Kuliah Desain Komunikasi Visual. *Jurnal Ilmiah Dikdaya*, *12*(1), 268–273. DOI: 10.33087/dikdaya.v12i1.301

Irawan, A. (2022). Kreativitas Guru Dalam Memotivasi Belajar Peserta Didik. *SKULA: Jurnal Pendidikan Profesi Guru Madrasah, 2*(2), 199–210. https://doi.org/http://studentjournal.iaincurup.ac.id/index.php/skula

Kholiyanti, A. (2018). Pembelajaran Matematika dari Konkret ke Abstrak dalam Membangun Konsep Dasar Geometri Bagi Siswa Sekolah Dasar. *Pi: Mathematics Education Journal, 1*(2), 40–46. https://doi.org/https://doi.org/10.21067/pmej.v1i2.2322

Lestari, P., Dewi, R. S., & Junita, A. R. (2024). Menumbuhkan Kreativitas tanpa Batas : Strategi Inovatif Sekolah dalam Mengembangkan Karakter Kreatif Siswa. *Ainara Journal (Jurnal Penelitian Dan PKM Bidang Ilmu Pendidikan), 5*(3), 358–364. https://doi.org/https://doi.org/10.54371/ainj.v5i3.543

Mandasari, N. (2018). Elaborasi Kognitif dalam Proses Abstraksi Konsep Matematika. *Seminar Nasional Pendidikan Universitas PGRI Palembang*, 399–405.

Manurung, A. S., Halim, A., & Rosyid, A. (2020). Pengaruh Kemampuan Berpikir Kreatif untuk Meningkatkan Hasil Belajar Matematika di Sekolah Dasar. *Jurnal Basicedu, 4*(4), 1291–1301. https://doi.org/https://doi.org/10.31004/basicedu.v4i4.544

Maulana, A., & Rizki, S. N. (2018). Sistem pengambilan keputusan dalam penerimaan proyek pembuatan kapal menggunakan metode fuzzy. *Jurnal Simetris, 9*(2), 723–730. DOI: 10.24176/simet.v9i2.2110

Mutyati, A. M., Kartika, A. D., Dwitasari, B. D., Rahmadanti, A., Dewi, A. S., & Ibrahim. (2023). Pentingnya Pemahaman Emosi dalam Proses Pembelajaran di MI Al-Masrhi Pangkalan Balai-Banyuasin. *IMEIJ: Indo-MathEdu Intellectuals Journal, 4*(2), 1198–1208. https://doi.org/http://doi.org/10.54373/imeij.v4i2.340

Nafiati, D. A. (2021). Revisi taksonomi Bloom: Kognitif, afektif, dan psikomotorik. *Humanika. Kajian Ilmiah Mata Kuliah Umum, 21*(2), 151–172. DOI: 10.21831/hum.v21i2.29252

Nurjan, S. (2018). Pengembangan Berpikir Kreatif. *AL-ASASIYYA: Journal Basic Of Education, 3*(1), 105–116. https://doi.org/http://dx.doi.org/10.24269/ajbe.v3i1.1302

Papurungan, E., & Paputungan, F. (2023). Pendekatan dan Fungsi Afektif dalam Proses Pembelajaran. *Journal of Education and Culture (JEaC) Vol., 3*(1).

Pashar, I., & Dwiantoro, L. (2020). Pengaruh Empowerment Terhadap Pengambilan Keputusan Perawat : Kajian Literature Review. *Journal of Holistic Nursing Science, 7*(2), 124–132. https://doi.org/https://doi.org/10.31603/nursing. v7i2.3097

Patnani, M. (2013). Upaya Meningkatkan Kemampuan Problem Solving pada Mahasiswa. *Jurnal Psikogenesis, 1*(2), 130–142. DOI: 10.24854/jps.v1i2.43

Purwaningsih, I. Oktariani, Hernawati, L., Wardarita, R., & Utami, P. I. (2022). Pendidikan sebagai suatu Sistem. *Jurnal Visionary : Penelitian Dan Pengembangan Dibidang Administrasi Pendidikan, 10*(1), 21–26. https://doi.org/https://e-journal .undikma.ac.id/index.php/visionary

Rahayu, F. (2022). Pengembangan Kreativitas Anak melalui Strategi 4P (Person, Press, Process, Product). [JIME]. *Jurnal Ilmiah Mandala Education, 8*(3), 2406–2414. DOI: 10.58258/jime.v8i3.3779

Rahman, A., Munandar, S. A., Fitriani, A., Karlina, Y., & Yumriani. (2022). Pengertian pendidikan, ilmu pendidikan dan unsur-unsur pendidikan. *Al Urwatul Wutsqa: Kajian Pendidikan Islam, 2*(1), 1–8. https://doi.org/https://journal.unismuh.ac.id/ index.php/alurwatul/article/view/7757

Ramadanti, M., Sary, C. P., & Suarni. (2022). Psikologi kognitif. *ALDIN: Jurnal Dakwah Dan Sosial Keagamaan, 8*(1), 46–59. https://doi.org/http://dx.doi.org/10 .30863/ajdsk.v8i1.3205

Rindiantika, Y. (2021). Pentingnya Pengembangan Kreativitas dalam Keberhasilan Pembelajaran: Kajian Teoritik. *Jurnal Intelegensia, 6*(1), 53–63.

Santrock, J. W. (2018).. . *Educational Psychology.*

Sari, A. A., Ekita, A., Kirana, W., Amelia, R., Susilowati, J., & Kusuma, I. R. (2024). Teori Pengambilan Keputusan: Peran Emosi dalam Pengambilan Keputusan. *Musytari: Neraca Manajemen Ekonomi, 9*(11), 1–6. DOI: 10.8734/mnmae.v1i2.359

Setiawan, A. (2019). Pengambilan Keputusan untuk Menyeleksi Penerimaan Guru Matematika dengan Methode Topsis. *Methomika: Jurnal Manajemen Informatika & Komputerisasi Akuntansi, 3*(1), 14–20. https://doi.org/https://doi.org/10.46880/ jmika.Vol3No1.pp14-20

Skemp, R. R. (2012). The Psychology of learning mathematics: Expanded American edition. In *The Psychology of Learning Mathematics: Expanded American Edition* (pp. 1–218). DOI: 10.4324/9780203396391

Sudrajat. (2022). Pemahaman Relasional dan Intrumental: Bagaimana Pengaruhnya dalam Pembelajaran Matematika Ditinjai dari Pemecahan Masalah Matematis. *Elips: Jurnal Pendidikan Matematika, 3*(1), 45–52. https://doi.org/https://doi.org/ 10.47650/elips.v3i1.393

Sulaiman, & Neviyarni. (2021). Teori Belajar Menurut Aliran Psikologi Humanistik Serta Implikasinya Dalam Proses Belajar dan Pembelajaran Sulaiman. *Jurnal Sikola: Jurnal Kajian Pendidikan Dan Pembelajaran, 2*(3), 220–234. https://doi.org/https://doi.org/10.24036/sikola.v2i3.118 Teori

Wahyuddin, S. S., & Asfar, F. (2021). Analisis Kemampuan Menyelesaikan Soal High Order Thinking Skills Ditijau dari Kemampuan Berpikir Logis. *AKSIOMA: Jurnal Program Studi Pendidikan Matematika, 10*(2), 521–535. https://doi.org/https://doi.org/10.24127/ajpm.v10i2.3480

Wardani, D. S. (2020). Usaha Peningkatan Keterampilan Pemecahan Masalah melalui Model Problem Based Learning di Kelas V SDN Babatan V/460 Surabaya. *COLLASE: Creative of Learning Students Elementary Education*, *3*(4), 104–117.

Wiyono, H. D., Ardiansyah, T., & Rasul, T. (2020). Kreativitas dan Inovasi dalam Berwirausaha. *Jurnal Usaha, 1*(2), 19–25. https://doi.org/https://doi.org/10.30998/juuk.v1i2.503

Chapter 7
Transforming Workforce Development through AI-Driven Education Networks: A Pathway to Sustainable Economic Growth

Sri Wahyuny Mustafa
https://orcid.org/0009-0004-4955-8803
Universitas Muhammadiyah Palopo, Indonesia

Harmita Sari
https://orcid.org/0000-0002-7324-0764
Universitas Muhammadiyah Palopo, Indonesia

Asriany Asriany
Universitas Muhammadiyah Palopo, Indonesia

Hajeni Hajeni
Universitas Muhammadiyah Palopo, Indonesia

ABSTRACT

AI-driven educational networks affect workforce development and sustained economic growth, according to this study. Conventional schooling often fails to meet labor market demands, resulting in skills gaps that hinder productivity and creativity. Educational institutions can provide industry-specific, personalized learning experiences by using artificial intelligence—machine learning, predictive analytics,

DOI: 10.4018/979-8-3373-5786-7.ch007

and natural language processing. Effective case studies, curriculum development methods, and collaborative frameworks for educators, industry stakeholders, and policymakers are shown in the document. It addresses important issues including data privacy, equity, and accessibility. For inclusive and scalable execution, continual education, interdisciplinary collaboration, and policy endorsement are prioritized. AI-driven educational networks foster a resilient, skilled workforce that can adapt to a rapidly changing global economy.

INTRODUCTION TO WORKFORCE DEVELOPMENT AND AI

Understanding Workforce Development

Workforce development encompasses a systematic array of techniques and efforts designed to augment the skills and competencies of the workforce to align with labor market expectations. It includes diverse activities such as education, training, and professional development aimed at equipping individuals for present and future employment prospects (Li, 2024). Workforce development is crucial for fostering economic growth, decreasing unemployment, and providing firms with a competent labor force.

Historically, workforce development has progressed in tandem with shifts in the economy and labor market. In the early 20th century, the emphasis was predominantly on vocational training, designed to furnish persons with specialized skills for trades and manual work. With the industrialization of economies, the demand for a more proficient workforce emerged, resulting in the creation of official training programs and educational institutions (Ozkan-Ozen & Kazancoglu, 2022). The post-World War II period experienced substantial investments in education, leading to a burgeoning middle class and a strong job market.

The later portion of the 20th century signified a transition to knowledge-based economies, characterized by an increased need for higher education and sophisticated skills. This transformation required a reassessment of workforce development methods, highlighting lifelong learning and adaptation (Mohamed et al., 2021). The emergence of globalization and technological progress has transformed the work environment, necessitating continuous workforce development activities that address changing employment demands.

In recent years, the advent of artificial intelligence (AI) has significantly altered the workforce development paradigm. AI technologies can analyze labor market trends, identify skills deficiencies, and customize educational programs to address the specific requirements of industries (Johnson et al., 2021). Utilizing AI can render workforce development more data-driven and adaptive, guaranteeing that individuals possess the requisite abilities for success in an evolving labor market.

The use of AI into educational networks can provide tailored learning experiences, permitting learners to advance at their own speed and concentrate on areas requiring enhancement (Sundari et al.). This method improves individual results and fosters a more skilled and flexible workforce.

In conclusion, comprehending workforce development is crucial for tackling the issues of the contemporary economy. In the subsequent chapters, we will examine the convergence of AI and education, revealing how these innovations might foster sustainable economic growth and enhance worker resilience.

The Role of Education in Workforce Development

Education is essential for workforce development, serving as the foundation for individuals to establish their careers and enhance the economy. Conventional educational frameworks have historically been defined by rigid curricula, uniform assessments, and a universal approach to learning (Gleeson, 2022). These methods, predominantly centered on academic information, frequently emphasize theoretical comprehension over practical abilities, potentially resulting in a disparity between students' learning and the capabilities demanded by employers in the job market.

In recent years, the shortcomings of conventional education have become increasingly evident. A considerable number of graduates enter the market inadequately equipped for employment expectations, leading to a substantial skills gap. Employers sometimes encounter challenges in locating workers possessing requisite technical skills, critical thinking capabilities, and interpersonal skills, including communication and collaboration (Crone, 2023). The skills gap is especially evident in sectors like technology, healthcare, and advanced manufacturing, where swift innovations and changing industry norms necessitate ongoing learning and adaptation.

The disparity between educational attainment and job market requirements has substantial consequences for economic development. When individuals lack the competencies demanded by businesses, productivity diminishes, innovation halts, and unemployment rates may increase. To tackle this difficulty, there is an increasing acknowledgment of the necessity for educational systems to adapt and better align with workforce demands (Tan et al. 2021). This alignment is crucial to guarantee that graduates possess the skills desired by businesses, hence enhancing economic strength.

In reaction to these problems, novel educational models are arising that prioritize experiential learning, industrial collaborations, and skills-oriented training. Programs that include internships, apprenticeships, and practical projects enable students to acquire real-world experience while cultivating the abilities essential for their future professions. Moreover, these approaches promote collaboration between educational institutions and enterprises, establishing a feedback loop that guarantees courses stay pertinent and adaptable to labor market demands.

The use of artificial intelligence (AI) into educational systems can augment workforce development by delivering data-driven insights regarding skills deficiencies and labor market dynamics. AI technology can scrutinize extensive datasets to discern in-demand competencies, allowing educational institutions to customize their curriculum accordingly (Ng et al. 2023). Moreover, AI can enhance individualized learning experiences, enabling students to concentrate on areas for improvement, thereby augmenting their employability.

In summary, education is essential for workforce growth, effectively addressing the skills gap and fulfilling labor market demands. In the next chapters, we will analyze how the convergence of AI and education might revolutionize workforce development and establish avenues for sustainable economic growth.

Introduction to Artificial Intelligence

Artificial Intelligence (AI) denotes the emulation of human cognitive functions by technology, especially computer systems. These processes encompass learning, reasoning, problem-solving, perception, and language comprehension (Dai & Ke, 2022). Artificial intelligence systems can evaluate data, identify patterns, and render conclusions with limited human involvement. The domain of AI includes several sub-disciplines, such as machine learning, natural language processing, robotics, and computer vision, each facilitating the creation of intelligent systems capable of executing tasks that often necessitate human intelligence.

Fundamental concepts in AI encompass machine learning, wherein algorithms are trained on extensive datasets to discern patterns and generate predictions; deep learning, a branch of machine learning employing neural networks to evaluate intricate data; and natural language processing, which allows machines to comprehend and interpret human language (Khan et al. 2023). These technologies are progressively incorporated into diverse industries, revolutionizing our methods of work, communication, and education.

AI technologies are transforming the educational landscape and redefining workforce development tactics. A prominent application of AI in education is individualized learning. AI-driven systems can evaluate individual students' strengths, limitations, and learning styles, facilitating customized educational experiences that adjust to each learner's requirements (Ezzaim et al. 2024). This customization enables students to learn at their own speed, guaranteeing mastery of fundamental skills prior to progressing to more complex subjects.

Furthermore, AI can improve administrative efficiency in educational institutions (Han et al., 2024). AI-driven chatbots can offer immediate assistance to students by addressing inquiries about course material or administrative procedures, thereby allowing educators to concentrate on instruction. Moreover, AI can facilitate the grading of assessments and the provision of feedback, optimizing the evaluation process and allowing educators to allocate more time to instructional activities.

AI is essential in closing the skills gap by examining labor market trends and pinpointing sought-after abilities. Educational institutions can utilize this data to create curricula that correspond with industry demands, ensuring graduates possess the competences necessary by companies (Verma et al. 2022). Moreover, AI can enhance career advising by aligning students with prospective employment possibilities that correspond to their talents and interests.

The integration of AI with education offers a revolutionary prospect for workforce development. AI-driven education networks can cultivate a more skilled and flexible workforce by personalizing learning experiences, improving administrative efficiency, and matching educational outputs with labor market requirements. In the subsequent chapters, we will examine how the convergence of AI and workforce development facilitates sustainable economic growth.

THE INTERSECTION OF AI AND EDUCATION

AI Technologies in Education

Artificial Intelligence (AI) technologies are profoundly reshaping the educational landscape by offering revolutionary tools and techniques that improve teaching and learning processes (Alam, 2021). Two crucial domains in which AI is advancing considerably are machine learning and predictive analytics, alongside natural language processing (NLP) and chatbots. These technologies are enhancing educational outcomes while aligning learning experiences with the changing requirements of the workforce.

Machine Learning and Predictive Analytics

Machine learning, a branch of artificial intelligence, encompasses techniques that allow computers to learn from data and provide predictions. In educational contexts, machine learning can evaluate extensive student data, encompassing performance measures, engagement levels, and learning behaviors (Yağcı, 2022). By recognizing patterns and trends, educational institutions can get significant insights into student learning processes and areas of difficulty.

Predictive analytics, utilizing machine learning algorithms, can anticipate student outcomes, including the probability of course completion or timely graduation. This proactive strategy enables educators to intervene promptly with focused assistance for at-risk kids, consequently enhancing retention rates and overall student achievement (Sghir et al., 2023). Moreover, predictive analytics can guide curriculum development by identifying courses or skills that necessitate greater focus in accordance with labor market trends, so ensuring the relevance and efficacy of educational programs.

Natural Language Processing and Chatbots

Natural language processing (NLP) is a vital AI technology that improves educational experiences. Natural Language Processing (NLP) empowers robots to comprehend, interpret, and react to human language effectively. NLP applications in education can enable automated essay grading, delivering immediate feedback to students and alleviating the effort for educators (Pruneski et al. 2023). This not only optimizes the evaluation process but also enables pupils to learn from their errors in real time.

Chatbots, driven by natural language processing, are progressively utilized in educational institutions to offer prompt support to pupils. These AI-powered virtual assistants can respond to inquiries regarding course material, administrative processes, and offer study strategies. By providing round-the-clock help, chatbots improve student engagement and satisfaction, enabling learners to obtain knowledge at any time (Abbas et al. 2022). This accessibility is especially advantageous in online and hybrid learning contexts, where students may need supplementary assistance beyond conventional classroom hours.

In conclusion, the incorporation of AI technologies, including machine learning, predictive analytics, and natural language processing, is transforming the educational landscape. By utilizing these techniques, educational institutions may develop more individualized, efficient, and adaptive learning environments. The exploration of the interface between AI and education reveals that these breakthroughs are crucial for cultivating a proficient workforce equipped to succeed in a swiftly evolving economic environment.

Benefits of AI-Driven Education Networks

AI-driven educational networks are transforming student learning, providing many advantages that improve the educational experience and better equip individuals for the workforce (Luckin, 2025). Two of the primary benefits of these networks are customized learning experiences and improved engagement and retention.

Personalized Learning Experiences

A significant advantage of AI in education is its capacity to deliver individualized learning experiences customized to the distinct needs of each student. Conventional educational programs frequently employ a uniform approach, thereby neglecting certain children while inadequately challenging others (Davis et al. 2024). AI-driven systems employ data analytics and machine learning algorithms to evaluate individual learning styles, preferences, and performance metrics.

Through the analysis of this data, AI systems may tailor learning pathways that adjust in real time to the development of each learner. For instance, if a learner encounters difficulty with a specific subject, the AI can provide further resources, practice exercises, or alternate explanations to enhance comprehension (Naseer et al., 2024). If a student excels in a subject, the system can provide more sophisticated resources to maintain their engagement. This customized method enhances comprehension of the material and enables students to assume responsibility for their education, resulting in better academic performance.

Enhanced Engagement and Retention

AI-powered educational networks substantially improve student involvement and retention. Students that are engaged are more inclined to persevere in their studies and attain superior outcomes. AI technology can enhance interactive and immersive learning experiences that engage students' attention (Rapaka et al. 2025). Gamification components, like incentives and challenges, can be included into educational systems to enhance enjoyment and motivation in learning.

Moreover, AI may evaluate engagement measures, like time allocated to activities and involvement in discussions, to discern when students could be losing interest or experiencing difficulties in maintaining pace (Archibald et al. 2023). Educators might subsequently intervene beforehand, providing assistance or modifying the curriculum to sustain student engagement.

The capacity to deliver prompt and pertinent feedback is another essential element in improving retention. AI systems provide immediate evaluations and recommendations, assisting students in comprehending their advancement and locations needing enhancement (Hooda et al. 2022). This ongoing feedback mechanism cultivates a sense of achievement and motivates students to stay dedicated to their academic pursuits.

In conclusion, AI-powered educational networks provide tailored learning experiences and improve student engagement and retention. By accommodating individual requirements and promoting a more engaging educational atmosphere, these networks equip students for both academic achievement and the expectations of the contemporary labor market. The exploration of AI's revolutionary impact on education reveals that these developments are crucial for developing a trained and adaptive workforce required for fostering sustainable economic growth.

Case Studies of Successful AI Integration

The incorporation of artificial intelligence (AI) in educational institutions has produced favorable outcomes, revolutionizing the learning experience and improving workforce preparedness (Bucea-Manea- oniş et al. 2022). Numerous case studies demonstrate the effective implementation of AI technology, highlighting their influence on student results and the alignment of education with labor market demands.

Example 1: Georgia State University

Georgia State University (GSU) has instituted an extensive AI system aimed at enhancing student retention and success rates. Employing predictive analytics, GSU's AI platform examines data from several sources, encompassing student demographics, academic achievement, and engagement measures (Shoaib et al. 2024). By identifying students at risk of attrition, the university can implement targeted interventions, including individualized advising and academic resources.

The outcomes have been remarkable. Following the adoption of this AI-driven methodology, GSU has experienced a notable enhancement in graduation rates, evidenced by a 22% increase in the number of students graduating within six years. This achievement not only improves individual student results but also fosters a more proficient workforce, as graduates are better equipped to satisfy the requirements of the labor market.

Example 2: Carnegie Mellon University

Carnegie Mellon University (CMU) has adopted AI via its “Open Learning Initiative,” providing courses augmented by intelligent tutoring technologies. These systems employ machine learning algorithms to deliver real-time feedback to students, tailoring teaching materials according to individual performance (D'Mello &

Graesser, 2023). Through the analysis of student interactions, the AI may discern prevalent misconceptions and modify the curriculum accordingly.

The effect on student results has been significant. Students utilizing the AI-enhanced courses at CMU have exhibited superior learning outcomes relative to conventional classroom environments. This method cultivates profound comprehension and equips pupils for the intricacies of the workforce by enhancing critical thinking and problem-solving abilities vital in the contemporary job market (Al-Zarkani et al. 2024).

Example 3: Duolingo

Duolingo, a prominent language-learning program, shows the effective incorporation of artificial intelligence in education. The platform utilizes natural language processing and machine learning to develop customized learning experiences for users (Phanwiriyarat et al. 2025). Duolingo customizes lessons based on user data, aligning them with individual competence levels to guarantee that learners remain both challenged and engaged.

The platform's efficacy is demonstrated by its swift expansion and user contentment. Duolingo, with over 500 million users globally, has demonstrated that artificial intelligence can render language acquisition both accessible and efficient. As individuals develop new language competencies, they enhance their competitiveness in the global labor market, hence improving their employability and workforce preparedness (Shortt et al. 2023).

In conclusion, these case studies illustrate the revolutionary potential of AI integration in education. Utilizing predictive analytics, intelligent tutoring systems, and personalized learning platforms, educational institutions can markedly enhance student results and more effectively equip individuals for the workforce. The exploration of the interface between AI and education reveals that these breakthroughs are essential for cultivating a trained workforce that can propel sustained economic growth.

DESIGNING AI-DRIVEN EDUCATION NETWORKS

Framework for AI-Driven Learning Environments

Creating efficient AI-driven educational networks necessitates a thorough framework that integrates essential components and architecture, alongside collaboration among many stakeholders, including educators, industry leaders, and governmental bodies (Kim et al., 2022). This cooperative strategy guarantees that the educational framework is attuned to the requirements of students and synchronized with labor market needs.

Key Components and Architecture

An AI-driven learning environment comprises several fundamental components that collaborate to establish a unified educational experience. The components comprise:

1. Data Infrastructure: A robust data infrastructure is essential for any AI-driven system, facilitating the collection, storage, and analysis of extensive information from many sources. This data encompasses student performance measures, engagement levels, and demographic information (Desai et al. 2021). An effectively structured data architecture facilitates real-time analytics, empowering educators to make informed decisions grounded in actionable findings.
2. AI Algorithms and Instruments: The essence of AI-driven education resides in the algorithms and tools that analyze data and provide tailored learning experiences (Sundari et al.). Machine learning algorithms can examine student interactions to discern patterns, while natural language processing technologies can enhance communication and feedback. These technologies provide personalized learning trajectories customized to the specific requirements of each student.
3. User Interface: The user interface is essential for facilitating seamless navigation of the AI-driven platform for students, educators, and administrators. A user-centric and accessible design fosters engagement and promotes the adoption of the technology (Eswaran and Eswaran 2025). Interactive dashboards offer educators insights into student progress, while learners can obtain individualized tools and feedback.

A dynamic content management system is essential for curating and delivering instructional materials that correspond with individual learning pathways (Pierce et al. 2022). This system must accommodate many material types, including videos, interactive simulations, and assessments, to address varying learning preferences.

Collaboration Between Stakeholders

Collaboration among stakeholders is vital to optimize the efficacy of AI-driven educational networks. Educators are essential in formulating curriculum that incorporate AI tools and approaches, guaranteeing that learning experiences are pertinent and significant (Kim et al., 2022). Their understanding of student requirements and teaching methodologies is essential for informing the creation of AI systems.

Industry partners supply data on labor market trends and in-demand skills, enabling educational institutions to connect their curriculum with actual requirements (Johnson et al. 2021). Collaborative programs, including internships and apprenticeships, can effectively connect education and work by providing students with actual experience in their selected sectors.

Government organizations can bolster these activities by formulating regulations that foster innovation in education, financing research endeavors, and enabling collaborations between educational institutions and industry (Pandey et al. 2022). By establishing an ecosystem that fosters collaboration, stakeholders can jointly develop AI-driven educational networks that equip students for the demands of the contemporary workforce.

In summary, the framework for AI-enhanced learning environments must include essential elements and promote collaboration among educators, industry, and government. By utilizing the skills of each stakeholder, we can develop efficient educational systems that improve learning outcomes and foster sustainable economic growth.

Curriculum Development for AI Integration

The incorporation of artificial intelligence (AI) into educational systems requires a deliberate strategy for curriculum development that matches with industry demands and integrates both technical and interpersonal abilities (Khosravi et al. 2022). This connection is vital for equipping students to succeed in a swiftly changing employment environment where adaptability and a varied skill set are crucial.

Synchronizing Curriculum with Industry Requirements

To maintain the relevance and efficacy of educational programs, curricula must be meticulously linked with labor market demands. Engaging with industry stakeholders is essential in this process. Educational institutions ought to collaborate with employers to ascertain the existing and emerging skills necessary across various sectors (Aljohani et al. 2022). This collaboration may manifest in several formats, such as advisory boards, internships, and collaborations that promote knowledge transfer.

An effective technique involves performing regular labor market analyses to discern trends and skill deficiencies. Through the analysis of job listings, workforce surveys, and industry forecasts, educators can modify their courses to meet the specific competencies desired by employers (Alibasic et al. 2022). In the technology sector, curricula should incorporate training in data analytics, machine learning, and cybersecurity to equip students for in-demand positions.

Furthermore, integrating real-world projects and case studies into the curriculum helps augment students' comprehension of industrial methods (Popli & Singh, 2024). Engaging in projects that replicate professional issues enables students to apply their knowledge in practical contexts, so bridging the divide between theory and practice.

Incorporating Soft Skills and Technical Skills

In the current work market, technical abilities alone are inadequate for professional success. Employers are increasingly seeking people with robust soft skills, including communication, teamwork, problem-solving, and adaptability. Consequently, curriculum must incorporate both technical and interpersonal abilities to deliver a comprehensive education (Hirudayaraj et al., 2021).

Artificial intelligence can substantially contribute to the development of these talents. Collaborative learning platforms enhanced by AI can enable group projects, fostering collaboration and communication skills among students (Issa & Hall, 2024). Furthermore, AI-driven simulations can provide students with authentic settings that necessitate critical thinking and problem-solving, allowing them to hone these vital abilities in a secure setting.

Furthermore, educators want to underscore the significance of lifelong learning and adaptability in their instruction. As industries progress, the capacity to acquire new skills and adjust to change becomes progressively vital (Park & Park, 2021). By fostering a growth attitude in kids, educators may equip them to manage the intricacies of their future professions.

In conclusion, curriculum development for AI integration must prioritize the alignment of educational programs with industrial requirements, while integrating both technical and interpersonal abilities. By promoting collaboration between educational institutions and industry stakeholders and prioritizing the cultivation of a diverse skill set, we can produce a workforce that is proficient in technical domains and possesses the crucial soft skills required for success in a dynamic job market. This comprehensive educational strategy is essential for fostering sustainable economic growth and equipping graduates to confront future problems.

Challenges and Considerations

As educational institutions progressively incorporate artificial intelligence (AI) into their systems, certain obstacles and issues must be addressed to guarantee the effective implementation of AI-driven educational networks (Okunlaya et al., 2022). The major problems are data privacy and ethical considerations, with accessibility and equity in education.

Data Privacy and Ethical Concerns

The application of AI in education sometimes entails the aggregation and examination of extensive student data, encompassing personal information, academic performance, and behavioral tendencies. This data can augment individualized learning experiences and promote educational outcomes, but it also presents considerable privacy problems (Ismail and Aloshi 2025). Educational institutions must manage the intricacies of data protection requirements, including the Family Educational Rights and Privacy Act (FERPA) in the United States and the General Data Protection Regulation (GDPR) in Europe.

To mitigate these issues, universities must establish stringent data governance policies that promote student privacy. This entails guaranteeing that data is gathered, retained, and processed securely, accompanied by transparent consent protocols (Yang & Beil, 2024). Moreover, institutions have to implement ethical frameworks for AI utilization, guaranteeing that algorithms remain unbiased and do not perpetuate current disparities. Routine audits and evaluations of AI systems can assist in recognizing and alleviating any ethical concerns, hence cultivating trust among students, parents, and instructors.

Accessibility and Equity in Education

A vital factor in the creation of AI-driven educational networks is the assurance of accessibility and equity for all students. Although AI possesses the capacity to improve educational experiences, it also poses a risk of intensifying pre-existing inequalities in education (Kunjumuhammed, 2024). Students from marginalized or impoverished backgrounds may have restricted access to technology and internet connectivity, impeding their capacity to utilize AI-driven educational resources.

To foster equity, educational institutions must emphasize diversity in their AI programs. This entails investing in infrastructure that guarantees all pupils access to essential technology and resources (Roshanaei, 2024). Moreover, AI systems must be engineered to address multiple learning requirements, catering to students with disabilities and varying learning modalities. It is imperative to offer training for educators on the efficient use of AI tools to assist different learners.

Furthermore, collaborations with community organizations and governmental entities can facilitate the bridging of the digital gap by offering resources and assistance to marginalized communities. By cultivating an inclusive atmosphere, educational institutions may guarantee that all students have the potential to excel in an AI-enhanced learning landscape (Grieco-Page et al. 2021).

In conclusion, whereas the incorporation of AI into education holds transformative promise, it also poses obstacles that must be meticulously addressed. Addressing data privacy and ethical issues, along with guaranteeing accessibility and equity, is essential for developing effective AI-driven educational networks. By emphasizing these factors, educational institutions can leverage AI to improve learning outcomes and foster sustainable economic growth, ultimately equipping all students for success in the workforce.

IMPLEMENTING AI-DRIVEN WORKFORCE DEVELOPMENT PROGRAMS

Strategies for Effective Implementation

The effective execution of AI-driven workforce development initiatives necessitates strategic strategy and implementation. Essential measures encompass launching pilot programs, expanding effective models, and delivering extensive training for educators and workforce development specialists (Md et al. 2025). These characteristics are essential for the proper integration of AI technology into educational frameworks and for addressing the growing demands of the labor market.

Pilot Programs and Scaling Successful Models

Initiating pilot programs is a crucial initial phase in executing AI-driven workforce development efforts. Pilot projects enable educational institutions and organizations to evaluate AI technologies in a controlled setting, facilitating the assessment of their efficacy and the identification of potential issues prior to a wider implementation (Quan et al. 2022). The preliminary experiments may concentrate on certain industries or skill sets, yielding significant insights into the practical applications of AI in workforce development.

In the pilot phase, it is essential to define explicit success indicators, including enhancements in student engagement, learning outcomes, and employment rates. Gathering and evaluating data from these initiatives will assist stakeholders in comprehending the effects of AI interventions and enhancing their methodologies (Ikudayisi et al. 2022). According to the findings, effective models can be expanded to engage a broader audience, guaranteeing that the advantages of AI-driven education are distributed across diverse sectors and demographics.

Expanding successful models necessitates engagement with industry partners to guarantee that the programs correspond with contemporary labor market demands. Interacting with employers can yield insights on the requisite skills and capabilities, enabling educational institutions to modify their curricula accordingly (Hung et al., 2023). Additionally, collaborations with community organizations can enhance access to marginalized populations, guaranteeing that AI-driven workforce development initiatives are inclusive and equitable.

Training Educators and Workforce Development Professionals

The successful execution of AI-driven initiatives relies on the training and professional advancement of educators and workforce development specialists. As AI technologies are incorporated into educational systems, it is crucial for educators to have the skills and expertise to utilize these tools effectively (Jenkins & Khanna, 2025). Extensive training programs must be established to acquaint educators with AI technologies, data analytics, and individualized learning methodologies.

Professional development must prioritize cultivating a growth mentality in educators, motivating them to adopt innovation and adjust to novel teaching approaches (Lin et al., 2022). Workshops, seminars, and collaborative learning communities offer continuous support and resources for educators as they incorporate AI into their teaching methodologies.

Moreover, workforce development experts must receive training to comprehend the ramifications of AI on job preparedness and career guidance. This involves providing them with the abilities to monitor labor market trends and identify future industries, so enabling them to successfully lead students in their career trajectories (Li, 2024).

In conclusion, the implementation of AI-driven workforce development programs necessitates a comprehensive strategy encompassing pilot initiatives, the scaling of successful models, and the training of educators and workforce development professionals. By implementing these tactics, educational institutions can develop effective programs that improve learning outcomes and equip students for the requirements of the contemporary workforce, thereby fostering sustained economic growth.

Measuring Impact and Success

Assessing the efficacy and outcomes of AI-driven workforce development programs is essential for guaranteeing that these initiatives adequately equip students for the requirements of the labor market. Establishing key performance indicators (KPIs) and establishing feedback mechanisms are vital elements of this evaluation process (Gafni et al. 2024). Collectively, they offer significant insights into program efficacy and promote ongoing enhancement.

Essential Performance Metrics for Workforce Preparedness

Key Performance Indicators (KPIs) function as measurable indicators that evaluate the efficacy of workforce development initiatives. Various KPIs can be employed to assess workforce readiness for AI-driven initiatives:

1. work Rates: Monitoring the proportion of program graduates who obtain work within a designated period following completion is a critical KPI. Elevated employment rates signify that the program successfully prepares students with the requisite skills for the labor market.
2. Job Placement in Relevant Fields: Assessing the percentage of alumni securing employment in their area of study offers insight into the program's congruence with industry demands. This KPI assesses the curriculum's effectiveness in preparing students for designated career trajectories.
3. Skill Acquisition: Evaluating the competencies students attain during the program is essential. This can be quantified via pre- and post-assessments, industry certifications, or competency evaluations, confirming that graduates possess requisite technical and interpersonal abilities.
4. Employer Satisfaction: Collecting input from companies about the performance and readiness of graduates can yield significant insights into the program's efficacy. Surveys and interviews can be utilized to assess employer satisfaction and pinpoint areas for enhancement.
5. Student Retention and Completion Rates: Assessing the retention rates of students in the program might reflect the program's engagement and pertinence. Elevated completion rates indicate that students perceive the education offered as valuable.

Feedback Loops and Continuous Improvement

Establishing feedback loops is essential for cultivating a culture of ongoing enhancement in AI-driven workforce development initiatives. Feedback loops entail the systematic collection of data and insights from diverse stakeholders, such as students, instructors, employers, and industry experts (Sjödin et al., 2021). This information can evaluate the program's efficacy and pinpoint areas for improvement.

Systematic evaluations and assessments must be performed to analyze the gathered data. This may encompass focus groups, surveys, and performance evaluations, which yield qualitative and quantitative data regarding the program's strengths and flaws (Nevedal et al. 2021). Educational institutions can make informed revisions to curricula and teaching approaches by requesting input from students about their learning experiences and from employers regarding the performance of graduates.

Furthermore, utilizing AI analytics can improve the feedback mechanism. AI systems may examine extensive information to discern trends and find areas for enhancement, enabling educators to proactively address emerging difficulties.

In conclusion, assessing the efficacy and outcomes of AI-driven workforce development initiatives necessitates the formulation of key performance measures and the construction of comprehensive feedback mechanisms. By concentrating on these factors, educational institutions can guarantee that their programs adequately equip students for the workforce, promoting ongoing enhancement and facilitating sustainable economic growth.

Building Partnerships for Sustainability

Establishing sustainable collaborations is crucial for the efficacy of AI-driven workforce development initiatives. Partnerships with enterprises and community organizations, coupled with efficient finance and resource distribution techniques, are essential for ensuring these programs are adequately supported, pertinent, and influential.

Collaboration with Businesses and Community Organizations

Collaborating with businesses is essential for synchronizing educational curricula with labor market demands. Through collaborations with local and regional employers, educational institutions can acquire knowledge regarding the requisite skills and abilities in demand. These interactions may manifest in several formats, including advisory boards, internships, apprenticeships, and job placement programs (Atwell et al. 2022). Businesses can provide real-world projects for students, enabling them to apply their knowledge in realistic environments while concurrently supplying companies with a source of competent people.

Community organizations are essential in establishing sustainable workforce development initiatives. They can facilitate the connection between educational institutions and marginalized populations, guaranteeing that programs are accessible to all community members (Abiddin et al., 2022). Through collaboration with these organizations, educational institutions can engage a wider audience, especially individuals who encounter obstacles to education and employment. Community organizations can provide support services, including counseling, mentoring, and job ready training, thereby augmenting the efficacy of workforce development projects.

Strategies for Funding and Resource Allocation

Effective funding and resource allocation techniques frequently underpin sustainable collaborations. Acquiring financial support from many sources, including as government grants, private sector investments, and philanthropic donations, is crucial for the advancement and sustainability of AI-driven workforce initiatives (Kalyanaraman et al. 2022). Educational institutions must proactively seek varied financing sources to guarantee a consistent influx of resources.

Alongside securing finances, it is imperative to use resources strategically to optimize impact. This encompasses investment in technological infrastructure, educator training, and program development. By prioritizing resource allocation according to data-driven evaluations of program requirements and community needs, institutions may guarantee that their workforce development activities are both responsive and effective (Menon and Suresh 2022).

Furthermore, utilizing in-kind contributions from commercial partners can improve program sustainability. Businesses can provide access to buildings, technology, or knowledge, alleviating the financial strain on educational institutions and enhancing the learning experience for students (Thompson, 2021).

In summary, establishing collaborations with enterprises and community organizations, coupled with the execution of efficient funding and resource distribution methods, is crucial for the sustainability of AI-driven workforce development initiatives. These collaborations boost the relevance and efficacy of educational activities while ensuring accessibility for all community members. By cultivating strong collaborations and obtaining varied financing sources, educational institutions can establish effective workforce development programs that promote sustainable economic growth and equip individuals for success in the contemporary job market.

FUTURE TRENDS AND THE PATH FORWARD

Emerging Technologies in Workforce Development

As workforce development advances, emerging technologies including virtual reality (VR), augmented reality (AR), and blockchain are set to assume transformative roles (Saranya et al. 2024). These technologies provide novel solutions that improve training, credentialing, and the overall learning experience, rendering them indispensable elements of AI-driven educational networks.

Virtual Reality (VR) and Augmented Reality (AR) in Training

Virtual reality and augmented reality are transforming training and education by offering immersive, interactive experiences that improve learning results. Virtual reality generates entirely immersive environments that enable learners to interact with content in a simulated context, facilitating skill practice in a secure and regulated environment (Coban et al., 2022). In healthcare, virtual reality can replicate surgical operations, allowing medical students to acquire practical experience without the dangers of actual practice. This practical learning promotes enhanced comprehension and retention of intricate concepts.

Augmented reality enhances this by superimposing digital information onto the physical environment. In vocational training, augmented reality can aid learners by offering immediate assistance and feedback during job execution. In manufacturing, augmented reality (AR) can project sequential instructions onto machinery, thereby enhancing trainees' comprehension of operations and reducing errors (Carretero et al. 2021). These technologies not only improve engagement but also cater to various learning styles, rendering training more accessible and effective.

Blockchain for Credentialing and Skills Verification

Blockchain technology is developing as a potent instrument for credentialing and skills verification, tackling the difficulties linked to conventional means of authenticating educational accomplishments. Utilizing blockchain, educational institutions can establish secure, immutable digital credentials that offer a transparent record of learners' qualifications and competencies. This technology enables companies to swiftly and effectively verify candidates' credentials, minimizing the time and resources allocated to background checks (Jha, 2023).

Furthermore, blockchain can enable the development of digital portfolios that exhibit a learner's competencies, credentials, and experiences. These portfolios can be readily disseminated to prospective employers, offering a thorough overview of a candidate's competencies (Yadav, 2024). As the labor market grows more competitive, possessing a verified and readily accessible record of abilities will be essential for job seekers.

Moreover, blockchain can facilitate lifelong learning by allowing individuals to compile and preserve a digital record of their ongoing education and training (Bjelobaba et al., 2023). This method fosters a culture of continuous learning, enabling employees to adjust to evolving job demands and seek new possibilities throughout their careers.

In conclusion, emerging technologies like virtual reality, augmented reality, and blockchain are poised to revolutionize workforce development by augmenting training experiences and refining credentialing processes. As educational institutions incorporate these technologies into their AI-driven teaching frameworks, they will be more adept at preparing students for the exigencies of the contemporary workforce. By adopting these technologies, we can cultivate a more proficient, versatile, and competitive workforce, thereby fostering sustained economic growth.

Policy Recommendations for Supporting AI-Driven Education

As AI-driven educational networks advance, it is imperative for policymakers to foster an environment that promotes innovation while upholding ethical standards and ensuring fair access (Berson et al.). This chapter delineates essential policy ideas, emphasizing governmental activities, financial prospects, and the creation of a regulatory framework for artificial intelligence in education.

Government Initiatives and Funding Opportunities

To properly leverage AI's promise in education, governmental initiatives must prioritize funding for research and development in AI technology. This funding can facilitate initiatives that investigate innovative applications of AI in educational environments, including personalized learning platforms, intelligent tutoring systems, and data analytics for workforce preparedness (de Silva, 2024). Through investment in research, governments can promote collaboration among educational institutions, technological firms, and industry players, thereby advancing the creation of viable AI solutions.

Furthermore, governments ought to establish grant programs that encourage educational institutions to implement AI-driven technologies. These awards can assist in financing the implementation of AI tools, the training of educators, and the development of AI-integrated curriculum. Governments can reduce entrance barriers for institutions, especially in disadvantaged regions, by offering financial support, so guaranteeing that all students can receive the advantages of AI-enhanced educational experiences (Yu et al., 2022).

Moreover, activities designed to enhance digital literacy and artificial intelligence proficiency among instructors are essential. Training programs must be developed to enable instructors to proficiently incorporate AI tools into their classrooms (Chiu et al. 2024). By cultivating a cadre of educators skilled in AI technology, governments can guarantee that kids have superior instruction and assistance.

Creating a Regulatory Framework for AI in Education

Creating a legislative framework for AI in education is crucial to tackle ethical issues, data protection, and the fair application of AI technologies. Policymakers must establish criteria to guarantee openness and accountability in AI systems utilized in educational environments (Nguyen et al. 2023). This encompasses establishing criteria for data acquisition, preservation, and utilization, in addition to guaranteeing that AI algorithms are devoid of bias and discrimination.

Furthermore, regulations must advocate for the ethical utilization of AI, underscoring the significance of student privacy and data protection (Ferhataj et al. 2025). Educational institutions must develop stringent data governance regulations that protect student information while facilitating the appropriate utilization of AI analytics to improve learning results.

The regulatory framework should promote collaboration among stakeholders, including educators, technologists, and policymakers (Ifenthaler et al. 2021). Through the promotion of discourse and collaboration, stakeholders may together tackle obstacles and ascertain optimal practices for the ethical application of AI in education.

In summary, endorsing AI-driven education necessitates thorough policy suggestions encompassing government initiatives, financial options, and a well articulated regulatory framework. By emphasizing these domains, policymakers may foster an atmosphere that promotes innovation while guaranteeing the ethical and equitable use of AI technologies. These initiatives will ultimately improve workforce development, equipping students for success in a dynamic labor market and fostering sustainable economic growth.

Vision for a Sustainable Economic Growth

The incorporation of artificial intelligence (AI) into educational systems offers a transformative possibility for promoting sustainable economic development. In contemplating the future, it is imperative to acknowledge the enduring advantages of AI-driven educational systems and the vital importance of lifelong learning in adjusting to the changing labor market (Mhlanga, 2021).

Enduring Advantages of AI-Enhanced Educational Networks

AI-driven educational networks possess the capacity to cultivate a more proficient, versatile, and inventive workforce. By customizing educational experiences, these networks guarantee that individuals obtain the requisite skills to excel in many industries. This focused strategy not only improves individual employability but also mitigates the skills gap encountered by numerous employers today (Tavakoli et al. 2022). Graduating students with skills that meet labor market requirements enhances the talent pool for firms, resulting in heightened productivity and economic expansion.

Furthermore, AI technology can enhance lifetime learning by granting learners perpetual access to educational resources and training opportunities. As industries progress and novel technologies arise, the capacity to upskill and reskill becomes essential (Ahsan, 2025). AI-driven systems provide customized learning trajectories that enable individuals to adjust to evolving employment demands, hence maintaining their competitiveness in the labor market. This adaptability cultivates a culture of innovation, as a proficient workforce is more capable of adopting new technology and advancing economic development.

The Role of Continuous Learning in the Evolving Job Market

In the current dynamic employment landscape, ongoing education is crucial for both individuals and businesses. The half-life of skills is diminishing, indicating that knowledge and competencies may become obsolete more rapidly than ever. Consequently, cultivating a lifelong learning attitude is essential for maintaining economic growth. Educational institutions and workforce development programs must underscore the significance of lifelong learning, motivating individuals to engage in continual training and professional advancement throughout their careers (Berchin & de Aguiar Dutra…, 2021).

AI-driven educational networks are essential for fostering continuous learning by providing flexible, accessible, and customized educational experiences. These platforms offer real-time feedback, adaptable learning pathways, and an abundance of materials that enable learners to assume control of their education (Singh et al., 2025). Organizations can utilize AI to detect skills deficiencies within their staff and create focused training programs to meet these requirements, ensuring personnel remain pertinent and efficient.

In summary, the aspiration for sustainable economic growth via AI-driven educational networks relies on the enduring advantages of individualized learning and the encouragement of lifelong education. By providing workers with the necessary skills to adapt to a changing labor market and promoting a culture of continuous learning, we can cultivate a resilient workforce capable of encouraging innovation and economic growth. By adopting these developments, we facilitate a future in which education and workforce development are cohesively intertwined, thereby fostering sustainable economic growth.

CONCLUSION

The incorporation of AI-driven educational networks into workforce development plans offers a significant opportunity to rectify skills mismatches, improve employability, and foster inclusive economic growth. This research illustrates that artificial intelligence facilitates individualized, data-driven learning experiences that better correspond with current job market requirements. By utilizing technologies such as machine learning, predictive analytics, and intelligent tutoring systems, educational institutions may more effectively prepare learners with the technical and interpersonal skills necessary for a swiftly evolving labor market.

Case studies from prominent colleges and platforms such as Duolingo illustrate the beneficial effects of AI-enhanced programs on student performance and workforce preparedness. Furthermore, the establishment of collaborative ecosystems—integrating government, industry, and academia—becomes essential for guaranteeing relevance, scalability, and sustainability. AI facilitates continuous learning, enabling employees to enhance and acquire new skills throughout their careers, thus promoting innovation and resilience within the workforce.

For these technologies to flourish, concerns related to equity, data privacy, and access must be proactively resolved. Investments in infrastructure, educator training, and the ethical implementation of artificial intelligence are crucial. Policymakers must provide supportive frameworks that guarantee both opportunities and protections for learners across all levels.

In summary, AI-driven educational networks signify a crucial transformation in workforce development, connecting education with employment. When developed inclusively and executed strategically, these systems can boost individual career opportunities and promote long-term, sustainable economic development globally. The future of employment necessitates a synergy of technology, education, and human potential.

REFERENCES

Abbas, N., Whitfield, J., Atwell, E., Bowman, H., Pickard, T., & Walker, A. (2022). Online chat and chatbots to enhance mature student engagement in higher education. [tandfonline.com]. *International Journal of Lifelong Education, 41*(3), 308–326. DOI: 10.1080/02601370.2022.2066213

Abiddin, N. Z., Ibrahim, I., & Abdul Aziz, S. A. (2022). Non-governmental organisations (NGOs) and their part towards sustainable community development. Sustainability. mdpi.com

Ahsan, M. J. (2025). Cultivating a culture of learning: The role of leadership in fostering lifelong development. [HTML]. *The Learning Organization, 32*(2), 282–306. DOI: 10.1108/TLO-03-2024-0099

Al-Zarkani, K. H., Al-Atabi, A. R. J., & Al-Jubouri, M. T. A. (2024, July). The Use of Artificial Intelligence Analytics to Understand Learning Behaviors and Improve Student Outcomes in E-Learning. In International Conference on Intelligent Systems, Blockchain, and Communication Technologies (pp. 523-530). Cham: Springer Nature Switzerland. [HTML]

Alam, A. (2021, November). Possibilities and apprehensions in the landscape of artificial intelligence in education. In 2021 International conference on computational intelligence and computing applications (ICCICA) (pp. 1-8). IEEE. [HTML] DOI: 10.1109/ICCICA52458.2021.9697272

Alibasic, A., Upadhyay, H., Simsekler, M. C. E., Kurfess, T., Woon, W. L., & Omar, M. A. (2022). Evaluation of the trends in jobs and skill-sets using data analytics: A case study. [springer.com]. *Journal of Big Data, 9*(1), 32. DOI: 10.1186/s40537-022-00576-5

Aljohani, N. R., Aslam, A., Khadidos, A. O., & Hassan, S. U. (2022). Bridging the skill gap between the acquired university curriculum and the requirements of the job market: A data-driven analysis of scientific literature. [sciencedirect.com]. *Journal of Innovation & Knowledge, 7*(3), 100190. DOI: 10.1016/j.jik.2022.100190

Archibald, A., Hudson, C., Heap, T., Thompson, R. R., Lin, L., DeMeritt, J., & Lucke, H. (2023). A validation of AI-enabled discussion platform metrics and relationships to student efforts. [springer.com]. *TechTrends, 67*(2), 285–293. DOI: 10.1007/s11528-022-00825-7 PMID: 36711121

Atwell, A., Ecton, W., Klein, S., D'Amico, M. M., & Sublett, C. (2022). Community college responses to align career and technical education programs with changing labor markets. [wiley.com]. *New Directions for Community Colleges, 2022*(197), 45–58. DOI: 10.1002/cc.20496

Berchin, I. I. & Aguiar Dutra, A. R. (2021). How do higher education institutions promote sustainable development? A literature review. Sustainable …. [HTML]

Berson, I. R., Berson, M. J., & Luo, W. Innovating responsibly: ethical considerations for AI in early childhood education. AI. springer.com

Bjelobaba, G., Savić, A., Tošić, T., Stefanović, I., & Kocić, B. (2023). Collaborative learning supported by Blockchain Technology as a model for improving the Educational process. Sustainability. mdpi.com

Bucea-Manea- oniş, R., Kuleto, V., Gudei, S. C. D., Lianu, C., Lianu, C., Ilić, M. P., & Păun, D. (2022). Artificial intelligence potential in higher education institutions enhanced learning environment in Romania and Serbia. [mdpi.com]. *Sustainability (Basel), 14*(10), 5842. DOI: 10.3390/su14105842

Carretero, M. D. P., García, S., Moreno, A., Alcain, N., & Elorza, I. (2021). Methodology to create virtual reality assisted training courses within the Industry 4.0 vision. [HTML]. *Multimedia Tools and Applications, 80*(19), 29699–29717. DOI: 10.1007/s11042-021-11195-2

Chiu, T. K., Ahmad, Z., Ismailov, M., & Sanusi, I. T. (2024). What are artificial intelligence literacy and competency? A comprehensive framework to support them. [sciencedirect.com]. *Computers and Education Open, 6*, 100171. DOI: 10.1016/j.caeo.2024.100171

Coban, M., Bolat, Y. I., & Goksu, I. (2022). The potential of immersive virtual reality to enhance learning: A meta-analysis. [HTML]. *Educational Research Review, 36*, 100452. DOI: 10.1016/j.edurev.2022.100452

Crone, V. C. A. (2023). A mismatch: Why non-tenured teachers are ill-prepared to deal with the perceived job insecurity of students in the humanities. Arts and Humanities in Higher Education. sagepub.com

D'Mello, S. K., & Graesser, A. (2023). Intelligent tutoring systems: How computers achieve learning gains that rival human tutors. Handbook of educational psychology. [HTML]

Dai, C. P. & Ke, F. (2022). Educational applications of artificial intelligence in simulation-based learning: A systematic mapping review. Computers and Education: Artificial Intelligence. sciencedirect.com

Davis, C., Bush, T., & Wood, S. (2024). Artificial intelligence in education: Enhancing learning experiences through personalized adaptation. [iaic-publisher.org]. *International Journal of Cyber and IT Service Management*, *4*(1), 26–32. DOI: 10.34306/ijcitsm.v4i1.146

Desai, R. J., Matheny, M. E., Johnson, K., Marsolo, K., Curtis, L. H., Nelson, J. C., Heagerty, P. J., Maro, J., Brown, J., Toh, S., Nguyen, M., Ball, R., Dal Pan, G., Wang, S. V., Gagne, J. J., & Schneeweiss, S. (2021). Broadening the reach of the FDA Sentinel system: A roadmap for integrating electronic health record data in a causal analysis framework. [nature.com]. *NPJ Digital Medicine*, *4*(1), 170. DOI: 10.1038/s41746-021-00542-0 PMID: 34931012

Eswaran, U., & Eswaran, V. (2025). AI-Driven Cross-Platform Design: Enhancing Usability and User Experience. In Navigating Usability and User Experience in a Multi-Platform World (pp. 19-48). IGI Global. [HTML]

Ezzaim, A., Dahbi, A., Aqqal, A., & Haidine, A. (2024). AI-based learning style detection in adaptive learning systems: A systematic literature review. [HTML]. *Journal of Computers in Education*, •••, 1–39. DOI: 10.1007/s40692-024-00328-9

Ferhataj, A., Memaj, F., Sahatcija, R., Ora, A., & Koka, E. (2025). Ethical concerns in AI development: analyzing students' perspectives on robotics and society. Journal of Information, Communication and Ethics in Society. [HTML]

Gafni, R., Aviv, I., Kantsepolsky, B., Sherman, S., Rika, H., Itzkovich, Y., & Barger, A. (2024). Objectivity by design: The impact of AI-driven approach on employees' soft skills evaluation. [HTML]. *Information and Software Technology*, *170*, 107430. DOI: 10.1016/j.infsof.2024.107430

Gleeson, J. (2022). Evolution of Irish curriculum culture: Understandings, policy, reform and change. Irish Educational Studies. tandfonline.com

Grieco-Page, H., Black, C. J., Berent, J. M., Gautam, B., & Betancourt, T. S. (2021). Beyond the pandemic: Leveraging rapid expansions in US telemental health and digital platforms to address disparities and resolve the digital divide. [frontiersin.org]. *Frontiers in Psychiatry*, *12*, 671502. DOI: 10.3389/fpsyt.2021.671502 PMID: 34421669

Han, X., Xiao, S., Sheng, J., & Zhang, G. (2024). Enhancing efficiency and decision-making in higher education through intelligent commercial integration: Leveraging artificial intelligence. [HTML]. *Journal of the Knowledge Economy*, *16*(1), 1546–1582. DOI: 10.1007/s13132-024-01868-2

Hirudayaraj, M., Baker, R., Baker, F., & Eastman, M. (2021). Soft skills for entry-level engineers: What employers want. Education Sciences. mdpi.com

Hooda, M., Rana, C., Dahiya, O., Rizwan, A., & Hossain, M. S. (2022). Artificial intelligence for assessment and feedback to enhance student success in higher education. [wiley.com]. *Mathematical Problems in Engineering*, *2022*(1), 5215722. DOI: 10.1155/2022/5215722

Hung, B. K. H., To, C. C. N., Fung, R. K. H., & Chan, C. C. S. (2023). Addressing proficiency gaps in future skills between employers and learners through data visualization. SN computer science. springer.com

Ifenthaler, D., Gibson, D., Prasse, D., Shimada, A., & Yamada, M. (2021). Putting learning back into learning analytics: Actions for policy makers, researchers, and practitioners. [springer.com]. *Educational Technology Research and Development*, *69*(4), 2131–2150. DOI: 10.1007/s11423-020-09909-8

Ikudayisi, A. E., Chan, A. P., Darko, A., & Adegun, O. B. (2022). Integrated design process of green building projects: A review towards assessment metrics and conceptual framework. [HTML]. *Journal of Building Engineering*, *50*, 104180. DOI: 10.1016/j.jobe.2022.104180

Ismail, I. A., & Aloshi, J. M. R. (2025). Data Privacy in AI-Driven Education: An In-Depth Exploration Into the Data Privacy Concerns and Potential Solutions. In AI Applications and Strategies in Teacher Education (pp. 223-252). IGI Global. [HTML]

Issa, T. & Hall, M. (2024). A teamwork framework for preventing breaches of academic integrity and improving students' collaborative skills in the AI era. Heliyon. cell.com

Jenkins, D., & Khanna, G. (2025). AI-Enhanced Training, Education, & Development: Exploration and Insights Into Generative AI's Role in Leadership Learning. [HTML]. *Journal of Leadership Studies*, *18*(4), 81–97. DOI: 10.1002/jls.70004

Jha, S. K. (2023). The counterfeit degree certificate: Application of blockchain technology in higher education in India. [HTML]. *Library Hi Tech News*, *40*(2), 20–24. DOI: 10.1108/LHTN-02-2022-0023

Johnson, M., Jain, R., Brennan-Tonetta, P., Swartz, E., Silver, D., Paolini, J., Mamonov, S., & Hill, C. (2021). Impact of big data and artificial intelligence on industry: Developing a workforce roadmap for a data driven economy. [HTML]. *Global Journal of Flexible Systems Managment*, *22*(3), 197–217. DOI: 10.1007/s40171-021-00272-y

Kalyanaraman, A., Burnett, M., Fern, A., Khot, L., & Viers, J. (2022). Special report: The AgAID AI institute for transforming workforce and decision support in agriculture. [sciencedirect.com]. *Computers and Electronics in Agriculture, 197*, 106944. DOI: 10.1016/j.compag.2022.106944

Khan, W., Daud, A., Khan, K., Muhammad, S., & Haq, R. (2023). Exploring the frontiers of deep learning and natural language processing: A comprehensive overview of key challenges and emerging trends. [sciencedirect.com]. *Natural Language Processing Journal, 4*, 100026. DOI: 10.1016/j.nlp.2023.100026

Khosravi, H., Shum, S. B., Chen, G., Conati, C., Tsai, Y. S., Kay, J., ... & Gašević, D. (2022). Explainable artificial intelligence in education. Computers and education: artificial intelligence, 3, 100074. sciencedirect.com

Kim, J., Lee, H., & Cho, Y. H. (2022). Learning design to support student-AI collaboration: Perspectives of leading teachers for AI in education. Education and information technologies. springer.com

Kunjumuhammed, S. K. (2024). Artificial Intelligence in Addressing Educational Inequality Dimensions in Higher Education Institutions (HEIs): A Critical Review. Risks and Challenges of AI-Driven Finance: Bias, Ethics, and Security, 146-164. [HTML]

Li, L. (2024). Reskilling and upskilling the future-ready workforce for industry 4.0 and beyond. Information Systems Frontiers. springer.com

Lin, W., Yin, H., & Liu, Z. (2022). The roles of transformational leadership and growth mindset in teacher professional development: The mediation of teacher self-efficacy. Sustainability. mdpi.com

Luckin, R. (2025). Nurturing human intelligence in the age of AI: Rethinking education for the future. [HTML]. *Development and Learning in Organizations, 39*(1), 1–4. DOI: 10.1108/DLO-04-2024-0108

Md, S., Md Saiful, I., & Jannatul, F. (2025). Harnessing AI Adoption in the Workforce A Pathway to Sustainable Competitive Advantage through Intelligent Decision-Making and Skill Transformation. *American Journal of Economics and Business Management, 8*(3), 954–976. umsida.ac.id

Menon, S., & Suresh, M. (2022). Assessment framework for workforce agility in higher education institutions. Higher Education [HTML]. *Skills and Work-Based Learning, 12*(6), 1169–1188. DOI: 10.1108/HESWBL-01-2022-0014

Mhlanga, D. (2021). Artificial intelligence in the industry 4.0, and its impact on poverty, innovation, infrastructure development, and the sustainable development goals: Lessons from …. Sustainability. mdpi.com

Mohamed, B. H., Ari, I., Al-Sada, M. S., & Koç, M. (2021). Strategizing human development for a country in transition from a resource-based to a knowledge-based economy. Sustainability. mdpi.com

Naseer, F., Khan, M. N., Tahir, M., Addas, A., & Aejaz, S. M. H. (2024). Integrating deep learning techniques for personalized learning pathways in higher education. Heliyon. cell.com

Nevedal, A. L., Reardon, C. M., Opra Widerquist, M. A., Jackson, G. L., Cutrona, S. L., White, B. S., & Damschroder, L. J. (2021). Rapid versus traditional qualitative analysis using the Consolidated Framework for Implementation Research (CFIR). [springer.com]. *Implementation Science : IS*, *16*(1), 67. DOI: 10.1186/s13012-021-01111-5 PMID: 34215286

Ng, D. T. K., Leung, J. K. L., Su, J., Ng, R. C. W., & Chu, S. K. W. (2023). Teachers' AI digital competencies and twenty-first century skills in the post-pandemic world. [springer.com]. *Educational Technology Research and Development*, *71*(1), 137–161. DOI: 10.1007/s11423-023-10203-6 PMID: 36844361

Nguyen, A., Ngo, H. N., Hong, Y., Dang, B., & Nguyen, B. P. T. (2023). Ethical principles for artificial intelligence in education. [springer.com]. *Education and Information Technologies*, *28*(4), 4221–4241. DOI: 10.1007/s10639-022-11316-w PMID: 36254344

Okunlaya, R. O., Syed Abdullah, N., & Alias, R. A. (2022). Artificial intelligence (AI) library services innovative conceptual framework for the digital transformation of university education. [HTML]. *Library Hi Tech*, *40*(6), 1869–1892. DOI: 10.1108/LHT-07-2021-0242

Ozkan-Ozen, Y. D., & Kazancoglu, Y. (2022). Analysing workforce development challenges in the Industry 4.0. [HTML]. *International Journal of Manpower*, *43*(2), 310–333. DOI: 10.1108/IJM-03-2021-0167

Pandey, N., de Coninck, H., & Sagar, A. D. (2022). Beyond technology transfer: Innovation cooperation to advance sustainable development in developing countries. [wiley.com]. *Wiley Interdisciplinary Reviews. Energy and Environment*, *11*(2), e422. DOI: 10.1002/wene.422

Park, S. & Park, S. (2021). How can employees adapt to change? Clarifying the adaptive performance concepts. Human Resource Development Quarterly. wiley.com

Phanwiriyarat, K., Anggoro, K. J., & Chaowanakritsanakul, T. (2025). Exploring AI-powered gamified flipped classroom in an English-speaking course: A case of Duolingo. [tandfonline.com]. *Cogent Education*, *12*(1), 2488545. DOI: 10.1080/2331186X.2025.2488545

Pierce, K., Sosa, L., Fredrickson, M., & Kenon, V. H. (2022). Content Management System Tools to Enhance Student Learning in Higher Education. [HTML]. *Journal of Higher Education Theory and Practice*, *22*(8).

Popli, N. K. & Singh, R. P. (2024). Enhancing academic outcomes through industry collaboration: our experience with integrating real-world projects into engineering courses. Discover Education. springer.com

Pruneski, J. A., Pareek, A., Nwachukwu, B. U., Martin, R. K., Kelly, B. T., Karlsson, J., Pearle, A. D., Kiapour, A. M., & Williams, R. J.III. (2023). Natural language processing: Using artificial intelligence to understand human language in orthopedics. [HTML]. *Knee Surgery, Sports Traumatology, Arthroscopy : Official Journal of the ESSKA*, *31*(4), 1203–1211. DOI: 10.1007/s00167-022-07272-0 PMID: 36477347

Quan, S. Y., Wei, M. T., Lee, J., Mohi-Ud-Din, R., Mostaghim, R., Sachdev, R., Siegel, D., Friedlander, Y., & Friedland, S. (2022). Clinical evaluation of a real-time artificial intelligence-based polyp detection system: A US multi-center pilot study. [nature.com]. *Scientific Reports*, *12*(1), 6598. DOI: 10.1038/s41598-022-10597-y PMID: 35449442

Rapaka, A., Dharmadhikari, S. C., Kasat, K., Mohan, C. R., Chouhan, K., & Gupta, M. (2025). Revolutionizing learning– A journey into educational games with immersive and AI technologies. [HTML]. *Entertainment Computing*, *52*, 100809. DOI: 10.1016/j.entcom.2024.100809

Roshanaei, M. (2024). Towards best practices for mitigating artificial intelligence implicit bias in shaping diversity, inclusion and equity in higher education. [HTML]. *Education and Information Technologies*, *29*(14), 18959–18984. DOI: 10.1007/s10639-024-12605-2

Saranya, S. M., Komarasamy, D., Mohanapriya, S., Iyapparaja, M., & Prabavathi, R. (2024). Industry 4.0: The Role of Industrial IoT, Big Data, AR/VR, and Blockchain in the Digital Transformation. In Smart Computing Techniques in Industrial IoT (pp. 11-39). Singapore: Springer Nature Singapore. [HTML]

Sghir, N., Adadi, A., & Lahmer, M. (2023). Recent advances in Predictive Learning Analytics: A decade systematic review (2012–2022). Education and information technologies. springer.com

Shoaib, M., Sayed, N., Singh, J., Shafi, J., Khan, S., & Ali, F. (2024). AI student success predictor: Enhancing personalized learning in campus management systems. [HTML]. *Computers in Human Behavior, 158*, 108301. DOI: 10.1016/j.chb.2024.108301

Shortt, M., Tilak, S., Kuznetcova, I., Martens, B., & Akinkuolie, B. (2023). Gamification in mobile-assisted language learning: A systematic review of Duolingo literature from public release of 2012 to early 2020. [tandfonline.com]. *Computer Assisted Language Learning, 36*(3), 517–554. DOI: 10.1080/09588221.2021.1933540

Singh, T. M., Reddy, C. K. K., Murthy, B. R., Nag, A., & Doss, S. (2025). Ai and education: Bridging the gap to personalized, efficient, and accessible learning. In *Internet of Behavior-Based Computational Intelligence for Smart Education Systems* (pp. 131–160). IGI Global. [HTML]

Sjödin, D., Parida, V., Palmié, M., & Wincent, J. (2021). How AI capabilities enable business model innovation: Scaling AI through co-evolutionary processes and feedback loops. Journal of Business Research. sciencedirect.com

Sundari, M. S., Penthala, H. R., & Nayyar, A. Transforming Education through AI-Enhanced Content Creation and Personalized Learning Experiences. In *Impact of Artificial Intelligence on Society* (pp. 98–118). Chapman and Hall/CRC. [HTML]

Tan, S. C., Chan, C., Bielaczyc, K., Ma, L., Scardamalia, M., & Bereiter, C. (2021). Knowledge building: Aligning education with needs for knowledge creation in the digital age. *Educational Technology Research and Development, 69*(4), 2243–2266. nie.edu.sg. DOI: 10.1007/s11423-020-09914-x

Tavakoli, M., Faraji, A., Vrolijk, J., Molavi, M., Mol, S. T., & Kismihók, G. (2022). An AI-based open recommender system for personalized labor market driven education. [sciencedirect.com]. *Advanced Engineering Informatics, 52*, 101508. DOI: 10.1016/j.aei.2021.101508

Thompson, B. S. (2021). Corporate payments for ecosystem services in theory and practice: Links to economics, business, and sustainability. Sustainability. mdpi.com

Verma, A., Lamsal, K., & Verma, P. (2022). An investigation of skill requirements in artificial intelligence and machine learning job advertisements. [HTML]. *Industry and Higher Education, 36*(1), 63–73. DOI: 10.1177/0950422221990990

Yadav, S. (2024). *Designing Effective E-Portfolios for Authentic Assessment: Encouraging Reflection and Promoting Student Ownership*. Cases on Authentic Assessment in Higher Education. [HTML] DOI: 10.4018/979-8-3693-1001-4.ch011

Yağcı, M. (2022). Educational data mining: prediction of students' academic performance using machine learning algorithms. Smart Learning Environments. springer.com

Yang, E., & Beil, C. (2024). Ensuring data privacy in AI/ML implementation. [HTML]. *New Directions for Higher Education, 2024*(207), 63–78. DOI: 10.1002/he.20509

Yu, H., Wei, W., Li, J., & Li, Y. (2022). The impact of green digital finance on energy resources and climate change mitigation in carbon neutrality: Case of 60 economies. [HTML]. *Resources Policy, 79*, 103116. DOI: 10.1016/j.resourpol.2022.103116

Chapter 8

Impact of AI on Students Mental Health and Well-Being

Lakshya Choudhary
https://orcid.org/0009-0004-1747-0209
Christ University Delhi-NCR, India

Sumin Samuel Sybol
https://orcid.org/0000-0002-4068-1635
Christ University, India

ABSTRACT

This chapter examines the transformative impact of artificial intelligence (AI) on students' mental health and well-being, addressing the urgent need for innovative solutions in response to escalating mental health challenges among this demographic. In recent years, mental health issues among students have surged due to a combination of factors, including increasing academic pressures, socio-economic disparities, and the pervasive influence of digital technologies. These challenges create a complex array of psychological and emotional difficulties that necessitate timely and effective interventions.AI technologies, particularly those leveraging natural language processing (NLP) and machine learning (ML), are emerging as scalable and accessible tools for mental health support in educational settings. Unlike traditional therapeutic methods, which often face geographical, financial, and logistical constraints, AI-powered tools provide round-the-clock assistance to users, transcending barriers of time and location.

DOI: 10.4018/979-8-3373-5786-7.ch008

INTRODUCTION

Artificial intelligence (AI) is drastically altering the field of mental health and education by providing inventive responses to the complex psychological and emotional issues that students run across. Rising academic expectations, social disparity, and the pervasive influence of digital technology have made students' mental health issues worse during the past ten years (Farrukh Shahzad et al., 2024). AI is now a potent weapon to meet the urgent demand for successful and scalable mental health treatments resulting from this explosion. Using technologies such natural language processing (NLP), machine learning (ML), and data analytics, artificial intelligence (AI) is offering potential paths for mental health care in educational settings.

Students today deal with a range of mental health problems, which are closely related to the changes in society and education are bringing about (Alsayed et al., 2024). Academic expectations have grown as students balance rigorous courses, tests, and ongoing performance requirements. Beyond the classroom, socioeconomic issues include uneven resource availability and unpredictable finances raise stress levels. Among the omnipresent digital tools that have caused even more psychological stress are social media, online learning settings, and virtual relationships. Problems include screen addiction, cyberbullying, and FOMO cause students nowadays often to feel anxious and depressed. This makes traditional mental health treatments often overwhelmed and unable to meet the growing need for quick, customized help.

HISTORICAL EVOLUTION

By offering creative, reasonably priced, scalable, and easily available solutions, artificial intelligence has evolved into a game-changing tool for reducing the gap in mental health care. AI-powered solutions provide users 24/7 help, overcoming time and geographical limits unlike conventional treatment approaches, which are sometimes constrained by logistical, financial, and geographic constraints (Woebot Health, n.d.). Thanks to tools like natural language processing (NLP), which makes them ideal for uses like chatbots and virtual therapists, artificial intelligence systems can understand and react to human language in a sophisticated way. On the other hand, machine learning methods enable these computers to search enormous volumes of data in order to identify trends, project mental health issues, and generate customized treatments to meet individual need. AI-enabled mood-monitoring systems—for example—can assess emotional states by looking at text inputs, speech tones, even facial expressions. They then can provide real-time remarks and coping mechanisms.

Integration of artificial intelligence in education takes psychological and emotional well-being into account beyond only academic help. By means of increasingly used AI-powered solutions, children are building emotional resilience, enhancing coping skills, and lowering stress. For example, AI-driven chatbots give children a safe space where they could share worries and obtain fast aid and advice. Replacing elements of human interaction, virtual therapists offer dynamic and interesting delivery of cognitive behavioral therapy (CBT) and other evidence-based interventions. Mood-monitoring devices measure mood swings, therefore helping to identify early on stress, anxiety, or sadness and the required treatment.

Notwithstanding these developments, the way artificial intelligence interacts with mental health causes ethical use, privacy problems, and limits of machine empathy (Chen et al., 2024; Alsayed et al., 2024). Artificial intelligence systems create big problems even in this regard even if they are excellent in data processing and reaction manufacturing on demand as they cannot totally understand human emotions. The application of artificial intelligence for emotional support begs issues regarding the effect of technology on students' emotional intelligence and interpersonal skills as well as on the danger of too great dependence on technology.

Particularly in educational situations where students encounter with different expectations and demands, changing AI systems for emotional awareness is a difficult task (Farrukh Shahzad et al., 2024). Academic criteria, society expectations, and the difficulties of human development generate sensitive interventions needed of a dynamic and smart environment. A general-use chatbot would not take into account the specific needs connected to test seasons, peer group dynamics, or college applications. Furthermore, greatly influenced by social and cultural elements are students' experiences and mental health requirements; so, contextualized and localized artificial intelligence solutions are rather crucial.

Currently under development are studies on the long-term consequences of depending on artificial intelligence for emotional assistance. Although it's not clear how artificial intelligence can assist long-term mental health, it can offer right now guidance and relief. Artificial intelligence systems raise questions about whether they could unintentionally hinder in-person interactions or underplay the value of personal ties in enabling emotional healing. Furthermore, defining the success of AI interventions is the quality and scope of the data applied to instruct these systems. Particularly for underrepresented or disadvantaged populations, prejudices in algorithm design and data collecting could generate unfair outcomes (Chen et al., 2024).

Alsayed et al. 2024; Woebot Health n.d.; claim that using artificial intelligence in mental health and education has complicated and wide ethical consequences. Privacy issues are especially important since artificial intelligence systems regularly exploit private data to offer customized solutions. Ensuring the privacy and security of this data will help to maintain users' confidence and protection of their welfare. Ethical questions also surface from worries about the responsibility and openness of artificial intelligence systems. Users might not completely understand, for instance, how suggestions created by artificial intelligence are developed or how their data is being used. To solve these issues, coordination among technologists, teachers, and mental health experts as well as strong legislative systems are required.

Another crucial ethical consideration is the likelihood that artificial intelligence might either magnify or exacerbate present inequities. Students from impoverished backgrounds may have restricted access to AI-powered resources, therefore creating a digital divide that distorts fair results. Moreover, cultural viewpoints on mental health and technology vary significantly, which influences the acceptance rate of artificial intelligence solutions and their successfulness. While in certain nations acceptance may be impeded by cynicism about technology, others may dissuade students from utilizing AI-based support systems due to the stigma attached with mental health.

THEORETICAL MODEL

Understanding how artificial intelligence (AI) influences students' mental health and overall well-being requires mostly theoretical support from the Technology Acceptance Model (TAM). This paradigm presents a disciplined approach for analyzing student opinions, acceptance, and finally classroom artificial intelligence technology application. More particularly in the sections that follow will be the basic elements of TAM, its adaptations to support artificial intelligence applications, and the integration of psychological theories that offer better understanding of the link between technological use and mental health consequences.

TAM, the Technology Acceptance Model:

Originally presented by Davis in 1989, the Technology Acceptance Model (TAM) has developed to be among the most influential conceptual frameworks for understanding human acceptance and use of technology. The model stresses that a person's inclination to employ a given technology is mostly influenced by two key factors: perceived usefulness (PU) and perceived ease of use (PEOU). This goal, sometimes referred to as behavioral intention (BI), thus regulates the actual technology use. TAM has been rather popular in many different domains, including organizational settings, education, and healthcare, mostly because to its simplicity of use and robustness. This broad research investigates TAM's basic concepts, applicability in learning contexts, and relevance in comprehending adoption of artificial intelligence in education.

Fundamental TAM Structures:

PU, or Perceived Usefulness

Perceived utility is the degree to which a person finds using a particular technology to enhance their performance. PU in educational environments is the degree to which teachers or students think that a technology improves the results of instruction or learning process. An artificial intelligence-powered learning system with adaptive learning paths and customized recommendations—for example—can be quite beneficial if it increases student performance or saves teachers time when designing lesson plans.

Adoption of a technology is more likely if consumers believe it immediately aids in their success.

Many times, people find technology to be useful in simplifying tough work or cutting the time required to do demanding projects.

Outcome Relevance: Technology becomes more valuable when its characteristics complement those of users.

PEOU—Perceived Simplicity of Usage

The extent to which one feels utilizing a technology to be straightforward is known as perceived ease of use. Adoption of a technology may be beneficial, but its complexity or lack of usability could impede it even if that is expected. Students as well as instructors are more likely to make use of a mobile app with basic design, smooth navigation, and easily available content in the classroom.

Simplicity of design serves to lower cognitive burden and increase usability, therefore impacting PEOU.

Availability of troubleshooting instruments or instructions facilitates uptake of technical support.

Generally general, people pick technology with less acute and shorter learning curves.

Intentional Activity (BI)

Behavioral intention is the element that helps to regulate the interaction of PU, PEOU, and actual technological use. Their views on the simplicity and practicality of the technology help one to appreciate their need to interact with it. Since it increases the probability of actual system usage, developers and teachers must give a good BI top priority if they want to inspire technology adoption.

TAM's Uses in Learning

Classroom use of TAM has produced some fascinating data on how teachers and students embrace and apply modern technologies. By means of PU, the PEOU, and BI interaction analysis, designers and researchers can identify adoption problems and develop solutions. Focusing artificial intelligence technology, this section investigates significant TAM applications in learning environments.

Learning environments based on web technologies

Especially in front with the COVID-19 epidemic, e-learning technologies have become indispensable tool in modern education. TAM has been used more and more to evaluate the acceptance of numerous platforms.

Studies show that PU significantly influences students' preferences to use e-learning materials since they value components like interactive tests, video courses, and real-time feedback that directly raise academic performance.

Furthermore, significantly influencing students' utilization of e-learning resources is PEOU. Research by Al-Samarraie et al. (2020) shows that students are more inclined to accept platforms with simple navigation and few technical problems. These two components affect behavioral intention, which drives consistent use of e-learning platforms and hence affects learning results.

USES OF MOBILE LEARNING

By offering accessibility and flexibility, applications for mobile learning—also known as m-learning—have raised the usage of technology in the classroom. TAM-based studies suggest that PU in m-learning environments is usually linked with characteristics including offline access, academic resource integration, and collaborative learning support. On smaller devices, on the other hand, PEOU is influenced by the simplicity of app design and the accessibility of content.

For instance, university students preferred easily set-up and used m-learning apps according to Huang et al. (2021). These findings emphasize how important user-centered design is to encouraging classroom acceptance of mobile technologies.

ARTIFICIAL INTELLIGENCE AND UNDERSTANDING

Especially examined through the prism of Technology Acceptance Models (TAM), artificial intelligence (AI) technology integration into education has changed conventional educational frameworks. Apart from improving education, artificial intelligence (AI) technologies include virtual teaching assistants, intelligent tutoring systems, and personalized learning platforms are inspiring a data-driven approach of learning. Examining the elements influencing the acceptance of various technologies using TAM offers a thorough approach including both user perceptions and technology efficiency.

A 2024 Yilmaz and Karaoglan Yilmaz study shows that students' behavioral intention to use AI tools—including ChatGPT—is much influenced by how valuable they believe them to be. Knowing how artificial intelligence might improve metacognitive self-regulated learning (MSRL) helps students to welcome it more easily. This is consistent with research by Wang et al. (2023), who demonstrated that by means of individualized learning experiences and adaptive feedback systems, AI-enabled solutions significantly assist international students overcoming language barriers and new educational systems.

Chen et al. (2024) claim that mental health and wellness are also ways in which artificial intelligence helps to improve learning results. The study claims that the ability of artificial intelligence to provide customized help via chatbots and other technologies can help to lower stress and increase focus, thereby enabling a complete educational process. These materials solve psychological problems in addition to intellectual ones, therefore offering a well-rounded and motivating classroom. In a same line, Gao (2025) underlined the potential of AI-driven emotional dialogue systems, which actively involve students and improve their educational experiences by means of sophisticated natural language processing.

AI technology can be used by educational institutions to create adaptable ecosystems that satisfy the needs of a broad spectrum of students while maintaining moral values about accessibility, privacy, and cultural sensitivity. Future studies and development should focus on enhancing these tools to promote emotional resonance and involvement thus ensuring that artificial intelligence serves as a pedagogical and compassionate resource.

Artificial Intelligence and Meta-Cognitive Self-Regulated Learning (MSRL)

Metacognitive self-regulated learning (MSRL) is the capacity of students to plan, monitor, and evaluate their own learning processes; it so fosters more autonomy and efficiency in accomplishing learning objectives. Since artificial intelligence (AI) tools let tailored feedback and adaptive learning approaches that meet the needs of every individual learner, they have proven revolutionary in helping MSRL.

Using features such intelligent tutoring systems, adaptive learning platforms, and predictive analytics, artificial intelligence technologies let MSRL These instruments assist students to detect knowledge gaps, recommend pertinent materials, and offer dynamic and customized coaching, so facilitating ongoing monitoring and enhancement of learning outcomes. By virtue of real-time feedback, AI-powered apps such as Grammarly and AutoTutor—which emphasize areas for development and track students over time—help to raise metacognitive awareness.

Studies centered around the Technology Acceptance Model (TAM) offer a methodical approach toward comprehending how artificial intelligence tools benefit MSRL. Important criteria influencing their acceptance are as follows:

PU: Perceived Usefulness

Students value artificial intelligence technologies when they effectively provide customized, useful knowledge. Artificial intelligence systems—like adaptive testing platforms—can help students focus on the areas that demand more attention by way of the tracking of personal performance patterns. This opens more important and concentrated learning opportunities.

Artificial intelligence interface perceived ease of use (PEOU) depends on their usability and simple design. Simple command structures, natural language interfaces, and interactive dashboards that reduce the learning curve assist a wider spectrum of students to use these technologies.

Students who prioritize simplicity of use (PEOU) and PU of AI products are quite more inclined to interact with them.

The 2024 results of Yilmaz and Karaoglan Yilmaz show that this higher intention leads to more engagement and better learning outcomes since they link AI technologies with improved metacognitive awareness and academic performance.

Importance

Artificial intelligence enhances mental and emotional health as well as intellectual ones, according to further research (Gao, 2024; Chen et al., 2024). AI guarantees, for example, that students stay inspired and targeted on achieving their educational goals and get sympathetic support by means of emotionally intelligent dialogue systems.

All things considered, adding artificial intelligence into MSRL helps students to become better independent learners and represents a paradigm change in education. Future studies should try to improve artificial intelligence systems to incorporate more strong emotional intelligence qualities and better customization of learning situations.

TAM's Problems and Educational Drawbacks. Although the Technology Acceptance Model (TAM) has shown to be a helpful tool for comprehending the acceptability of technology, various reasons limit its application in educational settings. Sometimes the intricacy of educational surroundings forces the paradigm outside its intended reach. Among important restrictions are:

As primary factors influencing technological adoption, TAM largely focuses on perceived usefulness (PU) and perceived ease of use (PEOU). This lowers, however, ignores important elements of learning environments such support from institutions, cultural attitudes, and social impact. Gao (2025), for example, emphasizes the need of emotional involvement and institutional support for the effective application of artificial intelligence in the education. Should these more broad components be missed, TAM might not be able to offer a whole understanding of technology acceptability.

Among the specific factors brought by educational environments TAM cannot totally control are curricular alignment, assessment integration, and the availability of teacher training programs. These elements greatly influence the adoption of technologies including learning systems based on artificial intelligence. In 2023, Wang et al., for instance, argue that AI's involvement in personalized learning must match institutional aims and assessment systems if we are to ensure significant adoption.

Dynamic Nature of Education: TAM has to be always changed to be relevant given the fast advancement of technology and changing teaching strategies. Emerging technologies like artificial intelligence-driven feedback tools and intelligent education systems bring new dimensions like emotional intelligence and ethical concerns that TAM does not naturally address. Chen et al. (2024) say that while still relevant to current educational challenges, AI applications in education must adapt to take these elements into consideration.

Overemphasizing Personal Views:

TAM regularly favors concentrating mostly on the opinions of individual users over the cooperative and systemic elements of educational decision-making. Usually involving many stakeholders, including legislators, teachers, and managers, adoption decisions Gao (2025) underlines the need of a joint strategy to their integration into institutional processes in order to maximize the influence of artificial intelligence technology.

Though TAM does a decent job of capturing initial acceptance, it offers little information on long-term consequences and continuous use. For educational technologies, iterative improvements, ongoing involvement, and integration into teaching and learning systems are all absolutely essential. According to Wang et al.

(2023), the length of adoption will depend on the degree to which AI technologies are included into more significant institutional projects and regularly upgraded to meet evolving needs.

Real-World Effects on Technology for Educators

Teachers and developers can use TAM findings to design and implement effective instructional technologies. Among the clever strategies are:

- Using case studies, success stories, and demonstrations, highlight the specific benefits of technology for both personal and intellectual growth.
- Improving Perceived Ease of Use: Give responsive technical assistance top priority; also, give careful user training and simple design great importance in lowering adoption obstacles.
- Promote good ideas of technology by including it into normal courses, collaborating on group projects, and obtaining peer endorsements.

Future Opportunities for TAM in Education

Future research and implementations should try to maximize TAM's power to guide the classroom technology adoption by means of:

- Increase the model to include trust, cultural context, and social impact among other things.
- Examining how TAM factors influence academic performance and long-term, consistent technology use can help one to emphasize on longitudinal studies.
- Analyze Cross-Cultural Variability: Particularly in international learning situations, investigate how cultural differences shape individuals's perspective of PU and PEOU.
- Integrate Emerging Technologies: Change TAM to look at virtual reality, augmented reality, and blockchain technologies among others.

TAM Extensions' Uses in Artificial Intelligence

Researchers have come to see that the original TAM framework must be enlarged as artificial intelligence technologies develop if we are to effectively manage the unique characteristics of AI applications. This involves components like:

- Adoption of AI systems that either make decisions on their own or provide customised recommendations depends much on trust in them. Studies reveal that students who trust more are more likely to be intending users of the service.
- Social Influence: One cannot stress the impact peers and social networks have on individuals's technological acceptance. Students often find influence from peers' experiences with artificial intelligence tools, which might inspire or deter them from using these tools.
- Students' inclination to use technology might be very much influenced by their level of enjoyment of it. If artificial intelligence tools appeal to students, they are more likely to be used.
- Personal Competence: The degree of a student's acceptance of technology depends on how competent they consider to be. Higher degrees of self-efficacy in using technology are linked to improved preparedness to engage with artificial intelligence applications.

THEORETICAL FRAMEWORKS

Relevant Models and Theory

Theory of Cognitive-behavioral Learning (CBT)

Cognitive-behavioral theory (CBT) is a well-known psychological model that emphasizes on identifying and modifying ineffective thought patterns and behaviors causing mental health problems. Developed in the middle of the 20th century by Aaron T. Beck and Albert Ellis, CBT is predicated on the idea that ideas, emotions, and behavior are all related. Negative or distorted thinking can lead to a vicious cycle aggravating mental health problems that might cause emotional pain and destructive actions. By means of structured interventions, cognitive behavioral therapy (CBT) helps people toward better coping strategies, identification and confrontation of their cognitive distortions, and more adaptive thought patterns. Therapists lead clients through a series of exercises, conversations, and homework assignments toward these objectives in regular cognitive behavioral therapy sessions. Though generally quite successful, standard cognitive behavioral therapy (CBT) sometimes requires a significant time commitment, financial outlay, and access to qualified mental health professionals—resources not always easily available to everyone, especially those in impoverished or highly sought-after educational environments. A game-changing technology enabling CBT-based mental health therapies to be more affordable, scalable, and easily available is artificial intelligence (AI). Artificial intelligence (AI) systems can duplicate some of the major tasks of a cognitive behavioural therapy (CBT) therapist by use of technologies including natural language processing (NLP), machine learning, and data analytics. These courses lead attendees through planned dialogues and activities aimed to combat cognitive distortions and promote more constructive mental processes.

Especially fitting for artificial intelligence-powered mental health technologies such virtual assistants, apps, and chatbots are students. Among the particular difficulties this generation often encounters are the changing nature of student life, social expectations, and academic obligations. Furthermore, many students may not be able to get traditional forms of treatment due of the stigma connected to mental health problems and their refusal to seek in-person counselling. AI technologies can close this disparity by providing discrete, on-demand help (Woebot Health, n.d.).

One shining illustration of how CBT ideas could be effectively used on a digital platform is the AI-powered chatbot Woebot. Designed by clinical psychologists and artificial intelligence experts, Woebot offers CBT-based therapy using conversation. Natural language processing (NLP) is used to spot cognitive distortions including all-or-nothing thinking, catastrophizing, and overgeneralizing. It then provides users with exercises and real-time direction to enable them to reinterpret their concepts.

Effect of Woebot on Mental Health:

Research on WoeBot's efficacy in reducing anxiety and depressed symptoms has revealed In a randomized controlled trial, Fitzpatrick et al. (2017) for instance found that Woebot users dramatically lowered their depressive symptoms following two weeks when compared to a control group. The study showed how effective mental health therapies on a big scale may be offered by AI-driven chatbots.

For students in classroom settings specifically, Woebot has been quite useful. It is unobtrusive and accessible anytime needed, thereby meeting the needs of young people who might be afraid to start conventional treatment. By providing quick advice during trying circumstances—including test seasons or college applications—Woebot helps children develop resilience and coping skills.

The Theory of Ecological Systems:

Originally developed in 1979 by developmental psychologist Urie Bronfenbrenner, Ecological Systems Theory provides a complete framework for understanding human development in respect to their environment. The theory holds that many interrelated systems, ranging from their local surroundings to more widespread social aspects, affect a person's development and mental well-being. These systems are seen as layers of influence, each of which dynamically shapes a person's experiences, behavior, and general well-being via interacting.

Bronfenbrenner broke out these strata into five systems:

- Microsystem: Direct contacts occur in the immediate surroundings—that of the family, friends, community, and educational institution.
- Mesosystem: The interactions among the elements of the microsystem—that is, the relationships between family members and teachers or between parents and colleagues.
- Exosystem: Direct external elements influencing a person, such as parental work stress or community rules.
- Macrosystem: More wide-ranging cultural and socioeconomic elements include societal values, customs, and financial situation.
- The chronological system is the time dimension including historical events, changes in one's personal or environmental circumstances, and life transitions.

Ecological Systems Theory emphasizes how important it is to consider these linked layers if one wants to build a whole picture of each individual's mental development and wellness. This idea provides a solid foundation for designing treatments targeting both internal and environmental factors thereby improving well-being.

The Place of Artificial Intelligence in Ecological Systems Theory

In the field of mental health, artificial intelligence (AI) has evolved into a transforming tool for operationalizing Ecological Systems Theory (EST.). EST gives great importance on how a person interacts with their complicated circumstances, which comprise social, private, and more general society aspects. Artificial intelligence systems might be able to identify trends, assess dangers, and offer specific treatments to help mental health by means of data from many domains.

Using a suite of data sources including social media activity, behaviors, academic achievement measures, and interaction histories, artificial intelligence (AI) systems investigate the complex interactions between an individual's surroundings and mental health. For example, Gao (2025) highlights how artificial intelligence systems leverage multidimensional data to offer at-risk populations predictive analytics and customized emotional assistance.

Putting EST into artificial intelligence-powered psychological systems promotes a multiple approach to wellness. These techniques evaluate more general contextual factors such family ties, scholastic obligations, and society influences that result in stress, anxiety, or depression than they would focus solely on particular symptoms. Chen et al., 2024 Studies this all-encompassing point of view with which underline the need of considering systematic elements while developing mental health treatments for college students.

Applying in Learning Settings

In educational environments, where pupils regularly come into difficult problems, the combining of artificial intelligence with EST is quite helpful. Affecting mental health is the interaction of personal challenges, social expectations, and academic pressure. AI systems designed with an EST architecture can examine these connected layers to generate insightful analysis. For instance, according to Wang et al. (2023), AI systems that offer tailored learning paths boost academic performance while also lowering related stress.

EST has one fascinating use in artificial intelligence systems: it helps to prevent student fatigue. Common in high-stress learning contexts, burnout is typified by emotional tiredness, depersonalization, which and poor academic achievement. By looking at data from many ecological layers, predictive analytics in intelligent systems can spot early burnout warning indicators. Microsystem data, for instance, cover attendance records, grades, and involvement patterns.

Social media connections or peer networks reveal mesosystem data.

Ecosystem data contain course load and test schedules, among institutional elements.

Case Study: Practical implementation of Ecological Systems In artificial intelligence systems, theory is the decrease of student burnout attained by means of artificial intelligence. Common in learning situations, burnout is defined by depersonalization, emotional tiredness, and low academic performance. Artificial intelligence systems could find pupils at danger and offer customized treatments by way of data analysis across several ecological layers.

In order to spot burnout symptoms such negative self-talk or withdrawment, artificial intelligence systems track academic performance indicators including grades, attendance, and project proposals as well as social media activity.

AI systems help educators, counselors, and parents to interact with one another so guaranteeing a coordinated approach for burnout control.

Artificial intelligence (AI) systems evaluate external stress such family financial problems or limited access to leisure activities that could lead burnout.

Macrosystem Analysis: AI systems take sociocultural elements including cultural perspectives on academic success or the stigma related with the development of intervention techniques or support requests under consideration.

Using longitudinal data, artificial intelligence (AI) systems track student well-being over time and identify trends pointing to a burnout path.

Combining this information lets artificial intelligence identify youngsters at risk and offer customised remedies include academic assistance, mindfulness coaching, or counsellor referrals.

. Gao (2025) also highlighted similar applications whereby AI-driven insights significantly improved methods of student mental health care.

Artificial Intelligence and Maslow's Hierarchy of Needs

Maslow's Hierarchy of Needs provides a structure for understanding human motivation since it underlines that fulfilling fundamental needs comes first in reaching self-actualization. Particularly in the domains of education and mental health, artificial intelligence (AI) technology might be rather beneficial in fulfilling these needs by means of inclusive and motivating digital environments.

Dealing with basic psychological demands like safety and belonging, AI systems can help to satisfy these by designing environments that support collaboration and community development. Students feel safer, for example, when they use tools designed to stop cyberbullying or spot distress signals in correspondence. In a similar line, AI-powered solutions that facilitate group interactions or peer relationships underline how important belongingness is for maintaining mental health. These digital technologies help Maslow's theory—that people must feel safe and valued in their group before they can ascend to greater levels of development.

Online discussion boards or study groups, among other AI-powered systems that inspire peer involvement, help students feel more of community and belonging. Recommendation engines and AI-powered chatbots, for instance, can match students with social circles or study partners based on shared interests or challenges. Gao (2025) stressed the need of artificial intelligence in building emotional dialogue systems allowing students to connect with one another, hence promoting social cohesiveness and group problem-solving.

Once more basic needs have been satisfied, AI systems can free students to concentrate on their cognitive and personal growth. Students can achieve self-actualization and excel academically using technology like intelligent tutors and customized learning platforms, which offer resources matched to the student's need. If one intends to advance personally, these systems also inspire introspection including goal-setting and self-evaluation.

Digital Communities and Well-Being as a Reference Point

Apart from meeting psychological demands, educational artificial intelligence systems emulating supportive communities improve engagement and retention as well. Including artificial intelligence-driven sentiment research into technologies like Slack or Microsoft Teams, for example, could help to find students who might feel isolated and offer rapid engagement options. Chen et al. (2024) also emphasized the need of belongingness for both academic and personal success, noting how AI tools in mental health platforms support emotional resilience and community-driven solutions.

Modern Models

Seq2Seq, or Sequence-to--Sequence:

Natural language processing (NLP) depends fundamentally on sequence-to- sequence (Seq2Seq) models because of their ability to generate responses organized, logical, and relevant to context. Using deep learning architectures including transformers, long short-term memory networks (LSTMs), or recurrent neural networks (RNNs), these models move an input sequence to a similar output sequence. Their versatility makes them absolutely essential for uses including machine translation, summarizing, and chatbot development.

Virtual counseling and mental health support benefit much from Sequ2Seq models since they let for scalable, empathetic, and tailored interactions. These models are able to:

- Train on emotionally challenging datasets to enable Sequence 2 Sequence models to replicate counselor-like encounters, therefore giving consumers immediate assistance. Gao (2025), for example, highlights how Seq2Seq models may provide college students coping with mental health problems personalized and emotionally relevant dialogues.
- Combining AI-driven personalization with Seq2Seq models helps answers to be dynamically changed depending on the emotional state of the user, hence improving emotional support and involvement.

The Use of Sequence2Seq Models in Online Counseling

Emotionally Sensitive DialogueSeq2Seq models can provide unique and empathetic responses by being trained on sets rich in emotional and conversational environments. When a user says they feel lonely, for example, *"It's normal to feel this way during tough times, but you're not alone. Let's explore ways to improve your situation together."* These kinds of exchanges help to validate and connect the user, both of which are crucial elements of mental health support.

- Among the primary advantages of Seq2Seq models are scalability. While artificial intelligence-driven solutions can help numerous people at once without compromising response times, traditional counseling services have few tools at hand.
- Seq2Seq models ensure constant use of therapeutic frameworks, unlike human counselors who could have varied approaches. This dependability is quite helpful in environments when consistent mental health therapies are needed.
- By addressing language, cultural, and socioeconomic variation, AI systems are becoming inclusive, therefore enabling broader access to mental health services. For instance, multilingual chatbots and culturally conscious algorithms can ensure that students from many backgrounds get relevant and helpful assistance. Customized interventions for local environments help to increase acceptance and efficacy of them.
- These hybrid models, which combine human monitoring with artificial intelligence efficiency, ensure accurate and sensitive interventions. A human counselor might review chatbot interactions to provide additional help in more complex circumstances. This approach keeps the scaling benefits of artificial intelligence while lowering the risk of erroneous diagnosis or inappropriate response.

LITERATURE REVIEW

Research Trend Lines

Research on mental health emphasizes artificial intelligence's promise for early identification, intervention, and tailored assistance. Chen et al. (2024) noted hotspots including machine learning applications for depression and anxiety in their bibliometric evaluation of worldwide research trends in AI and mental health. Gao (2025) expanded this knowledge by improving AI models like Seq2Seq for more emotionally sensitive counseling services. Talaue et al. (2018) discussed how students' mental health and academic performance indirectly suffer on social media and other digital platforms.

Crucial Findings

Thanks to the work of fields including public health, computer science, and psychology, artificial intelligence has become rather popular in mental health recently.

Wearable technologies and chatbots are being increasingly included into mental health services in order to offer scalable and efficient solutions.

Implementation of AI-based mental health treatments presents still main challenges including privacy issues, limited emotional interaction capacity, ethical constraints, and privacy concerns.

Advancements in Technology

Programs as Wysa and Woebot use natural language processing (NLP) to replicate sympathetic human interactions, therefore offering conversational therapy. These chatbots have shown to reduce anxiety and depression by providing fast, conveniently available help. Moreover, its inclusion into learning contexts has demonstrated to be cost-effective, hence increasing access to mental health resources.

Wearable technology tracks physiological data driven by artificial intelligence to expose trends in stress and mood. Devices like the Apple Watch and Fitbit use heart rate variability, for example, to detect stress levels and recommend restful activities. These approaches give objective data points for emotional analysis, hence improving artificial intelligence systems.

Sentiment Analysis Tools: At-risk children can get early intervention by use of advanced natural language processing models evaluating user input. When combined with social media data mining, these techniques can spot tendencies of anxiety or loneliness in student populations.

Challenges

- Two still major ethical concerns are informed permission and data privacy. For instance, students worried about data breaches or exploitation may be reluctant to supply artificial intelligence systems vital information. Clear policies and safe data management techniques are absolutely necessary if one is to overcome these challenges.
- limits in emotional involvement since artificial intelligence cannot exactly replicate human empathy. Despite progress in sentiment analysis, artificial intelligence systems often find it difficult to understand context-dependent subtleties, including cultural expressions of suffering (Shimada, 2023). This emotional limitation raises concerns about the effectiveness of AI in replacing traditional therapeutic relationships.

- Adoption challenges in low-resource settings, where infrastructure and internet access may limit the practicality of artificial intelligence systems. Fair access calls for creative solutions such AI tools operating offline or community-based assistance models as well as others.

IMPORTANT RESULTS FROM PRESENT STUDIES

Literary Views

Emphasizing the treatment of anxiety and depression, notable developments in artificial intelligence applications for mental health have been noted, expanding on the bibliometric research Chen et al. (2024). Key tools in these studies now are machine learning and other artificial intelligence methods since they allow one to study complex psychological trends and improve intervention strategies. This emphasizes the need of including artificial intelligence in many different contexts and is compatible with the requirement of cooperative, multidisciplinary approaches in mental health research.

Empathy in AI Systems

By improving conversational empathy and emotional understanding, artificial intelligence models such as Seq2Seq topologies could transform mental health counseling as Gao (2025) shows. These advancements enable AI-powered goods to replicate human-like interactions, therefore enhancing user relationships and offering scalable mental health care options. Focusing on emotional intelligence in artificial intelligence, researchers are extending the possibilities of conversational agents in therapeutic settings.

Social Media and Students's Welfare

Talaue et al. (2018) looked at how social media influences mental health and academic performance of students. Their findings emphasize the need of finding a balance between time management and internet activity. This point of view is crucial when creating AI-powered tools since these systems have to consider each individual digital activity if they are to support students' well-being and improve their educational experiences.

Key Lessons Learned

- Behavioral and academic data analysis driven by artificial intelligence for early mental health disorder diagnosis. This proactive strategy lets counselors and teachers intervene before problems get worse.
- better counseling outcomes via AI-enhanced dialogues Virtual counselors can provide quick help, therefore freeing part of the burden of genuine professionals.
- Digital platforms both help to lower and raise student stress depending on their nature. While artificial intelligence could be beneficial, depending too much on technology too great can cause digital weariness. Maintaining wellness calls for balancing contacts both online and in person.

CONCEPTS' DEVELOPMENT

Including artificial intelligence (AI) into mental health and educational initiatives has several benefits that could completely change the way help is given.

Instant, round-the-clock treatment provided by artificial intelligence has substantially improved access to mental health resources. Universities have begun using AI-powered chatbots to give round-the-clock access to self-help tools or counseling services to assist students who are struggling academically or emotionally. These tools ensure that students may access help when most needed by removing traditional barriers to asking for it, such shame or unavailability.

By analyzing vast amounts of data, artificial intelligence systems may create tailored treatments for every individual's need. Adaptive learning systems, for instance, change the delivery of materials based on a student's performance, learning preferences, and emotional state. Apart from raising academic performance, this degree of personalization fosters accomplishment and competency, both of which are crucial for maintaining good mental health. Gao (2025) claims that students' welfare and involvement could be much improved by AI's ability to react dynamically to emotional stimuli.

AI programs can track pupils' emotional moods by means of their digital contacts. Examining behavioral patterns, such changes in involvement or communication style, helps teachers and mental health professionals identify at-risk children early on and act before crises get more severe. Research suggests that machine learning algorithms could effectively identify mental health problems including depression and suicide thoughts, therefore offering students a proactive approach to their well-being.

Reduced Stigma: By means of AI-powered mental health solutions, the anonymity provided helps to mitigate the stigma usually associated with seeking treatment. Students may feel more comfortable interacting with AI systems—such as chatbots or virtual counselors—than with traditional in-person offerings. Farrukh Shahzad et al. (2024) claim that this seeming anonymity encourages openness and drives more students to seek therapy, hence normalizing dialogues on mental health.

CHALLENGES

Negative Consequences of Artificial Intelligence on Mental Health

While artificial intelligence shows great potential to help with mental health, including technology into classrooms presents challenges. One should consider some unfavorable effects some more.

Artificial intelligence systems may unintentionally make students more anxious even when they might improve access to school and offer academic support. Sometimes the constant connectivity of AI-driven systems causes burnout and stress by demanding users to be always efficient or performing. This "always-on" lifestyle aggravates mental health issues especially for students currently under a lot of social or intellectual load.

If we want to apply artificial intelligence in mental health, sensitive personal data has to be obtained and investigated; so, consent and privacy become ethical concerns. Many students from exposing their personal data to artificial intelligence systems (Farrukh Shahzad et al., 2024) are driven from by fear of data breaches, misuse, or illegal access. These issues show how important it is to have transparent policies and strong data security mechanisms if one is to guarantee confidence in AI uses.

Increased sensitivity of students to cyberbullying brought on by the widespread use of AI-powered digital communication platforms reflects present trends. Although AI-generated conversations and automated content monitoring are supposed to provide helpful settings, they can not help to stop bad behavior. Moreover, artificial intelligence generated content could be used to spread racist or harassing messages, therefore seriously affecting students's mental health.

Students who depend too much on artificial intelligence technologies for academic success or emotional support may find it more difficult to acquire important self-regulation and coping methods. Gao (2025) argues that this reliance could make it more difficult for pupils to address issues on their own and leave them defenseless in circumstances when technology aid is not accessible. This dependence emphasizes the need of balancing employing more conventional approaches of skill development and human communication against artificial intelligence.

Institutions must use moral artificial intelligence methods, set strong privacy policies, and inspire students' digital literacy if they are to meet these obstacles. Moreover, combining artificial intelligence with human-led therapy provides a well-rounded approach using the advantages of both technology and conventional support systems.

Case Studies Illustrating Favorable Results

Case Study: How a University Uses a Chatbot

A well-known California university debuted WellnessBot, an artificial intelligence-powered chatbot, to improve students' access to tools for mental wellness. Designed as a sort of virtual assistant, WellnessBot offers information about campus counseling facilities, delivers self-help advice depending on user questions, and runs mood checks to track mental wellness.

Outcomes:

Thirty percent more students used mental health resources following the launch of WellnessBot, according to the institution. This growing connection revealed how readily available and simple AI-powered tools for mental health support are.

Students valued having immediate support, especially after hours when regular counseling sessions were not accessible. The bot's quick replies closed the availability gap for mental health care.

Post-implementation polls show that 85% of users of WellnessBot said they felt more at ease asking for help. Students appreciated the chatbot's stress-free environment and privacy, which helped to reduce the customary challenges in personally seeking assistance.

Implications:

This case study shows how chatbots driven by artificial intelligence could increase campus culture's positive impact and access to mental health treatments. By providing quick, customized, stigma-free support, tools like WellnessBot can significantly raise students' eagerness to seek mental health treatments and engage in proactive efforts toward well-being.

Case Study:

Tracking Mental Health with Predictive Analytics

The University of Manchester in the United Kingdom uses machine learning techniques to support predictive analytics, therefore enhancing its mental health monitoring system. Examining data points including attendance, academic performance, and classroom participation helps one to identify early signs of pupils' mental health problems.

Conclusion:

Early Interventions: The predictive analytics system found at-risk teenagers using signs including declining grades, less participation in school events, and inconsistent attendance. These realizations helped the institution to act early and prevent little problems from becoming large mental health crises. Armed with data, academic advisers and mental health counselors often approached students who had been identified. Plans for customized support included tutoring, helping students contact campus mental health resources, and emotionally supporting them depending on their needs.

Among students deemed to be at-risk, the proactive approach raised retention rates by 15%. Early settlement of specific problems let the institution strengthen its general system of student care and improve academic achievement, so promoting a more friendly and accommodating environment.

Implications: This case study shows how greatly student welfare may be improved by predictive analytics. By combining data-driven insights with traditional support systems, schools could create powerful early intervention systems that support academic success and mental health. The positive outcomes also indicate how predictive technologies can help long-term institutional goals like higher student satisfaction and retention.

Challenges Educational Institutions Deal With

Though many problems still exist, several case studies have demonstrated positive results:

Many companies struggle to include artificial intelligence capabilities into their present systems either from a lack of infrastructure or staff training.

The second is Institutions must act early to allay worries about algorithmic bias and data privacy.

The third is Implementing AI solutions that function requires a significant outlay in technology and training resources.

Rational Justifications and Examples

- AI watches behavioral data like academic performance and social media activity to spot early warning signs of mental illness. Wearable technology that picks out odd sleep patterns, for example, can set off quick interventions. Combining behavioral patterns with academic schedules helps one to find students who are at danger during periods of great stress.
- AI systems evaluate individual needs to offer tailored solutions including mindfulness training or workload changes. At schools, for example, AI dashboards can identify students who are at risk and recommend customized help programs such tutoring or counseling. Customizing helps to develop trust and raises adherence to recommended strategies.
- AI allows one to access mental health resources anonymously and around-the-clock, therefore enabling a great reduction of stigma. Students who might be reluctant to visit traditional therapy can engage with AI-powered tools in a confidential, nonjudging environment. AI's ability to operate across several communication channels—text, audio, and visual as well as others—improves accessibility even more.
- AI can identify tendencies in student populations, such a generalised anxiousness during test times, at community level. Schools can use these results to implement specific interventions including stress management programs. By addressing structural issues, institutions help to foster a more motivating intellectual environment.

Potential Uses

- Academic environments can utilize artificial intelligence to create mental health dashboards tracking students' welfare in real time. These technologies give managers and counselors insightful analysis by compiling data from several sources. One of the typical pressures these tools help schools to proactively handle is exam periods.
- AI systems can detect trends in student populations including group tension or anxiety surrounding significant events, therefore enabling community-level interventions. Using these insights can help organizations design tools or seminars especially meant to increase community resilience.
- Individualized learning environments are created by means of programs for personalized learning and well-being artificial intelligence-powered analysis of behavioral and academic data. For students who are experiencing academic burnout, for example, tailored recommendations for stress management

and leisure activities will help to improve their academic performance and mental health.

FUTURE RESEARCH AND CONSEQUENCES

Possible Consequences

- Data-driven insights enable academic institutions to look at long-term trends and patterns in the mental health of their students, therefore enhancing their service provision. By looking at data across several semesters to pinpoint high-stress times, such test seasons, colleges might more effectively allocate resources like counseling staff members and wellness initiatives. Ultimately, this deliberate use of data benefits institutions as well as students since it ensures quick interventions and best service delivery.
- Enhanced International Cooperation on AI Tools for Mental Health: Creation and standardizing of AI tools for mental health benefits from multidisciplinary, worldwide cooperation. By use of research results and best practices, institutions can create frameworks that operate in several cultural and educational contexts. Academics from industrialized and underdeveloped countries, for example, can work together to provide inclusive and culturally sensitive AI solutions that satisfy the particular needs of many individuals.
- Global Perspective and Adaptability: Multidisciplinary collaborations between institutions all around provide the adaptability of artificial intelligence research in many institutional and cultural settings as well as their progress. For example, AI systems developed in Western countries could have to be changed to meet the cultural standards and mental health needs of students in Asia, Africa, or Latin America. This global perspective ensures the equity, scalability, and efficacy of artificial intelligence solutions.
- Encouragement of ethical AI practices is necessary given the possibility of millions of lives being changed by AI technologies to be more included into mental health treatments. Inter-institutional collaboration can help to ensure that artificial intelligence is a tool for good by driving the creation of ethical norms addressing algorithmic bias, data protection, and fair access.
- AI-driven mental health solutions can help to close resource gaps in underfunded areas where traditional counseling services are not easily available. For instance, predictive algorithms or AI chatbots can help students in undeveloped areas where access to mental health professionals could be limited. This assures for every student, regardless of their location quick and effective assistance.

Future Research Routes

Using artificial intelligence in mental health treatment depends on its ability to identify and respond to challenging emotional inputs. Many times, the intricacy needed to replicate real empathy is absent in present models. Future research should mostly focus on methods such emotional-driven dialogue systems, multimodal sentiment analysis (which includes text, tone, and facial recognition), and reinforcement learning. These advances will raise artificial intelligence's emotional intelligence and hence increase its ability to help consumers. Gao (2025) says that building sympathetic and human-like AI interactions depends on applying such enhancements.

Respecting moral AI practices and safeguarding user data in sensitive mental health settings is absolutely vital. Research should first give great attention to the development of robust frameworks for data privacy with an eye toward encryption, anonymizing, and safe storing. Moreover, clear governance rules help to build user confidence by themselves. Farrukh Shahzad et al. (2024) underline how important it is to manage privacy concerns in order to soothe user worries and assure the general application of AI solutions.

Confirming the long-term success of AI treatments requires longitudinal investigations. These studies should evaluate indicators like academic performance, social integration, emotional resilience, and retention rates in order to present a whole picture of the consequences of artificial intelligence. This kind of research will direct little improvements and help companies maximize their mental health projects driven by artificial intelligence. Chen et al. (2024), for example, support long-term assessments to ensure that artificial intelligence projects yield notable and long-lasting effects.

Future research specifically for students with disabilities and those in low-resource contexts should focus on making AI mental health tools more inclusive and easily available. This means designing accessible user interfaces, improving language localization, and ensuring assistive technology fits. Innovations in these domains will ensure that every student, from all walks of life, has access to AI solutions and help close equity discrepancies.

CONCLUSION

Final Thoughts

Emphasizing its transforming ability, this chapter has investigated the theoretical and conceptual foundations of artificial intelligence in tackling student mental health problems. By offering unique ideas in early diagnosis, customized treatments, and more accessibility, artificial intelligence is transforming the way mental health treatments are given in learning environments. Its inherent limitations—which include data biases, emotional nuance, and ethical questions—should be addressed even if its impacts are obviously positive.

The larger relevance of this study results from its effects on academic institutions, policymakers, and mental health professionals striving to create a friendly environment for students. Combining artificial intelligence with traditional counseling methods allows educational institutions to design more effective, fair, long-lasting mental health care systems.

The inclusion of artificial intelligence into mental health services marks a paradigm change in student well-being approaches since it allows one to address problems at scale and adapt treatments to fit each individual. As the field grows, this chapter stresses the need of constant research, multidisciplinary cooperation, and ethical awareness. Only these projects will allow artificial intelligence to fully realize its possibilities in mental health, therefore ensuring a time when every student will have access to the tools needed for success.

REFERENCES

Al-Samarraie, H., Shamsuddin, A., & Alzahrani, A. I. (2020). A systematic review of the integration of learning management systems and social media in higher education. *Education and Information Technologies*, *25*(6), 5431–5449. DOI: 10.1007/s10639-020-10259-1

Alsayed, S., Assayed, S. K., Alkhatib, M., & Shaalan, K. (2024). Impact of Artificial Intelligence Chatbots on Student Well-being and Mental Health: A Systematic Review. *People and Behavior Analysis*, *2*(2), 1–13. DOI: 10.31098/pba.v2i2.2411

Chen, J., Yuan, D., Dong, R., Cai, J., Ai, Z., & Zhou, S. (2024). Artificial intelligence significantly facilitates development in the mental health of college students: A bibliometric analysis. *Frontiers in Psychology*, *15*, 1375294. Advance online publication. DOI: 10.3389/fpsyg.2024.1375294 PMID: 38515973

Davis, F. (1989). Perceived Usefulness, Perceived Ease of Use, and User Acceptance of Information Technology. *Management Information Systems Quarterly*, *13*, 319–340. DOI: 10.2307/249008

Farrukh Shahzad, M., Xu, S., Lim, W. M., Yang, X., & Khan, Q. R. (2024). Artificial intelligence and social media on academic performance and mental well-being: Student perceptions of positive impact in the age of smart learning. *Heliyon*, *10*(8), e29523. DOI: 10.1016/j.heliyon.2024.e29523 PMID: 38665566

Fitzpatrick, K. K., Darcy, A., & Vierhile, M. (2017). Delivering cognitive behavior therapy to young adults with symptoms of depression and anxiety using a fully automated conversational agent (Woebot): A randomized controlled trial. *JMIR Mental Health*, *4*(2), e19. https://doi.org/10.2196/mental.7785

Gao, Y. (2025). The impact and application of artificial intelligence technology on mental health counseling services for college students. *Journal of Computational Methods in Sciences and Engineering*, *25*(2), 1686–1701.

Shimada, K. (2023). The role of artificial intelligence in mental health: A review. *Science Insights*, *43*(5), 1119–1127. DOI: 10.15354/si.23.re820

Talaue, G. M., AlSaad, A., AlRushaidan, N., AlHugail, A., & AlFahhad, S. (2018). The impact of social media on academic performance of selected college students. *International Journal of Advanced Information Technology*, *8*(4/5), 27–35. DOI: 10.5121/ijait.2018.8503

Velastegui-Hernandez, D. C., Salazar-Garcés, L. F., & Rodriguez-Pérez, M. L. (2023). Impact of artificial intelligence on learning behaviors and psychological well-being of college students. *Salud, Ciencia y Tecnología - Serie de Conferencias, 2,* 582. https://doi.org/DOI: 10.56294/sctconf2023582

Wang, T., Lund, B. D., Marengo, A., Pagano, A., Mannuru, N. R., Teel, Z. A., & Pange, J. (2023). Exploring the Potential Impact of Artificial Intelligence (AI) on International Students in Higher Education: Generative AI, Chatbots, Analytics, and International Student Success. *Applied Sciences (Basel, Switzerland), 13*(11), 6716.

Woebot Health. (n.d.). Woebot: Your mental health ally. https://woebothealth.com

Yilmaz, R. M., & Karaoglan Yilmaz, F. G. (2024). Students' acceptance of AI-powered educational tools: Exploring the impact of metacognitive self-regulation. *Computers & Education, 205,* 104900.

Compilation of References

Abbas, N., Whitfield, J., Atwell, E., Bowman, H., Pickard, T., & Walker, A. (2022). Online chat and chatbots to enhance mature student engagement in higher education. [tandfonline.com]. *International Journal of Lifelong Education, 41*(3), 308–326. DOI: 10.1080/02601370.2022.2066213

Abdulah, D. M., Zaman, B. A., Mustafa, Z. R., & Hassan, L. H. (2024). Artificial Intelligence Integration in Academic Writing: Insights from the University of Duhok. *ARO (Koya), 12*(2), 194–200. DOI: 10.14500/aro.11794

Abiddin, N. Z., Ibrahim, I., & Abdul Aziz, S. A. (2022). Non-governmental organisations (NGOs) and their part towards sustainable community development. Sustainability. mdpi.com

Abu Bakar, N. F., Yusof, A. F. A., Iahad, N., & Ahmad, N. (2018). The Implementation of Gamification in Massive Open Online Courses (MOOC) Platform. In Abdullah, N., Wan Adnan, W. A., & Foth, M. (Eds.), *User Science and Engineering* (Vol. 886, pp. 183–193). Springer Singapore., DOI: 10.1007/978-981-13-1628-9_17

Aderamo, A. T., Olisakwe, H. C., Adebayo, Y. A., & Esiri, A. E. (2024). AI-powered pandemic response framework for offshore oil platforms: Ensuring safety during global health crises. Comprehensive Research and Reviews in Engineering and Technology, 2(1), 044-063.

Aguiar, M. F., Mesa, J. A., Jugend, D., Pinheiro, M. A. P., & Fiorini, P. D. C. (2022). Circular product design: Strategies, challenges and relationships with new product development. [HTML]. *Management of Environmental Quality, 33*(2), 300–329. DOI: 10.1108/MEQ-06-2021-0125

Ahsan, M. J. (2025). Cultivating a culture of learning: The role of leadership in fostering lifelong development. [HTML]. *The Learning Organization, 32*(2), 282–306. DOI: 10.1108/TLO-03-2024-0099

Akhtar, M. A. K., Kumar, M., & Nayyar, A. (2024). The Role of Human-Centered Design in Developing Explainable AI. In Towards Ethical and Socially Responsible Explainable AI: Challenges and Opportunities (pp. 99-126). Cham: Springer Nature Switzerland. [HTML] DOI: 10.1007/978-3-031-66489-2_4

Alam, A. (2021, November). Possibilities and apprehensions in the landscape of artificial intelligence in education. In 2021 International conference on computational intelligence and computing applications (ICCICA) (pp. 1-8). IEEE. [HTML] DOI: 10.1109/ICCICA52458.2021.9697272

Al-Ansi, A. M., Jaboob, M., Garad, A., & Al-Ansi, A. (2023). Analyzing augmented reality (AR) and virtual reality (VR) recent development in education. [sciencedirect.com]. *Social Sciences & Humanities Open*, *8*(1), 100532. DOI: 10.1016/j.ssaho.2023.100532

Albantakis, L., Barbosa, L., Findlay, G., Grasso, M., Haun, A. M., Marshall, W., Mayner, W. G. P., Zaeemzadeh, A., Boly, M., Juel, B. E., Sasai, S., Fujii, K., David, I., Hendren, J., Lang, J. P., & Tononi, G. (2023). Integrated information theory (IIT) 4.0: Formulating the properties of phenomenal existence in physical terms. [plos.org]. *PLoS Computational Biology*, *19*(10), e1011465. DOI: 10.1371/journal.pcbi.1011465 PMID: 37847724

Alharbi, W. (2023). AI in the Foreign Language Classroom: A Pedagogical Overview of Automated Writing Assistance Tools. *Education Research International*, *2023*, 1–15. DOI: 10.1155/2023/4253331

Alibasic, A., Upadhyay, H., Simsekler, M. C. E., Kurfess, T., Woon, W. L., & Omar, M. A. (2022). Evaluation of the trends in jobs and skill-sets using data analytics: A case study. [springer.com]. *Journal of Big Data*, *9*(1), 32. DOI: 10.1186/s40537-022-00576-5

Aljohani, N. R., Aslam, A., Khadidos, A. O., & Hassan, S. U. (2022). Bridging the skill gap between the acquired university curriculum and the requirements of the job market: A data-driven analysis of scientific literature. [sciencedirect.com]. *Journal of Innovation & Knowledge*, *7*(3), 100190. DOI: 10.1016/j.jik.2022.100190

Allioui, H. & Mourdi, Y. (2023). Exploring the full potentials of IoT for better financial growth and stability: A comprehensive survey. Sensors. mdpi.com

Almenara, A. P., Elich, J. H., & Saltiveri, T. G. (2024). Past, present and future of user-centred design methodologies that empathise with the user and generate better accessible experiences. from theory to practice. In Future Perspectives on Human-Computer Interaction Research: Towards the Year 2030 (pp. 17-43). Cham: Springer Nature Switzerland. [HTML]

Almulla, M. A. & Al-Rahmi, W. M. (2023). Integrated social cognitive theory with learning input factors: The effects of problem-solving skills and critical thinking skills on learning performance sustainability. Sustainability. mdpi.com

Almusaed, A., Almssad, A., Yitmen, I., & Homod, R. Z. (2023). Enhancing student engagement: Harnessing "AIED"'s power in hybrid education—A review analysis. Education Sciences. mdpi.com

Alotaibi, N. S., & Alshehri, A. H. (2023). Prospers and Obstacles in Using Artificial Intelligence in Saudi Arabia Higher Education Institutions—The Potential of AI-Based Learning Outcomes. *Sustainability (Basel)*, *15*(13), 10723. DOI: 10.3390/su151310723

Al-Samarraie, H., Shamsuddin, A., & Alzahrani, A. I. (2020). A systematic review of the integration of learning management systems and social media in higher education. *Education and Information Technologies*, *25*(6), 5431–5449. DOI: 10.1007/s10639-020-10259-1

Alsayed, S., Assayed, S. K., Alkhatib, M., & Shaalan, K. (2024). Impact of Artificial Intelligence Chatbots on Student Well-being and Mental Health: A Systematic Review. *People and Behavior Analysis*, *2*(2), 1–13. DOI: 10.31098/pba.v2i2.2411

AlTwijri, L. & Alghizzi, T. M. (2024). Investigating the integration of artificial intelligence in English as foreign language classes for enhancing learners' affective factors: A systematic review. Heliyon. cell.com

Alvarez-Vargas, D., Lopez Perez, J. P., Bermudez, V. N., Beltrán-Grimm, S., Santana, E., Begolli, K., & Bustamante, A. S. (2023). Evidence-based designs for physically active and playful math learning. [HTML]. *Theory into Practice*, *62*(2), 166–180. DOI: 10.1080/00405841.2023.2202131

Al-Zarkani, K. H., Al-Atabi, A. R. J., & Al-Jubouri, M. T. A. (2024, July). The Use of Artificial Intelligence Analytics to Understand Learning Behaviors and Improve Student Outcomes in E-Learning. In International Conference on Intelligent Systems, Blockchain, and Communication Technologies (pp. 523-530). Cham: Springer Nature Switzerland. [HTML]

Amaliah, N., Limbong, S., Syam, N. I., Room, F., & Bashar, K. (2022). Using Technology as Learning Media to Enrich ESP Students' Speaking Skill for Indonesian Higher Education Students. IJOLEH. *International Journal of Education and Humanities*, *2*(1), 43–51.

Aminah, S., Ramawani, N., Azura, N., Fronika, S., Hasanah, S. M., & Salsabillah, T. (2022). Pengaruh Metode Belajar Sambil Bermain Terhadap Perkembangan Kognitif Anak Usia Sekolah Dasar. *SICEDU : Science and Education Journal, 1*(2), 465–471. https://doi.org/https://doi.org/10.31004/sicedu.v1i2.66

Amores-Valencia, A., Burgos, D., & Branch-Bedoya, J. W. (2022). Influence of motivation and academic performance in the use of Augmented Reality in education. A systematic review. [frontiersin.org]. *Frontiers in Psychology*, *13*, 1011409. DOI: 10.3389/fpsyg.2022.1011409 PMID: 36304863

Archibald, A., Hudson, C., Heap, T., Thompson, R. R., Lin, L., DeMeritt, J., & Lucke, H. (2023). A validation of AI-enabled discussion platform metrics and relationships to student efforts. [springer.com]. *TechTrends*, *67*(2), 285–293. DOI: 10.1007/s11528-022-00825-7 PMID: 36711121

Ardiana, R. (2022). Strategi Guru dalam Mengembangkan Kemampuan Kognitif Anak Usia 5-6 Tahun di Taman Kanak Kanak. *Murhum: Jurnal Pendidikan Anak Usia Dini*, *3*(2), 1–10. DOI: 10.37985/murhum.v3i2.116

Armstrong, A. (2022). Technological practices of middle years students with mathematics learning disabilities. [HTML]. *Canadian Journal of Science, Mathematics and Technology Education = Revue Canadienne de l'Enseignement des Sciences, des Mathématiques et de la Technologie*, *22*(2), 376–391. DOI: 10.1007/s42330-022-00208-3

Asdar, A., Hamsiah, A., Sujarwo, S., Lutfin, N., & Sukmawati, S. (2024). Integrative Approach for Reading Comprehension Espousing Information Communication Technology Literacy. [IJERE]. *International Journal of Evaluation and Research in Education, 13*(6), 4384. DOI: 10.11591/ijere.v13i6.29461

Ashford, M., Abraham, A., & Poolton, J. (2021). Understanding a player's decision-making process in team sports: a systematic review of empirical evidence. Sports. mdpi.com

Atoum, I. (2023). Measurement of key performance indicators of user experience based on software requirements. [HTML]. *Science of Computer Programming*, *226*, 102929. DOI: 10.1016/j.scico.2023.102929

Atwell, A., Ecton, W., Klein, S., D'Amico, M. M., & Sublett, C. (2022). Community college responses to align career and technical education programs with changing labor markets. [wiley.com]. *New Directions for Community Colleges*, *2022*(197), 45–58. DOI: 10.1002/cc.20496

Auernhammer, J., & Roth, B. (2021). The origin and evolution of Stanford University's design thinking: From product design to design thinking in innovation management. *Journal of Product Innovation Management, 38*(6), 623–644. DOI: 10.1111/jpim.12594

Autin, K. L., Herdt, M. E., Garcia, R. G., & Ezema, G. N. (2022). Basic psychological need satisfaction, autonomous motivation, and meaningful work: A self-determination theory perspective. [HTML]. *Journal of Career Assessment, 30*(1), 78–93. DOI: 10.1177/10690727211018647

Avsec, S., Jagiełło-Kowalczyk, M., Żabicka, A., Gil-Mastalerczyk, J., & Gawlak, A. (2024). Human-Centered Systems Thinking in Technology-Enhanced Sustainable and Inclusive Architectural Design. [mdpi.com]. *Sustainability (Basel), 16*(22), 9802. DOI: 10.3390/su16229802

Babu, M. S., Raj, K. B., & Devi, D. A. (2021). Data security and sensitive data protection using privacy by design technique. In *2nd EAI International Conference on Big Data Innovation for Sustainable Cognitive Computing: BDCC 2019* (pp. 177-189). Springer International Publishing. [HTML] DOI: 10.1007/978-3-030-47560-4_14

Bagai, R., & Mane, V. (2023). Designing an AI-Powered Mentorship Platform for Professional Development: Opportunities and Challenges. *International Journal of Computer Trends and Technology, 71*(4), 108–114. DOI: 10.14445/22312803/IJCTT-V71I4P114

Bahroun, Z., Anane, C., Ahmed, V., & Zacca, A. (2023). Transforming education: A comprehensive review of generative artificial intelligence in educational settings through bibliometric and content analysis. Sustainability. mdpi.com

Balaji, K. (2025). Human-Centric Innovation: Building Sustainable Organizations for Industry 5.0. In Human-Centric, Sustainable, and Resilient Organizations in the Digital Age (pp. 101-124). IGI Global Scientific Publishing. [HTML]

Baldassarre, B., Calabretta, G., Karpen, I. O., Bocken, N., & Hultink, E. J. (2024). Responsible Design Thinking for Sustainable Development: Critical Literature Review, New Conceptual Framework, and Research Agenda. [springer.com]. *Journal of Business Ethics, 195*(1), 25–46. DOI: 10.1007/s10551-023-05600-z PMID: 39507515

Bassachs, M., Serra, T., Bubnys, R., Cañabate, D., & Colomer, J. (2022). Multimodal approaches to math and physical education within cooperative learning to enhance social attitudes. [mdpi.com]. *Sustainability (Basel), 14*(24), 16961. DOI: 10.3390/su142416961

Bass, M., Dompierre, K. A. B., & McAlister, M. (2023). Creating transformative interdisciplinary learning opportunities for college students. [sagepub.com]. *Journal of Transformative Education*, *21*(1), 118–137. DOI: 10.1177/15413446211066934

Baumer, B. S. & Matthews, G. J. (2023). Big ideas in sports analytics and statistical tools for their investigation. Wiley Interdisciplinary …. [PDF]

Beagan, J. R. (2021). A Phenomenological Study of How Transformational Leadership Is Influenced by the Human-Centered Design Approach in Developing Organizational Synergy. [HTML]

Bellido, D., García-García, C., Talluri, A., Lukaski, H. C., & García-Almeida, J. M. (2023). Future lines of research on phase angle: Strengths and limitations. [springer.com]. *Reviews in Endocrine & Metabolic Disorders*, *24*(3), 563–583. DOI: 10.1007/s11154-023-09803-7 PMID: 37043140

Berchin, I. I. & Aguiar Dutra, A. R. (2021). How do higher education institutions promote sustainable development? A literature review. Sustainable …. [HTML]

Berson, I. R., Berson, M. J., & Luo, W. Innovating responsibly: ethical considerations for AI in early childhood education. AI. springer.com

Bhardwaj, R. (2024, May). AI Integrated Model Design for Education System for Analytical Computation (Mathematics). In 2024 4th International Conference on Advance Computing and Innovative Technologies in Engineering (ICACITE) (pp. 1412-1417). IEEE. [HTML]

Bjelobaba, G., Savić, A., Tošić, T., Stefanović, I., & Kocić, B. (2023). Collaborative learning supported by Blockchain Technology as a model for improving the Educational process. Sustainability. mdpi.com

Borges, P. H., Ueda, L. S. C., de Souza, P. V., Binda, M. E. V., da Silva, J. F., Ribeiro, J., & Guilherme, J. (2024). Original actions performed by a beginner attacker modify defensive dispersion in small-sided soccer games. [nature.com]. *Scientific Reports*, *14*(1), 28489. DOI: 10.1038/s41598-024-79741-0 PMID: 39558083

Bouschery, S., Blazevic, V., & Pillar, F. (2023). Augmenting human innovation teams with artificial intelligence: Exploring transformer-based language modes. *Journal of Product Innovation Management*, *40*(2), 139–153. DOI: 10.1111/jpim.12656

Bozkurt, A., Karadeniz, A., Baneres, D., Guerrero-Roldán, A. E., & Rodríguez, M. E. (2021). Artificial intelligence and reflections from educational landscape: A review of AI studies in half a century. [mdpi.com]. *Sustainability (Basel)*, *13*(2), 800. DOI: 10.3390/su13020800

Brem, A., Giones, F., & Werle, M. (2021). The AI digital revolution in innovation: A conceptual framework of artificial intelligence technologies for the management of innovation. *IEEE Transactions on Engineering Management, 70*(2), 770–776. DOI: 10.1109/TEM.2021.3109983

Brown, T. (2009). *Change by Design: How Design Thinking Transforms Organizations and Inspires Innovation*. HarperCollins.

Bucea-Manea- oniş, R., Kuleto, V., Gudei, S. C. D., Lianu, C., Lianu, C., Ilić, M. P., & Păun, D. (2022). Artificial intelligence potential in higher education institutions enhanced learning environment in Romania and Serbia. [mdpi.com]. *Sustainability (Basel), 14*(10), 5842. DOI: 10.3390/su14105842

Cao, F., Xiang, M., Chen, K., & Lei, M. (2022). Intelligent physical education teaching tracking system based on multimedia data analysis and artificial intelligence. Mobile Information Systems. wiley.com

Carayannis, E. G., Dezi, L., Gregori, G., & Calo, E. (2022). Smart environments and techno-centric and human-centric innovations for Industry and Society 5.0: A quintuple helix innovation system view towards smart, sustainable, and inclusive solutions. [springer.com]. *Journal of the Knowledge Economy, 13*(2), 926–955. DOI: 10.1007/s13132-021-00763-4 PMID: 40477337

Carretero, M. D. P., García, S., Moreno, A., Alcain, N., & Elorza, I. (2021). Methodology to create virtual reality assisted training courses within the Industry 4.0 vision. [HTML]. *Multimedia Tools and Applications, 80*(19), 29699–29717. DOI: 10.1007/s11042-021-11195-2

Carrió-Pastor, M. L. (Ed.). (2016). *Technology Implementation in Second Language Teaching and Translation Studies: New Tools, New Approaches*. Springer Singapore., DOI: 10.1007/978-981-10-0572-5

Casado-Robles, C., Viciana, J., Guijarro-Romero, S., & Mayorga-Vega, D. (2022). Effects of consumer-wearable activity tracker-based programs on objectively measured daily physical activity and sedentary behavior among school-aged children: A systematic review and meta-analysis. [springer.com]. *Sports Medicine - Open, 8*(1), 18. DOI: 10.1186/s40798-021-00407-6 PMID: 35099630

Castro-Alonso, J. C., de Koning, B. B., Fiorella, L., & Paas, F. (2021). Five strategies for optimizing instructional materials: Instructor-and learner-managed cognitive load. [springer.com]. *Educational Psychology Review, 33*(4), 1379–1407. DOI: 10.1007/s10648-021-09606-9 PMID: 33716467

Cen, C., Luo, G., Li, L., Liang, Y., Li, K., Jiang, T., & Xiong, Q. (2023). User-Centered software design: user interface redesign for Blockly–Electron, artificial intelligence educational software for primary and secondary schools. Sustainability. mdpi.com

Chang, L. & Zhang, X. (2022). A Method of Improving College Students' Physical Fitness Test Based on Fuzzy Comprehensive Evaluation of Information Fusion. Advances in Multimedia. wiley.com

Chang-Tik, C. (2023). Collaborative spaces: Investigating the relationships between students' group-based learning and lecturers' approaches. [HTML]. *Educational Research*, *65*(4), 409–427. DOI: 10.1080/00131881.2023.2256747

Chang, Y., Lee, S., Wong, S. F., & Jeong, S. (2022). AI-powered learning application use and gratification: An integrative model. *Information Technology & People*, *35*(7), 2115–2139. DOI: 10.1108/ITP-09-2020-0632

Chaudhry, I. S., Sarwary, S. A. M., El Refae, G. A., & Chabchoub, H. (2023). Time to revisit existing student's performance evaluation approach in higher education sector in a new era of ChatGPT—A case study. [tandfonline.com]. *Cogent Education*, *10*(1), 2210461. DOI: 10.1080/2331186X.2023.2210461

Chen, H., Rao, F., Chen, R., & Lin, Z. (2023). Teaching STEAM in the shaolin staff program: ways to stimulate student engagement in learning. Frontiers in Psychology. frontiersin.org

Cheng, L., Han, J., & Nasirov, J. (2024). Ethical considerations related to personal data collection and reuse: trust and transparency in language and speech technologies. International Journal of Legal Discourse. [HTML]

Chen, J., Yuan, D., Dong, R., Cai, J., Ai, Z., & Zhou, S. (2024). Artificial intelligence significantly facilitates development in the mental health of college students: A bibliometric analysis. *Frontiers in Psychology*, *15*, 1375294. Advance online publication. DOI: 10.3389/fpsyg.2024.1375294 PMID: 38515973

Chiu, T. K., Ahmad, Z., Ismailov, M., & Sanusi, I. T. (2024). What are artificial intelligence literacy and competency? A comprehensive framework to support them. [sciencedirect.com]. *Computers and Education Open*, *6*, 100171. DOI: 10.1016/j.caeo.2024.100171

Choukaier, D. (2024). Integrating AI In English Language Pedagogy: Innovations And Outcomes In Teaching English As Second /Foreign Language. *Educational Administration: Theory and Practice, 30*(5), 3811–3822. https://doi.org/Doi: DOI: 10.53555/kuey.v30i5.3538

Christensen, J., Ekelund, N., Melin, M., & Widén, P. (2021). The beautiful risk of collaborative and interdisciplinary research. A challenging collaborative and critical approach toward sustainable learning processes in academic …. Sustainability. mdpi.com

Coban, M., Bolat, Y. I., & Goksu, I. (2022). The potential of immersive virtual reality to enhance learning: A meta-analysis. [HTML]. *Educational Research Review*, *36*, 100452. DOI: 10.1016/j.edurev.2022.100452

Creely, E. (2024). Exploring the Role of Generative AI in Enhancing Language Learning: Opportunities and Challenges. *International Journal of Changes in Education*, *1*(3), 158–167. DOI: 10.47852/bonviewIJCE42022495

Creswell, J. W. (2013). *Educational research: Planning, conducting, and evaluating quantitative and qualitative research* (Fourth Indian edition). PHI Learning Private Limited.

Crone, V. C. A. (2023). A mismatch: Why non-tenured teachers are ill-prepared to deal with the perceived job insecurity of students in the humanities. Arts and Humanities in Higher Education. sagepub.com

D'Mello, S. K., & Graesser, A. (2023). Intelligent tutoring systems: How computers achieve learning gains that rival human tutors. Handbook of educational psychology. [HTML]

Dai, C. P. & Ke, F. (2022). Educational applications of artificial intelligence in simulation-based learning: A systematic mapping review. Computers and Education: Artificial Intelligence. sciencedirect.com

Damaševičius, R., & Zailskaitė-Jakštė, L. (2023, November). From STEAM to STREAM: Integrating Research as a Part of STEAM Education. In International Conference on New Media Pedagogy (pp. 318-335). Cham: Springer Nature Switzerland. [HTML]

Davis, C., Bush, T., & Wood, S. (2024). Artificial intelligence in education: Enhancing learning experiences through personalized adaptation. [iaic-publisher.org]. *International Journal of Cyber and IT Service Management*, *4*(1), 26–32. DOI: 10.34306/ijcitsm.v4i1.146

Davis, F. (1989). Perceived Usefulness, Perceived Ease of Use, and User Acceptance of Information Technology. *Management Information Systems Quarterly*, *13*, 319–340. DOI: 10.2307/249008

De Silva, C. S. B., & Taherdoost, H. (2025). *E-Business: Strategic Approaches to E-Business Transformation*. Mastering Innovation in Business. [HTML]

Deák, C. & Kumar, B. (2024). A systematic review of STEAM education's role in nurturing digital competencies for sustainable innovations. Education Sciences. mdpi.com

Dehbozorgi, M. H., Postell, J., Ward, D., Leardi, C., Sullivan, B. P., & Rossi, M. (2024). Human in the loop: Revolutionizing industry 5.0 with design thinking and systems thinking. [cambridge.org]. *Proceedings of the Design Society*, *4*, 245–254. DOI: 10.1017/pds.2024.27

Demirdis, B. (2025). Integrating Digital Literacy to Enhance Emotional and Social Skills in Education. In Innovative Educational Frameworks for Future Skills and Competencies (pp. 1-38). IGI Global Scientific Publishing. [HTML]

Desai, R. J., Matheny, M. E., Johnson, K., Marsolo, K., Curtis, L. H., Nelson, J. C., Heagerty, P. J., Maro, J., Brown, J., Toh, S., Nguyen, M., Ball, R., Dal Pan, G., Wang, S. V., Gagne, J. J., & Schneeweiss, S. (2021). Broadening the reach of the FDA Sentinel system: A roadmap for integrating electronic health record data in a causal analysis framework. [nature.com]. *NPJ Digital Medicine*, *4*(1), 170. DOI: 10.1038/s41746-021-00542-0 PMID: 34931012

Dewi, A. R. T., Mayasarokh, M., & Gustiana, E. (2020). Perilaku Sosial Emosional Anak Usia Dini. *Jurnal Golden Age*, *4*(1), 181–190.

Du, M., & Yuan, X. (2021). A survey of competitive sports data visualization and visual analysis. [HTML]. *Journal of Visualization / the Visualization Society of Japan*, *24*(1), 47–67. DOI: 10.1007/s12650-020-00687-2

Dutta, S., Ranjan, S., Mishra, S., Sharma, V., Hewage, P., & Iwendi, C. (2024, February). Enhancing educational adaptability: A review and analysis of AI-driven adaptive learning platforms. In 2024 4th International Conference on Innovative Practices in Technology and Management (ICIPTM) (pp. 1-5). IEEE. [HTML]

Eapen, T., Finkenstadt, D. J., Folk, H., & Venkataswamy, L. (2024). How Generative AI Can Augment Human Creativity. *SSRN*, (Fall), 25–32. DOI: 10.2139/ssrn.4759930

Ejjami, R. (2024). The future of learning: AI-based curriculum development. *International Journal for Multidisciplinary Research*, *6*(4).

Ekaningtyas, N. L. D. (2022). Psikologi dalam Dunia Pendidikan. *Padma Sari: Jurnal Ilmu Pendidikan*, *2*(1), 29–38. DOI: 10.53977/ps.v2i01.526

Ekawati, M. (2019). Teori Belajar Menurut Aliran Psikologi Kognitif serta Implikasinya dalam Proses Belajar dan Pembelajaran. *Jurnal E-Tech*, *7*(4), 1–12. DOI: 10.1007/XXXXXX-XX-0000-00

Eki, K. A. O., Sulang, M., Sari, P. N., & Lawalata, M. (2024). Penerapan Logika Dalam Kehidupan Pemuda : Sebuah Refleksi. *Sinar Kasih: Jurnal Pendidikan Agama Dan Filsafat, 2*(2), 209–224. https://doi.org/https://doi.org/10.55606/sinarkasih.v2i2.323

Elahi, M., Afolaranmi, S. O., Martinez Lastra, J. L., & Perez Garcia, J. A. (2023). A comprehensive literature review of the applications of AI techniques through the lifecycle of industrial equipment. [springer.com]. *Discover Artificial Intelligence*, *3*(1), 43. DOI: 10.1007/s44163-023-00089-x

Elfert, M. (2023). Humanism and democracy in comparative education. Comparative Education. tandfonline.com

Elsbach, K. D., & Stigliani, I. (2018). Design thinking and organizational culture: Aa review and framework for future research. *Journal of Management*, *44*(6), 2274–2306. DOI: 10.1177/0149206317744252

Eltahir, M. E. & Babiker, F. M. E. (2024). The influence of artificial intelligence tools on student performance in e-learning environments: Case study. Electronic Journal of e-Learning. academic-publishing.org

Estheriani, N. G. N., & Muhid, A. (2020). Pengembangan Kreativitas Berpikir Siswa di Era Industri 4.0 melalui Perangkat Pembelajaran dengan Media Augmented Reality. *Insight: Jurnal Ilmiah Psikologi, 22*(2), 118–129. https://doi.org/https://dx .doi.org/10.26486/psikologi.v22i2.1206

Estrada, M., Monferrer, D., Rodríguez, A., & Moliner, M. (2021). Does emotional intelligence influence academic performance? The role of compassion and engagement in education for sustainable development. Sustainability. mdpi.com

Eswaran, U., & Eswaran, V. (2025). AI-Driven Cross-Platform Design: Enhancing Usability and User Experience. In Navigating Usability and User Experience in a Multi-Platform World (pp. 19-48). IGI Global. [HTML]

Evanick, D. J. (2024). Implementing Mobile-First Strategies in Online Education. *The Learning Ideas Conference*. [HTML]

Exel, J. & Dabnichki, P. (2024). Precision sports science: what is next for data analytics for athlete performance and well-being optimization?. Applied Sciences. mdpi.com

Ezzaim, A., Dahbi, A., Aqqal, A., & Haidine, A. (2024). AI-based learning style detection in adaptive learning systems: A systematic literature review. [HTML]. *Journal of Computers in Education*, •••, 1–39. DOI: 10.1007/s40692-024-00328-9

Fang, F., Liu, S., Basak, A., Zhu, Q., Kiekintveld, C. D., & Kamhoua, C. A. (2021). Introduction to game theory. Game theory and machine learning for cyber security, 21-46. [HTML]

Farrukh Shahzad, M., Xu, S., Lim, W. M., Yang, X., & Khan, Q. R. (2024). Artificial intelligence and social media on academic performance and mental well-being: Student perceptions of positive impact in the age of smart learning. *Heliyon*, *10*(8), e29523. DOI: 10.1016/j.heliyon.2024.e29523 PMID: 38665566

Ferhataj, A., Memaj, F., Sahatcija, R., Ora, A., & Koka, E. (2025). Ethical concerns in AI development: analyzing students' perspectives on robotics and society. Journal of Information, Communication and Ethics in Society. [HTML]

Fernández-Batanero, J. M., Montenegro-Rueda, M., Fernández-Cerero, J., & García-Martínez, I. (2022). Assistive technology for the inclusion of students with disabilities: A systematic review. [springer.com]. *Educational Technology Research and Development*, *70*(5), 1911–1930. DOI: 10.1007/s11423-022-10127-7

Fitzpatrick, K. K., Darcy, A., & Vierhile, M. (2017). Delivering cognitive behavior therapy to young adults with symptoms of depression and anxiety using a fully automated conversational agent (Woebot): A randomized controlled trial. *JMIR Mental Health*, *4*(2), e19. https://doi.org/10.2196/mental.7785

Folgieri, R., Gil, M., Bait, M., & Lucchiari, C. (2024). AI-Powered Personalised Learning Platforms for EFL Learning: Preliminary Results: *Proceedings of the 16th International Conference on Computer Supported Education*, 255–261. DOI: 10.5220/0012672000003693

Fraidan, A. A. (2024). Integrating AI-Powered Library Systems to Enhance Research and Learning in English Language Departments: A Case Study of Faculty and Student Perceptions. *Library Progress International*, *44*(3), 12058–12065.

Furlong, L. A., Girginov, V., & McErlain-Naylor, S. (). Key Concepts in Sports Biomechanics. api.taylorfrancis.com. [HTML]

Gafni, R., Aviv, I., Kantsepolsky, B., Sherman, S., Rika, H., Itzkovich, Y., & Barger, A. (2024). Objectivity by design: The impact of AI-driven approach on employees' soft skills evaluation. [HTML]. *Information and Software Technology*, *170*, 107430. DOI: 10.1016/j.infsof.2024.107430

Gandedkar, N. H., Wong, M. T., & Darendeliler, M. A. (2021). Role of virtual reality (VR), augmented reality (AR) and artificial intelligence (AI) in tertiary education and research of orthodontics: An insight. [HTML]. *Seminars in Orthodontics*, *27*(2), 69–77. DOI: 10.1053/j.sodo.2021.05.003

Gao, Y. (2025). The impact and application of artificial intelligence technology on mental health counseling services for college students. *Journal of Computational Methods in Sciences and Engineering*, *25*(2), 1686–1701.

George, B. & Wooden, O. (2023). Managing the strategic transformation of higher education through artificial intelligence. Administrative Sciences. mdpi.com

Geszten, D., Hámornik, B. P., & Hercegfi, K. (). Empirical study of Team Usability Testing: a laboratory experiment. Cognition. springer.com

Ghanbaripour, A. N., Talebian, N., Miller, D., Tumpa, R. J., Zhang, W., Golmoradi, M., & Skitmore, M. (2024). A Systematic Review of the Impact of Emerging Technologies on Student Learning, Engagement, and Employability in Built Environment Education. [mdpi.com]. *Buildings (Basel, Switzerland)*, *14*(9), 2769. DOI: 10.3390/buildings14092769

Gibson, L., Obiakor, F. E., & Obi, S. O. (2023). Using technology to enhance learning for students from culturally and linguistically diverse backgrounds. In *Using technology to enhance special education* (pp. 199–214). Emerald Publishing Limited. [HTML] DOI: 10.1108/S0270-401320230000037012

Gimbert, B. G., Miller, D., Herman, E., Breedlove, M., & Molina, C. E. (2023). Social emotional learning in schools: The importance of educator competence. [sagepub.com]. *Journal of Research on Leadership Education*, *18*(1), 3–39. DOI: 10.1177/19427751211014920

Gleeson, J. (2022). Evolution of Irish curriculum culture: Understandings, policy, reform and change. Irish Educational Studies. tandfonline.com

Gligorea, I., Cioca, M., Oancea, R., Gorski, A. T., Gorski, H., & Tudorache, P. (2023). Adaptive learning using artificial intelligence in e-learning: A literature review. [mdpi.com]. *Education Sciences*, *13*(12), 1216. DOI: 10.3390/educsci13121216

Gonzalez-DeHass, A. R., Willems, P. P., Powers, J. R., & Musgrove, A. T. (2022). Parental involvement in supporting students' digital learning. [HTML]. *Educational Psychologist*, *57*(4), 281–294. DOI: 10.1080/00461520.2022.2129647

Goyibova, N., Muslimov, N., Sabirova, G., Kadirova, N., & Samatova, B. (2025). Differentiation approach in education: Tailoring instruction for diverse learner needs. [sciencedirect.com]. *MethodsX*, *14*, 103163. DOI: 10.1016/j.mex.2025.103163 PMID: 39897653

Grau, S. (2021). Using design thinking to drive human-centered innovation in marketing. In Pantano, E. (Ed.), *Creativity + Marketing: The Fuel for Success* (pp. 85–99). Emerald Publishing. DOI: 10.1108/978-1-80071-330-720211006

Grau, S., & Rockett, T. (2022). Creating Student Centered Experiences Using Design Thinking to Create Student Engagement. *The Journal of Entrepreneurship, 31*(25), 1355–1395.

Gredin, N. V., Bishop, D. T., Williams, A. M., & Broadbent, D. P. (2023). The use of contextual priors and kinematic information during anticipation in sport: Toward a Bayesian integration framework. [tandfonline.com]. *International Review of Sport and Exercise Psychology, 16*(1), 286–310. DOI: 10.1080/1750984X.2020.1855667

Grieco-Page, H., Black, C. J., Berent, J. M., Gautam, B., & Betancourt, T. S. (2021). Beyond the pandemic: Leveraging rapid expansions in US telemental health and digital platforms to address disparities and resolve the digital divide. [frontiersin.org]. *Frontiers in Psychiatry, 12*, 671502. DOI: 10.3389/fpsyt.2021.671502 PMID: 34421669

Grill, L., & Pedota, M. (2024). Creativity and artificial intelligence: A multilevel perspective. *Creativity and Innovation Management, 33*(2), 234–247. DOI: 10.1111/caim.12580

Gruber, M., De Leon, N., George, G., & Thompson, P. (2015). Managing by Design. *Academy of Management Journal, 58*(1), 1–7. DOI: 10.5465/amj.2015.4001

Guay, F. (2022). Applying self-determination theory to education: Regulations types, psychological needs, and autonomy supporting behaviors. Canadian Journal of School Psychology. sagepub.com

Guerrini, A., Ferri, G., Rocchi, S., Cirelli, M., Piña, V., & Grieszmann, A. (2023). Personalization@ scale in airlines: Combining the power of rich customer data, experiential learning, and revenue management. [springer.com]. *Journal of Revenue and Pricing Management, 22*(2), 171–180. DOI: 10.1057/s41272-022-00404-8

Güner, P., & Erbay, H. N. (2021). Prospective mathematics teachers' thinking styles and problem-solving skills. [HTML]. *Thinking Skills and Creativity, 40*, 100827. DOI: 10.1016/j.tsc.2021.100827

Guo, Y., & Wang, Y. (2024). Exploring the Effects of Artificial Intelligence Application on EFL Students' Academic Engagement and Emotional Experiences: A Mixed-Methods Study. *European Journal of Education, 12812*. Advance online publication. DOI: 10.1111/ejed.12812

Gutierrez, A., & Boero, P. (2006). *Handbook of Research on the Psychology of Mathematics Education*. DOI: 10.1163/9789087901127

Halb, F., & Seebacher, U. G. (2021). User experience and touchpoint management: A touchpoint performance management toolkit for the buyer journey. In *B2B Marketing: A Guidebook for the Classroom to the Boardroom* (pp. 285–315). Springer International Publishing. [HTML] DOI: 10.1007/978-3-030-54292-4_12

Haleem, A., Javaid, M., Qadri, M. A., Singh, R. P., & Suman, R. (2022). Artificial intelligence (AI) applications for marketing: A literature-based study. [sciencedirect.com]. *International Journal of Intelligent Networks*, *3*, 119–132. DOI: 10.1016/j.ijin.2022.08.005

Halkiopoulos, C. & Gkintoni, E. (2024). Leveraging AI in e-learning: Personalized learning and adaptive assessment through cognitive neuropsychology—A systematic analysis. Electronics. mdpi.com

Hamamra, B., Mayaleh, A., & Khlaif, Z. N. (2024). Between tech and text: The use of generative AI in Palestinian universities - a ChatGPT case study. *Cogent Education*, *11*(1), 2380622. DOI: 10.1080/2331186X.2024.2380622

Han, A., Zhou, X., Cai, Z., Han, S., Ko, R., Corrigan, S., & Peppler, K. A. (2024). Teachers, Parents, and Students' perspectives on Integrating Generative AI into Elementary Literacy Education. *Proceedings of the CHI Conference on Human Factors in Computing Systems*, 1–17. DOI: 10.1145/3613904.3642438

Hanna, M., Pantanowitz, L., Jackson, B., Palmer, O., Visweswaran, S., Pantanowitz, J., & Rashidi, H. (2024). Ethical and Bias considerations in artificial intelligence (AI)/machine learning. [sciencedirect.com]. *Modern Pathology*, •••, 100686. PMID: 39694331

Han, X., Xiao, S., Sheng, J., & Zhang, G. (2024). Enhancing efficiency and decision-making in higher education through intelligent commercial integration: Leveraging artificial intelligence. [HTML]. *Journal of the Knowledge Economy*, *16*(1), 1546–1582. DOI: 10.1007/s13132-024-01868-2

Harison, E. (2024). Educating to Innovate: Fostering Innovation Through Interdisciplinary Collaboration Between Design and Engineering Students. In Preconceptions of Policies, Strategies, and Challenges in Education 5.0 (pp. 51-62). IGI Global. [HTML]

Harrison, T. & Laco, D. (2022). Where's the character education in online higher education? Constructivism, virtue ethics and roles of online educators. E-Learning and Digital Media. sagepub.com

Haryono, E., Suprihatiningsih, S., Septian, D., Widodo, J., Ashar, A., & Sariman, S. (2024). New Paradigm Metode Penelitian Kepustakaan (Library Research) di Perguruan Tinggi. An-Nuur, 14(1).

Hasanain, B. (2024). The role of ergonomic and human factors in sustainable manufacturing: A review. Machines. mdpi.com

Hasan, B. (2020). Proses Kognitif Siswa Field Independent dan Field Dependent dalam Menyelesaikan Masalah Matematika. [Jurnal Pembelajaran Matematika Inovatif]. *JPMI*, *3*(4), 323–332. DOI: 10.22460/jpmi.v3i4.323-332

Hasyim, N., Arismunandar, , Butarbutar, R., Ramli, A. M., & Malik Nur, I. D. (2024). Mind Mapping of Teachers' Readiness for Online Teaching and Learning: A Reflective Study of Urban and Suburban Areas. *Cogent Education*, *11*(1), 2292864. DOI: 10.1080/2331186X.2023.2292864

Herbert, C. (2022). Enhancing mental health, well-being and active lifestyles of university students by means of physical activity and exercise research programs. Frontiers in public health. frontiersin.org

Hirudayaraj, M., Baker, R., Baker, F., & Eastman, M. (2021). Soft skills for entry-level engineers: What employers want. Education Sciences. mdpi.com

Hong, S. W., Lee, J., & Lee, J. K. (2024). Human behaviour simulation for promoting usefulness and user-centric values in parametric design. [HTML]. *Automation in Construction*, *162*, 105386. DOI: 10.1016/j.autcon.2024.105386

Hooda, M., Rana, C., Dahiya, O., Rizwan, A., & Hossain, M. S. (2022). Artificial intelligence for assessment and feedback to enhance student success in higher education. [wiley.com]. *Mathematical Problems in Engineering*, *2022*(1), 5215722. DOI: 10.1155/2022/5215722

Hughes, J., & Gallus, S. (). Inciting incident causes student concerns over safety on campus. nsuworks.nova.edu. nova.edu

Hung, B. K. H., To, C. C. N., Fung, R. K. H., & Chan, C. C. S. (2023). Addressing proficiency gaps in future skills between employers and learners through data visualization. SN computer science. springer.com

Hunt, D. F., Bailey, J., Lennox, B. R., Crofts, M., & Vincent, C. (2021). Enhancing psychological safety in mental health services. [springer.com]. *International Journal of Mental Health Systems*, *15*(1), 1–18. DOI: 10.1186/s13033-021-00439-1 PMID: 33853658

Hutson, J., Jeevanjee, T., Graaf, V. V., Lively, J., Weber, J., Weir, G., Arnone, K., Carnes, G., Vosevich, K., Plate, D., Leary, M., & Edele, S. (2022). Artificial Intelligence and the Disruption of Higher Education: Strategies for Integrations across Disciplines. *Creative Education, 13*(12), 3953–3980. DOI: 10.4236/ce.2022.1312253

Huynh, T., Madsen, A., McKagan, S., & Sayre, E. (2021). Building personas from phenomenography: A method for user-centered design in education. [emerald.com]. *Information and Learning Science, 122*(11/12), 689–708. DOI: 10.1108/ILS-12-2020-0256

IDEO The intersection of Design Thinking and AI: Enhancing Innovation, IDEO blog www.ideou.com/blogs/inspiration/ai-and-design-thinking/

Ifenthaler, D., Gibson, D., Prasse, D., Shimada, A., & Yamada, M. (2021). Putting learning back into learning analytics: Actions for policy makers, researchers, and practitioners. [springer.com]. *Educational Technology Research and Development, 69*(4), 2131–2150. DOI: 10.1007/s11423-020-09909-8

Ikudayisi, A. E., Chan, A. P., Darko, A., & Adegun, O. B. (2022). Integrated design process of green building projects: A review towards assessment metrics and conceptual framework. [HTML]. *Journal of Building Engineering, 50*, 104180. DOI: 10.1016/j.jobe.2022.104180

Imran, M. C., & Sulviana, S. (2022). Using BBC Web-Based Learning Courses to Improve Vocational High School (VHS) Students' Speaking Skill. Education. *Language and Culture Journal, 2*(1), 94–100.

Indrawijaya, S., & Siregar, A. P. (2022). Peningkatan Kreativitas melalui Penerapan Pembelajaran Team Based Project pada Mata Kuliah Desain Komunikasi Visual. *Jurnal Ilmiah Dikdaya, 12*(1), 268–273. DOI: 10.33087/dikdaya.v12i1.301

Irawan, A. (2022). Kreativitas Guru Dalam Memotivasi Belajar Peserta Didik. *SKULA: Jurnal Pendidikan Profesi Guru Madrasah, 2*(2), 199–210. https://doi.org/http://studentjournal.iaincurup.ac.id/index.php/skula

Isaksson, O., Wynn, D. C., & Eckert, C. (2023). Design perspectives, theories, and processes for engineering systems design. In *Handbook of engineering systems design* (pp. 1–47). Springer International Publishing. [HTML]

Islam, A., Ali, R., Singh, G., Islam, B., Islam, A., & Hossain, S. (2024, May). An Evaluation of AI-Enhanced Collaborative Learning Platforms. In 2024 International Conference on Communication, Computer Sciences and Engineering (IC3SE) (pp. 207-211). IEEE. [HTML]

Ismail, I. A., & Aloshi, J. M. R. (2025). Data Privacy in AI-Driven Education: An In-Depth Exploration Into the Data Privacy Concerns and Potential Solutions. In AI Applications and Strategies in Teacher Education (pp. 223-252). IGI Global. [HTML]

Issa, T. & Hall, M. (2024). A teamwork framework for preventing breaches of academic integrity and improving students' collaborative skills in the AI era. Heliyon. cell.com

Itonics www.intonics-innovation.com

Iuliano, E., Mazzilli, M., Zambelli, S., Macaluso, F., Raviolo, P., & Picerno, P. (2021). Satisfaction levels of sport sciences university students in online workshops for substituting practice-oriented activities during the COVID-19 lockdown. [mdpi.com]. *Education Sciences*, *11*(10), 600. DOI: 10.3390/educsci11100600

Jenkins, D., & Khanna, G. (2025). AI-Enhanced Training, Education, & Development: Exploration and Insights Into Generative AI's Role in Leadership Learning. [HTML]. *Journal of Leadership Studies*, *18*(4), 81–97. DOI: 10.1002/jls.70004

Jeon, J. E. (2021). The effects of user experience-based design innovativeness on user-metaverse platform channel relationships in South Korea. Journal of distribution science. koreascience.kr

Jha, S. K. (2023). The counterfeit degree certificate: Application of blockchain technology in higher education in India. [HTML]. *Library Hi Tech News*, *40*(2), 20–24. DOI: 10.1108/LHTN-02-2022-0023

Jia, P., & Stan, C. (2021). Artificial Intelligence Factory, Data Risk, and VCs' Mediation: The Case of ByteDance, an AI-Powered Startup. *Journal of Risk and Financial Management*, *14*(5), 203. DOI: 10.3390/jrfm14050203

Johansson-Sköldber, U., Woodilla, J., & Çetinkaya, M. (2013). Design Thinking: Past, Present and Possible Futures. *Creativity and Innovation Management*, *22*(2), 121–146. DOI: 10.1111/caim.12023

Johler, M. (2022). Collaboration and communication in blended learning environments. Frontiers in Education. frontiersin.org

Johnson, D. L. & Davis, C. G. (2024). Bridging the gap for underserved populations: Personalized AI solutions for college access and learning support. New Directions for Higher Education. wiley.com

Johnson, M., Jain, R., Brennan-Tonetta, P., Swartz, E., Silver, D., Paolini, J., Mamonov, S., & Hill, C. (2021). Impact of big data and artificial intelligence on industry: Developing a workforce roadmap for a data driven economy. [HTML]. *Global Journal of Flexible Systems Managment*, *22*(3), 197–217. DOI: 10.1007/s40171-021-00272-y

Juškevičienė, A., Stupurienė, G., & Jevsikova, T. (2021). Computational thinking development through physical computing activities in STEAM education. [HTML]. *Computer Applications in Engineering Education*, *29*(1), 175–190. DOI: 10.1002/cae.22365

Kaakandikar, R. M., Sakhare, A. A., & Prasad, N. (2025). Innovative Approaches to Teaching and Learning in the 21st Century: Leveraging Technology for Enhanced Outcomes. In New Technological Applications in the Flipped Learning Model (pp. 37-70). IGI Global Scientific Publishing. [HTML]

Kaddoura, S. & Al Husseiny, F. (2023). The rising trend of Metaverse in education: Challenges, opportunities, and ethical considerations. PeerJ Computer Science. peerj.com

Kakatkar, C., Bilgram, V., & Fuller, J. (2020). Innovation analytics: Leveraging artificial intelligence in the innovation process. *Business Horizons*, *63*(2), 171–181. DOI: 10.1016/j.bushor.2019.10.006

Kalyanaraman, A., Burnett, M., Fern, A., Khot, L., & Viers, J. (2022). Special report: The AgAID AI institute for transforming workforce and decision support in agriculture. [sciencedirect.com]. *Computers and Electronics in Agriculture*, *197*, 106944. DOI: 10.1016/j.compag.2022.106944

Kampakis, S. (2023). The limits of prediction (part b): Game theory, agent-based modeling and complexity (actions and reactions). In Predicting the Unknown: The History and Future of Data Science and Artificial Intelligence (pp. 183-208). Berkeley, CA: Apress. [HTML]

Kaswan, K. S., Dhatterwal, J. S., & Ojha, R. P. (2024). AI in personalized learning. In *Advances in technological innovations in higher education* (pp. 103–117). CRC Press. [HTML] DOI: 10.1201/9781003376699-9

Kavitha, R. K., Krupa, C. R., & Kaarthiekheyan, V. AI-Powered Digital Solutions for Smart Learning: Revolutionizing Education. In Cybersecurity and Data Science Innovations for Sustainable Development of HEICC (pp. 213-227). CRC Press. [HTML]

Kelley, T., & Kelley, D. (2013). *Creative Confidence: Unleashing the Creative Potential Within us all.* Random House.

Khamis, R. (2024). *AI-Powered Learning Experience Platforms: Investigating Personalized Learning in the Workplace: A Case of an International Company in Sweden.*

Khan, W., Daud, A., Khan, K., Muhammad, S., & Haq, R. (2023). Exploring the frontiers of deep learning and natural language processing: A comprehensive overview of key challenges and emerging trends. [sciencedirect.com]. *Natural Language Processing Journal, 4*, 100026. DOI: 10.1016/j.nlp.2023.100026

Kholiyanti, A. (2018). Pembelajaran Matematika dari Konkret ke Abstrak dalam Membangun Konsep Dasar Geometri Bagi Siswa Sekolah Dasar. *Pi: Mathematics Education Journal, 1*(2), 40–46. https://doi.org/https://doi.org/10.21067/pmej.v1i2.2322

Khorana, A., Pareek, A., Ollivier, M., Madjarova, S. J., Kunze, K. N., Nwachukwu, B. U., Karlsson, J., Marigi, E. M., & Williams, R. J.III. (2023). Choosing the appropriate measure of central tendency: Mean, median, or mode? [HTML]. *Knee Surgery, Sports Traumatology, Arthroscopy : Official Journal of the ESSKA, 31*(1), 12–15. DOI: 10.1007/s00167-022-07204-y PMID: 36322179

Khosravi, H., Shum, S. B., Chen, G., Conati, C., Tsai, Y. S., Kay, J., ... & Gašević, D. (2022). Explainable artificial intelligence in education. Computers and education: artificial intelligence, 3, 100074. sciencedirect.com

Kim, J., Lee, H., & Cho, Y. H. (2022). Learning design to support student-AI collaboration: Perspectives of leading teachers for AI in education. Education and information technologies. springer.com

Kimbell, L. (2011, November). Rethinking design thinking: Part 1. *Design and Culture, 3*(3), 285–306. DOI: 10.2752/175470811X13071166525216

Kim, J., Mathius, H., & Sent, D. (2024). Human-centered evaluation of explainable AI applications: A systematic review. *Frontiers in Artificial Intelligence, 7*, 1456486. https://www.frontiersin.org/journals/artificial-intelligence/articles/10.3389/frai.2024.1456486/full. DOI: 10.3389/frai.2024.1456486 PMID: 39484154

Kim, S., Jang, Y., Kim, W., Choi, S., Jung, H., Kim, S., & Kim, H. (2021, May). Why and what to teach: AI curriculum for elementary school. In *proceedings of the AAAI Conference on Artificial Intelligence* (Vol. 35, No. 17, pp. 15569-15576). DOI: 10.1609/aaai.v35i17.17833

Kock, F., Berbekova, A., & Assaf, A. G. (2021). Understanding and managing the threat of common method bias: Detection, prevention and control. [HTML]. *Tourism Management*, *86*, 104330. DOI: 10.1016/j.tourman.2021.104330

Kolko, J. (2010). Abductive thinking and sensemaking: The drivers of design synthesis. *Design Issues*, *26*(1), 15–28. DOI: 10.1162/desi.2010.26.1.15

Kolko, J. (2015, September). Design thinking comes of age. *Harvard Business Review*, *93*(9), 66–69.

Kopp, T., Baumgartner, M., & Kinkel, S. (2021). Success factors for introducing industrial human-robot interaction in practice: An empirically driven framework. [springer.com]. *International Journal of Advanced Manufacturing Technology*, *112*(3-4), 685–704. DOI: 10.1007/s00170-020-06398-0

Korteling, J. E., Paradies, G. L., & Sassen-van Meer, J. P. (2023). Cognitive bias and how to improve sustainable decision making. [frontiersin.org]. *Frontiers in Psychology*, *14*, 1129835. DOI: 10.3389/fpsyg.2023.1129835 PMID: 37026083

Koul, S., & Nayar, B. (2021). The holistic learning educational ecosystem: A classroom 4.0 perspective. [HTML]. *Higher Education Quarterly*, *75*(1), 98–112. DOI: 10.1111/hequ.12271

Kovari, A. (2025). A systematic review of AI-powered collaborative learning in higher education: Trends and outcomes from the last decade. Social Sciences & Humanities Open. sciencedirect.com

Krebs, D., & Rosenbaum, A. (2023). The use of generative AI tools in design thinking academic makeathon. *CERN ideaSquare Journal of Experimental Innovation*, *13*(1), 1470.

Krizea, M., Gialelis, J., Protopsaltis, G., Mountzouris, C., & Theodorou, G. (2022). Empowering people with a user-friendly wearable platform for unobtrusive monitoring of vital physiological parameters. [mdpi.com]. *Sensors (Basel)*, *22*(14), 5226. DOI: 10.3390/s22145226 PMID: 35890907

Kulal, A., Dinesh, S., Abhishek, N., & Anchan, A. (2024). Digital access and learning outcomes: A study of equity and inclusivity in distance education. [HTML]. *International Journal of Educational Management*, *38*(5), 1391–1423. DOI: 10.1108/IJEM-03-2024-0166

Kulkarni, A. R., La Rocca, G., Veldhuis, L. L. M., & Eitelberg, G. (2022). Subscale flight test model design: Developments, challenges and opportunities. [sciencedirect.com]. *Progress in Aerospace Sciences*, *130*, 100798. DOI: 10.1016/j.paerosci.2021.100798

Kumar, Y., Marchena, J., Awlla, A. H., Li, J. J., & Abdalla, H. B. (2024). The AI-Powered Evolution of Big Data. Applied Sciences. mdpi.com

Kunjumuhammed, S. K. (2024). Artificial Intelligence in Addressing Educational Inequality Dimensions in Higher Education Institutions (HEIs): A Critical Review. Risks and Challenges of AI-Driven Finance: Bias, Ethics, and Security, 146-164. [HTML]

Kurokawa, T. (2013). Design thinking education at universities and graduate schools. *Science & Technology Trends Quarterly Review*, *46*, 50–62.

Lakkala, S., Galkienė, A., Navaitienė, J., Cierpiałowska, T., Tomecek, S., & Uusiautti, S. (2021). Teachers supporting students in collaborative ways—An analysis of collaborative work creating supportive learning environments for every student in a school: Cases from Austria, Finland, Lithuania, and Poland. [mdpi.com]. *Sustainability (Basel)*, *13*(5), 2804. DOI: 10.3390/su13052804

Lampropoulos, G., Keramopoulos, E., Diamantaras, K., & Evangelidis, G. (2022). Augmented reality and virtual reality in education: Public perspectives, sentiments, attitudes, and discourses. [mdpi.com]. *Education Sciences*, *12*(11), 798. DOI: 10.3390/educsci12110798

Laupichler, M. C., Aster, A., Schirch, J., & Raupach, T. (2022). Artificial intelligence literacy in higher and adult education: A scoping literature review. *Computers and Education: Artificial Intelligence*, *3*, 100101. DOI: 10.1016/j.caeai.2022.100101

Lau, W. S., & Shea, M. (2024). Empowering English learners in the classroom through culturally responsive social-emotional teaching practices. [HTML]. *Journal of Multilingual and Multicultural Development*, *45*(7), 2880–2897. DOI: 10.1080/01434632.2022.2078337

Lee, H. S. & Lee, J. (2021). Applying artificial intelligence in physical education and future perspectives. Sustainability. mdpi.com

Lerner, R. E., Grolnick, W. S., Caruso, A. J., & Levitt, M. R. (2022). Parental involvement and children's academics: The roles of autonomy support and parents' motivation for involvement. [HTML]. *Contemporary Educational Psychology*, *68*, 102039. DOI: 10.1016/j.cedpsych.2021.102039

Lestari, P., Dewi, R. S., & Junita, A. R. (2024). Menumbuhkan Kreativitas tanpa Batas : Strategi Inovatif Sekolah dalam Mengembangkan Karakter Kreatif Siswa. *Ainara Journal (Jurnal Penelitian Dan PKM Bidang Ilmu Pendidikan)*, *5*(3), 358–364. https://doi.org/https://doi.org/10.54371/ainj.v5i3.543

Leyer, M., & Schneider, S. (2021). Decision augmentation and automation with artificial intelligence: Threat or opportunity for managers? [HTML]. *Business Horizons*, *64*(5), 711–724. DOI: 10.1016/j.bushor.2021.02.026

Li, L. (2024). Reskilling and upskilling the future-ready workforce for industry 4.0 and beyond. Information Systems Frontiers. springer.com

Liedtka, J. (2018). Exploring the Impact of Design Thinking in Action. Darden Working paper series.

Liedtka, J. (2020). Putting Technology in its place: Design thinking's social technology at work. *California Management Review*, *62*(2), 53–83. DOI: 10.1177/0008125619897391

Liedtka, J., & Ogilvie, T. (2011). *Design for Growth: A Design thinking toolkit for managers*. Columbia Business School Publishing.

Li, M. (2024). Adapting legal education for the changing landscape of regional emerging economies: A dynamic framework for law majors. [HTML]. *Journal of the Knowledge Economy*.

Limbong, S., Jabu, B., & Basri, M. (2022). The Impact of Synchronous Learning of Marlins in Teaching Maritime English. *Journal of Learning and Development Studies, 2*(3), 06–13. DOI: 10.32996/jlds.2022.2.3.2

Limbong, S., Nursyam, Asdar, Palayukan, N., & Tandibura, F. (2024). Synchronous Online Reading toward Digital Literacy and Higher-Order Thinking Skills Supporting Cadets' Self-Regulated Learning. *XLinguae, 17*(4), 317–335. DOI: 10.18355/XL.2024.17.04.19

Lin, M. P. C., Liu, A. L., Poitras, E., Chang, M., & Chang, D. H. (2024). An exploratory study on the efficacy and inclusivity of AI technologies in diverse learning environments. Sustainability. mdpi.com

Lin, W., Yin, H., & Liu, Z. (2022). The roles of transformational leadership and growth mindset in teacher professional development: The mediation of teacher self-efficacy. Sustainability. mdpi.com

Lin, W., Zaman, S. I., Jamil, S., & Khan, S. A. (2023). Students engagement in distant learning: How much influence do the critical factors have for success in academic performance? [HTML]. *Psychology in the Schools*, *60*(7), 2373–2394. DOI: 10.1002/pits.22858

Li, T., & Zhan, Z. (2022). A systematic review on design thinking integrated learning in K-12 education. *Applied Sciences (Basel, Switzerland)*, *12*(16), 8077. DOI: 10.3390/app12168077

Lopez-Fierro, S., Kollar, I., & Nguyen, H. (2024). Making Human-AI Contributions Transparent in Qualitative Coding. *17th International Conference on Computer-Supported Collaborative Learning (CSCL)*. ISLS Annual Meeting 2024 June 10-14, 2024 Learning as a Cornerstone of Healing, Resilience, and Community. DOI: 10.22318/cscl2024.352932

Luckin, R. (2025). Nurturing human intelligence in the age of AI: Rethinking education for the future. [HTML]. *Development and Learning in Organizations*, *39*(1), 1–4. DOI: 10.1108/DLO-04-2024-0108

Macenski, S., Foote, T., Gerkey, B., Lalancette, C., & Woodall, W. (2022). Robot operating system 2: Design, architecture, and uses in the wild. [science.org]. *Science Robotics*, *7*(66), eabm6074. DOI: 10.1126/scirobotics.abm6074 PMID: 35544605

MacKnight, C. (2021). Supporting critical thinking in interactive learning environments. The web in higher education. [HTML]

Makda, F. (2025). Digital education: Mapping the landscape of virtual teaching in higher education–a bibliometric review. Education and Information Technologies. springer.com

Makeleni, S., Mutongoza, B. H., & Linake, M. A. (2023). Language Education and Artificial Intelligence: An Exploration of Challenges Confronting Academics in Global South Universities. *Journal of Culture and Values in Education*, *6*(2), 158–171. DOI: 10.46303/jcve.2023.14

Makkonen, T., Tirri, K., & Lavonen, J. (2021). Engagement in learning physics through project-based learning: A case study of gifted Finnish upper-secondary-level students. [sagepub.com]. *Journal of Advanced Academics*, *32*(4), 501–532. DOI: 10.1177/1932202X211018644

Mandasari, N. (2018). Elaborasi Kognitif dalam Proses Abstraksi Konsep Matematika. *Seminar Nasional Pendidikan Universitas PGRI Palembang*, 399–405.

Manurung, A. S., Halim, A., & Rosyid, A. (2020). Pengaruh Kemampuan Berpikir Kreatif untuk Meningkatkan Hasil Belajar Matematika di Sekolah Dasar. *Jurnal Basicedu, 4*(4), 1291–1301. https://doi.org/https://doi.org/10.31004/basicedu.v4i4.544

Martin, R. L. (2009). *The design of business: Why design thinking is the next competitive advantage*. Harvard Business Press.

Matthee, M., & Turpin, M. (2019). Teaching critical thinking, problem solving, and design thinking: Preparing IS students for the future. *Journal of Information Systems Education*, *30*(4), 242–252.

Matysek, A. (2023). The use of one-on-one interviews in library and information science: A scoping review. [HTML]. *Journal of Information Science*, 01655515231171088. DOI: 10.1177/01655515231171088

Maulana, A., & Rizki, S. N. (2018). Sistem pengambilan keputusan dalam penerimaan proyek pembuatan kapal menggunakan metode fuzzy. *Jurnal Simetris*, *9*(2), 723–730. DOI: 10.24176/simet.v9i2.2110

Mavilidi, M. F. & Vazou, S. (2021). Classroom-based physical activity and math performance: Integrated physical activity or not?. Acta paediatrica. wiley.com

May, D., Terkowsky, C., Varney, V., & Boehringer, D. (2023). Between hands-on experiments and Cross Reality learning environments–contemporary educational approaches in instructional laboratories. [tandfonline.com]. *European Journal of Engineering Education*, *48*(5), 783–801. DOI: 10.1080/03043797.2023.2248819

McCampbell, M., Schumann, C., & Klerkx, L. (2022). Good intentions in complex realities: Challenges for designing responsibly in digital agriculture in low-income countries. Sociologia Ruralis. wiley.com

Md, S., Md Saiful, I., & Jannatul, F. (2025). Harnessing AI Adoption in the Workforce A Pathway to Sustainable Competitive Advantage through Intelligent Decision-Making and Skill Transformation. *American Journal of Economics and Business Management*, *8*(3), 954–976. umsida.ac.id

Mele, C., Spena, T. R., Kaartemo, V., & Marzullo, M. L. (2021). Smart nudging: How cognitive technologies enable choice architectures for value co-creation. [sciencedirect.com]. *Journal of Business Research*, *129*, 949–960. DOI: 10.1016/j.jbusres.2020.09.004

Mendelson, B. J., Ebersole, K. T., Brau, S. D., & Ebersole, N. T. (2025). Exploration of Heart Rate Recovery After Maximal Treadmill and Three-Minute All-Out Shuttle Tests in Firefighters. Fire. mdpi.com

Menon, S., & Suresh, M. (2022). Assessment framework for workforce agility in higher education institutions. Higher Education [HTML]. *Skills and Work-Based Learning*, *12*(6), 1169–1188. DOI: 10.1108/HESWBL-01-2022-0014

Meyer, J., & Seaman, J. (2021). Beyond experiential learning cycles. Outdoor environmental education in higher education: International perspectives, 75-87. [HTML]

Mhalanga, D. (2022). Human-Centered Artificial Intelligence: The Superlative Approach to Achieve Sustainable Development Goals in the Fourth Industrial Revolution. *Sustainability (Basel)*, *14*(13), 7804. DOI: 10.3390/su14137804

Mhlanga, D. (2021). Artificial intelligence in the industry 4.0, and its impact on poverty, innovation, infrastructure development, and the sustainable development goals: Lessons from …. Sustainability. mdpi.com

Mills, K. (2022). Consent and the Right to Privacy. Journal of Applied Philosophy. wiley.com

Mirabdolah, A., Alaeifard, M., & Marandi, A. (2023). User-Centered Design in HCl: Enhancing Usability and Interaction in Complex Systems. [ijahci.com]. *International Journal of Advanced Human Computer Interaction*, *1*(1), 16–33.

Miseliunaite, B., Kliziene, I., & Cibulskas, G. (2022). Can holistic education solve the world's problems: A systematic literature review. Sustainability. mdpi.com

Mohamad Hasim, S., Rosli, R., Halim, L., Capraro, M. M., & Capraro, R. M. (2022). STEM professional development activities and their impact on teacher knowledge and instructional practices. [mdpi.com]. *Mathematics*, *10*(7), 1109. DOI: 10.3390/math10071109

Mohamed, B. H., Ari, I., Al-Sada, M. S., & Koç, M. (2021). Strategizing human development for a country in transition from a resource-based to a knowledge-based economy. Sustainability. mdpi.com

Mondejar, M. E., Avtar, R., Diaz, H. L. B., Dubey, R. K., Esteban, J., Gómez-Morales, A., Hallam, B., Mbungu, N. T., Okolo, C. C., Prasad, K. A., She, Q., & Garcia-Segura, S. (2021). Digitalization to achieve sustainable development goals: Steps towards a Smart Green Planet. [sciencedirect.com]. *The Science of the Total Environment*, *794*, 148539. DOI: 10.1016/j.scitotenv.2021.148539 PMID: 34323742

Monteiro, V., Carvalho, C., & Santos, N. N. (2021). Creating a supportive classroom environment through effective feedback: Effects on students' school identification and behavioral engagement. Frontiers in Education. frontiersin.org

Morales, M., Amado-Salvatierra, H. R., Hernández, R., Pirker, J., & Gütl, C. (2016). A Practical Experience on the Use of Gamification in MOOC Courses as a Strategy to Increase Motivation. In Uden, L., Liberona, D., & Feldmann, B. (Eds.), *Learning Technology for Education in Cloud – The Changing Face of Education* (Vol. 620, pp. 139–149). Springer International Publishing., DOI: 10.1007/978-3-319-42147-6_12

Moustafa, A. W. (2023). Integrating User Experience in Practices of Human-Centered Design Process in Product Design. International Design Journal. ekb.eg

Muro, J. A. (2024). "The PTA intimidates": Racially segregated parent organizations in a dual immersion school. [HTML]. *Race, Ethnicity and Education*, *27*(1), 55–74. DOI: 10.1080/13613324.2023.2192915

Mutyati, A. M., Kartika, A. D., Dwitasari, B. D., Rahmadanti, A., Dewi, A. S., & Ibrahim. (2023). Pentingnya Pemahaman Emosi dalam Proses Pembelajaran di MI Al-Masrhi Pangkalan Balai-Banyuasin. *IMEIJ: Indo-MathEdu Intellectuals Journal*, *4*(2), 1198–1208. https://doi.org/http://doi.org/10.54373/imeij.v4i2.340

Nafiati, D. A. (2021). Revisi taksonomi Bloom: Kognitif, afektif, dan psikomotorik. *Humanika. Kajian Ilmiah Mata Kuliah Umum*, *21*(2), 151–172. DOI: 10.21831/hum.v21i2.29252

Nair, A. J., Manohar, S., Mittal, A., & Chaudhry, R. (2024). Unleashing Digital Frontiers: Bridging Realities of Augmented Reality, Virtual Reality, and the Metaverse. In The Metaverse Dilemma: Challenges and Opportunities for Business and Society (pp. 85-112). Emerald Publishing Limited. [HTML]

Namaziandost, E., Behbahani, H. K., & Naserpour, A. (2024). Peer support in language learning: Mitigating anxiety, enhancing achievement, cultivating growth mindsets, and increasing enjoyment. [researchgate.net]. *Journal of Applied Learning and Teaching*, *7*(2), 296–313.

Naseer, F., Khan, M. N., Tahir, M., Addas, A., & Aejaz, S. M. H. (2024). Integrating deep learning techniques for personalized learning pathways in higher education. Heliyon. cell.com

Nevedal, A. L., Reardon, C. M., Opra Widerquist, M. A., Jackson, G. L., Cutrona, S. L., White, B. S., & Damschroder, L. J. (2021). Rapid versus traditional qualitative analysis using the Consolidated Framework for Implementation Research (CFIR). [springer.com]. *Implementation Science : IS*, *16*(1), 67. DOI: 10.1186/s13012-021-01111-5 PMID: 34215286

Ng, D. T. K., Chan, E. K. C., & Lo, C. K. (2025). Opportunities, Challenges and School Strategies for Integrating Generative AI in Education. *Computers and Education: Artificial Intelligence*, 100373.

Ng, D. T. K., Lee, M., Tan, R. J. Y., Hu, X., Downie, J. S., & Chu, S. K. W. (2023). A review of AI teaching and learning from 2000 to 2020. *Education and Information Technologies*, *28*(7), 8445–8501. DOI: 10.1007/s10639-022-11491-w

Ng, D. T. K., Leung, J. K. L., Su, J., Ng, R. C. W., & Chu, S. K. W. (2023). Teachers' AI digital competencies and twenty-first century skills in the post-pandemic world. [springer.com]. *Educational Technology Research and Development, 71*(1), 137–161. DOI: 10.1007/s11423-023-10203-6 PMID: 36844361

Nguyen, A., Ngo, H. N., Hong, Y., Dang, B., & Nguyen, B. P. T. (2023). Ethical principles for artificial intelligence in education. [springer.com]. *Education and Information Technologies, 28*(4), 4221–4241. DOI: 10.1007/s10639-022-11316-w PMID: 36254344

Niemi, K. (2021). 'The best guess for the future?'Teachers' adaptation to open and flexible learning environments in Finland. Education Inquiry. tandfonline.com

Nurhikmah, H., & Ramli, A. M. (2024). Teachers' Readiness in Online Learning: Digital Literacy-Self-Efficacy, Pedagogical Competence, Attitude, Infrastructure, and Management Support. *Electronic Journal of e-Learning, 22*(8), 93–105. DOI: 10.34190/ejel.22.8.3358

Nurjan, S. (2018). Pengembangan Berpikir Kreatif. *AL-ASASIYYA: Journal Basic Of Education, 3*(1), 105–116. https://doi.org/http://dx.doi.org/10.24269/ajbe.v3i1.1302

Okunlaya, R. O., Syed Abdullah, N., & Alias, R. A. (2022). Artificial intelligence (AI) library services innovative conceptual framework for the digital transformation of university education. [HTML]. *Library Hi Tech, 40*(6), 1869–1892. DOI: 10.1108/LHT-07-2021-0242

Okwuduba, E. N., Nwosu, K. C., Okigbo, E. C., Samuel, N. N., & Achugbu, C. (2021). Impact of intrapersonal and interpersonal emotional intelligence and self-directed learning on academic performance among pre-university science students. Heliyon, 7(3). cell.com

O'Neill, G. & Short, A. (2025). Relevant, practical and connected to the real world: what higher education students say engages them in the curriculum. Irish Educational Studies. tandfonline.com

Osaba, E., Villar-Rodriguez, E., Del Ser, J., Nebro, A. J., Molina, D., LaTorre, A., Suganthan, P. N., Coello Coello, C. A., & Herrera, F. (2021). A tutorial on the design, experimentation and application of metaheuristic algorithms to real-world optimization problems. [PDF]. *Swarm and Evolutionary Computation, 64*, 100888. DOI: 10.1016/j.swevo.2021.100888

Ostojic, M., Winkler, P. W., Karlsson, J., Becker, R., & Prill, R. (2023). Minimal Clinically Important Difference: Don't just look at the "p-value". [springer.com]. *Knee Surgery, Sports Traumatology, Arthroscopy : Official Journal of the ESSKA, 31*(10), 4077–4079. DOI: 10.1007/s00167-023-07512-x PMID: 37460662

Owen, C. (2007). Design thinking: Notes on its nature and use. *Design research quarterly, 2*(1), 16-27.

Ozberk, E. H. (2025). *Learning Theories in Psychology From Philosophical Roots to Educational Measurement*. Exploring Adult Education Through Learning Theory. [HTML]

Özdere, M. (2023). The Integration of Artificial Intelligence in English Education: Opportunities and Challenges. [LET Journal]. *Language Education & Technology, 3*(2), 137–172.

Ozkan-Ozen, Y. D., & Kazancoglu, Y. (2022). Analysing workforce development challenges in the Industry 4.0. [HTML]. *International Journal of Manpower, 43*(2), 310–333. DOI: 10.1108/IJM-03-2021-0167

Pakdemirli, M. (2025). Calculation of the number of players in a defence wall for free kick in football. [HTML]. *International Journal of Mathematical Education in Science and Technology*, •••, 1–10. DOI: 10.1080/0020739X.2025.2464555

Pandey, N., de Coninck, H., & Sagar, A. D. (2022). Beyond technology transfer: Innovation cooperation to advance sustainable development in developing countries. [wiley.com]. *Wiley Interdisciplinary Reviews. Energy and Environment, 11*(2), e422. DOI: 10.1002/wene.422

Panke, S. (2019). Design thinking in education: Perspectives, opportunities and challenges. *Open Education Studies, 1*(1), 281–306. DOI: 10.1515/edu-2019-0022

Papastergiou, M., & Mastrogiannis, I. (2021). Design, development and evaluation of open interactive learning objects for secondary school physical education. [HTML]. *Education and Information Technologies, 26*(3), 2981–3007. DOI: 10.1007/s10639-020-10390-2

Papurungan, E., & Paputungan, F. (2023). Pendekatan dan Fungsi Afektif dalam Proses Pembelajaran. *Journal of Education and Culture (JEaC) Vol., 3*(1).

Paranjape, K., Schinkel, M., Panday, R. N., Car, J., & Nanayakkara, P. (2019). Introducing artificial intelligence training in medical education. *JMIR Medical Education, 5*(2), e16048. DOI: 10.2196/16048 PMID: 31793895

Park, S. & Park, S. (2021). How can employees adapt to change? Clarifying the adaptive performance concepts. Human Resource Development Quarterly. wiley.com

Pashaie, S., Mohammadi, S., & Golmohammadi, H. (2024). Unlocking athlete potential: The evolution of coaching strategies through artificial intelligence. Proceedings of the Institution of Mechanical Engineers, Part P: Journal of Sports Engineering and Technology, 17543371241300889. [HTML]

Pashar, I., & Dwiantoro, L. (2020). Pengaruh Empowerment Terhadap Pengambilan Keputusan Perawat : Kajian Literature Review. *Journal of Holistic Nursing Science, 7*(2), 124–132. https://doi.org/https://doi.org/10.31603/nursing. v7i2.3097

Patnani, M. (2013). Upaya Meningkatkan Kemampuan Problem Solving pada Mahasiswa. *Jurnal Psikogenesis, 1*(2), 130–142. DOI: 10.24854/jps.v1i2.43

Patrick, V. M., & Hollenbeck, C. R. (2021). Designing for all: Consumer response to inclusive design. [HTML]. *Journal of Consumer Psychology, 31*(2), 360–381. DOI: 10.1002/jcpy.1225

Phanwiriyarat, K., Anggoro, K. J., & Chaowanakritsanakul, T. (2025). Exploring AI-powered gamified flipped classroom in an English-speaking course: A case of Duolingo. [tandfonline.com]. *Cogent Education, 12*(1), 2488545. DOI: 10.1080/2331186X.2025.2488545

Pichler, S., Kohli, C., & Granitz, N. (2021). DITTO for Gen Z: A framework for leveraging the uniqueness of the new generation. Business horizons. sciencedirect.com

Pierce, K., Sosa, L., Fredrickson, M., & Kenon, V. H. (2022). Content Management System Tools to Enhance Student Learning in Higher Education. [HTML]. *Journal of Higher Education Theory and Practice, 22*(8).

Piñero Charlo, J. C., Belova, N., Quevedo Gutiérrez, E., Zapatera Llinares, A., Arboleya-García, E., Swacha, J., López-Serentill, P., & Carmona-Medeiro, E. (2022). Preface for the special issue "trends in educational gamification: Challenges and learning opportunities". [mdpi.com]. *Education Sciences, 12*(3), 179. DOI: 10.3390/educsci12030179

Plakias, S., Tsatalas, T., Armatas, V., Tsaopoulos, D., & Giakas, G. (2024). Tactical situations and playing styles as key performance indicators in soccer. [mdpi.com]. *Journal of Functional Morphology and Kinesiology, 9*(2), 88. DOI: 10.3390/jfmk9020088 PMID: 38804454

Pokrivcakova, S. (2019). Preparing teachers for the application of AI-powered technologies in foreign language education. *Journal of Language and Cultural Education, 7*(3), 135–153. DOI: 10.2478/jolace-2019-0025

Poleac, D. (2024). Design thinking with AI. *Proceedings of the International Conference on Business Excellence*, 18(1): June.

Polster, L., Bilgram, V., & Gortz, S. (2024). AI-Augmented Design Thinking: Potentials, Challenges, and Mitigation Strategies of Integrating Artificial Intelligence in Human-Centered Innovation Processes. *IEEE Engineering Management Review*, *99*, 1–36. DOI: 10.1109/EMR.2024.3512866

Pons, E., García-Calvo, T., Cos, F., Resta, R., Blanco, H., López del Campo, R., Díaz-García, J., & Pulido-González, J. J. (2021). Integrating video tracking and GPS to quantify accelerations and decelerations in elite soccer. [nature.com]. *Scientific Reports*, *11*(1), 18531. DOI: 10.1038/s41598-021-97903-2 PMID: 34535734

Popli, N. K. & Singh, R. P. (2024). Enhancing academic outcomes through industry collaboration: our experience with integrating real-world projects into engineering courses. Discover Education. springer.com

Pruneski, J. A., Pareek, A., Nwachukwu, B. U., Martin, R. K., Kelly, B. T., Karlsson, J., Pearle, A. D., Kiapour, A. M., & Williams, R. J.III. (2023). Natural language processing: Using artificial intelligence to understand human language in orthopedics. [HTML]. *Knee Surgery, Sports Traumatology, Arthroscopy : Official Journal of the ESSKA*, *31*(4), 1203–1211. DOI: 10.1007/s00167-022-07272-0 PMID: 36477347

Purwaningsih, I. Oktariani, Hernawati, L., Wardarita, R., & Utami, P. I. (2022). Pendidikan sebagai suatu Sistem. *Jurnal Visionary : Penelitian Dan Pengembangan Dibidang Administrasi Pendidikan, 10*(1), 21–26. https://doi.org/https://e-journal .undikma.ac.id/index.php/visionary

Qasmi, F., & Fatima, S. K. (2024, June). Enhancing education and well-being through artificial intelligence: opportunities and challenges. In International Conference on Breaking Barriers with Generative Intelligence (pp. 154-164). Cham: Springer Nature Switzerland. [HTML] DOI: 10.1007/978-3-031-65996-6_13

Qiu, Y., Guan, Y., & Liu, S. (2023). The analysis of infrared high-speed motion capture system on motion aesthetics of aerobics athletes under biomechanics analysis. Plos one. plos.org

Qi, Y., Sajadi, S. M., Baghaei, S., Rezaei, R., & Li, W. (2024). Digital technologies in sports: Opportunities, challenges, and strategies for safeguarding athlete wellbeing and competitive integrity in the digital era. [HTML]. *Technology in Society*, *77*, 102496. DOI: 10.1016/j.techsoc.2024.102496

Quan, S. Y., Wei, M. T., Lee, J., Mohi-Ud-Din, R., Mostaghim, R., Sachdev, R., Siegel, D., Friedlander, Y., & Friedland, S. (2022). Clinical evaluation of a real-time artificial intelligence-based polyp detection system: A US multi-center pilot study. [nature.com]. *Scientific Reports, 12*(1), 6598. DOI: 10.1038/s41598-022-10597-y PMID: 35449442

Quin, F., Weyns, D., Galster, M., & Silva, C. C. (2024). A/B testing: A systematic literature review. Journal of Systems and Software. sciencedirect.com

Rahayu, F. (2022). Pengembangan Kreativitas Anak melalui Strategi 4P (Person, Press, Process, Product). [JIME]. *Jurnal Ilmiah Mandala Education, 8*(3), 2406–2414. DOI: 10.58258/jime.v8i3.3779

Rahman, A., Munandar, S. A., Fitriani, A., Karlina, Y., & Yumriani. (2022). Pengertian pendidikan, ilmu pendidikan dan unsur-unsur pendidikan. *Al Urwatul Wutsqa: Kajian Pendidikan Islam, 2*(1), 1–8. https://doi.org/https://journal.unismuh.ac.id/index.php/alurwatul/article/view/7757

Rainio, O., Teuho, J., & Klén, R. (2024). Evaluation metrics and statistical tests for machine learning. Scientific Reports. nature.com

Ramadanti, M., Sary, C. P., & Suarni. (2022). Psikologi kognitif. *ALDIN: Jurnal Dakwah Dan Sosial Keagamaan, 8*(1), 46–59. https://doi.org/http://dx.doi.org/10.30863/ajdsk.v8i1.3205

Ramaila, S. M. (2025). Fostering Holistic Development: The Integral Role of Educators in Nurturing Student Growth and Learning. In Former Educators' Roles in Supporting Student Growth and Learning (pp. 117-146). IGI Global Scientific Publishing. [HTML]

Rapaka, A., Dharmadhikari, S. C., Kasat, K., Mohan, C. R., Chouhan, K., & Gupta, M. (2025). Revolutionizing learning– A journey into educational games with immersive and AI technologies. [HTML]. *Entertainment Computing, 52*, 100809. DOI: 10.1016/j.entcom.2024.100809

Rapanta, C., Botturi, L., Goodyear, P., Guàrdia, L., & Koole, M. (2021). Balancing technology, pedagogy and the new normal: Post-pandemic challenges for higher education. [springer.com]. *Postdigital Science and Education, 3*(3), 715–742. DOI: 10.1007/s42438-021-00249-1 PMID: 40477266

Rauschnabel, P. A., Babin, B. J., tom Dieck, M. C., Krey, N., & Jung, T. (2022). What is augmented reality marketing? Its definition, complexity, and future. [HTML]. *Journal of Business Research, 142*, 1140–1150. DOI: 10.1016/j.jbusres.2021.12.084

Rauth, I., Köppen, E., Jobst, B., & Meinel, C. (2010). Design thinking: An educational model towards creative confidence. In *DS 66-2: Proceedings of the 1st international conference on design creativity (ICDC 2010).*

Razzouk, R., & Shute, V. (2012). What is design thinking and why is it important? *Review of Educational Research, 82*(3), 330–348. DOI: 10.3102/0034654312457429

Rebolledo Font De La Vall, R., & González Araya, F. (2023). Exploring the Benefits and Challenges of AI-Language Learning Tools. *International Journal of Social Sciences and Humanities Invention, 10*(01), 7569–7576. DOI: 10.18535/ijsshi/v10i01.02

Redmond, P., Heffernan, A., Abawi, L., Brown, A., & Henderson, R. (2018). An Online Engagement Framework for Higher Education. *Online Learning : the Official Journal of the Online Learning Consortium, 22*(1). Advance online publication. DOI: 10.24059/olj.v22i1.1175

Renuka, O., RadhaKrishnan, N., Priya, B. S., Jhansy, A., & Ezekiel, S. (2025). Data Privacy and Protection: Legal and Ethical Challenges. Emerging Threats and Countermeasures in Cybersecurity, 433-465. [HTML]

Richard, B., Sivo, S. A., Orlowski, M., Ford, R. C., Murphy, J., Boote, D. N., & Witta, E. L. (2021). Qualitative research via focus groups: Will going online affect the diversity of your findings? [HTML]. *Cornell Hospitality Quarterly, 62*(1), 32–45. DOI: 10.1177/1938965520967769

Richards, K. A., Dauenhauer, B., Gaudreault, K., Jones, E. M., McMullen, J., Shiver, V. N., Wilson, W. J., & Wright, P. M. (2025). Intra-Institutional Collaborations to Promote Research and Scholarship: Examples from the Field. [HTML]. *International Journal of Kinesiology in Higher Education, 9*(1), 58–74. DOI: 10.1080/24711616.2024.2430027

Rindiantika, Y. (2021). Pentingnya Pengembangan Kreativitas dalam Keberhasilan Pembelajaran: Kajian Teoritik. *Jurnal Intelegensia, 6*(1), 53–63.

Rivadeneira, J. & Inga, E. (2023). Interactive peer instruction method applied to classroom environments considering a learning engineering approach to innovate the Teaching–Learning process. Education Sciences. mdpi.com

Roshanaei, M. (2024). Towards best practices for mitigating artificial intelligence implicit bias in shaping diversity, inclusion and equity in higher education. [HTML]. *Education and Information Technologies, 29*(14), 18959–18984. DOI: 10.1007/s10639-024-12605-2

Roy, D., & Putatunda, T. (2023). From Textbooks to Chatbots: Integrating AI in English literature classrooms of India. *Journal of E-Learning and Knowledge Society*, 65-73 Pages. DOI: 10.20368/1971-8829/1135860

Runcan, R., Ha egan, V., Toderici, O., Croitoru, G., Gavrila-Ardelean, M., Cuc, L. D., Rad, D., Costin, A., & Dughi, T. (2025). Ethical AI in Social Sciences Research: Are We Gatekeepers or Revolutionaries? [mdpi.com]. *Societies (Basel, Switzerland), 15*(3), 62. DOI: 10.3390/soc15030062

Sajja, R., Sermet, Y., Cikmaz, M., Cwiertny, D., & Demir, I. (2024). Artificial intelligence-enabled intelligent assistant for personalized and adaptive learning in higher education. Information. mdpi.com

Salas-Pilco, S. Z., Xiao, K., & Hu, X. (2022). Artificial intelligence and learning analytics in teacher education: A systematic review. Education Sciences. mdpi.com

Salmela-Aro, K., Tang, X., Symonds, J., & Upadyaya, K. (2021). Student engagement in adolescence: A scoping review of longitudinal studies 2010–2020. [wiley.com]. *Journal of Research on Adolescence, 31*(2), 256–272. DOI: 10.1111/jora.12619 PMID: 33991151

Santrock, J. W. (2018).. . *Educational Psychology.*

Saranya, S. M., Komarasamy, D., Mohanapriya, S., Iyapparaja, M., & Prabavathi, R. (2024). Industry 4.0: The Role of Industrial IoT, Big Data, AR/VR, and Blockchain in the Digital Transformation. In Smart Computing Techniques in Industrial IoT (pp. 11-39). Singapore: Springer Nature Singapore. [HTML]

Sari, A. A., Ekita, A., Kirana, W., Amelia, R., Susilowati, J., & Kusuma, I. R. (2024). Teori Pengambilan Keputusan: Peran Emosi dalam Pengambilan Keputusan. *Musytari: Neraca Manajemen Ekonomi, 9*(11), 1–6. DOI: 10.8734/mnmae.v1i2.359

Sarkar, S. B. (2024). *The Role of Leaders in Implementing Cross-Functional Business Processes: From Silos to Synergy*. BVIMSR Journal of Management Research. [HTML]

Sarlis, V. & Tjortjis, C. (2024). Sports analytics: data mining to uncover NBA player position, age, and injury impact on performance and economics. Information. mdpi.com

Sasabone, L., Limbong, S., Pongpalilu, F., Soepriadi, & Jubhari. (2022). Utilizing WhatsApp As An Educational Technology Tool In Improving Students' Speaking For ESP Instruction. *EDULEC : Education, Language, and Culture Journal, 2*(2). https://doi.org/DOI: 10.56314/edulec.v2i2

Saxena, K. (2025). *Emotive Intelligence and Interpersonal Skills: Key Drivers of Leadership Effectiveness and Personal Competence*. Pacific Business Review International. [HTML]

Schmidthaler, E., Schalk, M., Schmollmüller, M., Hinterplattner, S., Hörmann, C., Anđić, B., Rottenhofer, M., Lavicza, Z., & Sabitzer, B. (2023). The interdisciplinary implementation of poly-universe to promote computational thinking: Teaching examples from biological, physical, and digital education in Austrian secondary schools. [frontiersin.org]. *Frontiers in Psychology, 14*, 1139884. DOI: 10.3389/fpsyg.2023.1139884 PMID: 37008848

Setiawan, A. (2019). Pengambilan Keputusan untuk Menyeleksi Penerimaan Guru Matematika dengan Methode Topsis. *Methomika: Jurnal Manajemen Informatika & Komputerisasi Akuntansi, 3*(1), 14–20. https://doi.org/https://doi.org/10.46880/jmika.Vol3No1.pp14-20

Sghir, N., Adadi, A., & Lahmer, M. (2023). Recent advances in Predictive Learning Analytics: A decade systematic review (2012–2022). Education and information technologies. springer.com

Shaheen, N. L. (2022). Technology accessibility: How US K-12 schools are enacting policy and addressing the equity imperative. [HTML]. *Computers & Education, 179*, 104414. DOI: 10.1016/j.compedu.2021.104414

Shahid, R., Mozumder, M. A. S., Sweet, M. M. R., Hasan, M., Alam, M., Rahman, M. A., Prabha, M., Arif, M., Ahmed, M. P., & Islam, M. R. (2024). Predicting Customer Loyalty in the Airline Industry: A Machine Learning Approach Integrating Sentiment Analysis and User Experience. [comien.org]. *International Journal on Computational Engineering, 1*(2), 50–54. DOI: 10.62527/comien.1.2.12

Shanmugasundaram, M. & Tamilarasu, A. (2023). The impact of digital technology, social media, and artificial intelligence on cognitive functions: a review. Frontiers in Cognition. frontiersin.org

Sheehan, W. B., Tribolet, R., Watsford, M. L., Novak, A. R., Rennie, M., & Fransen, J. (2022). Tactical analysis of individual and team behaviour in professional Australian football: Original investigation. [HTML]. *Science & Medicine in Football, 6*(2), 172–180. DOI: 10.1080/24733938.2021.1923792 PMID: 35475736

Shih, H. P., Lai, K. H., & Cheng, T. C. E. (2023). Complied by belief consistency: The cognitive-information lens of user-generated persuasion. [mdpi.com]. *Journal of Theoretical and Applied Electronic Commerce Research, 18*(1), 372–393. DOI: 10.3390/jtaer18010020

Shimada, K. (2023). The role of artificial intelligence in mental health: A review. *Science Insights*, *43*(5), 1119–1127. DOI: 10.15354/si.23.re820

Shoaib, M., Sayed, N., Singh, J., Shafi, J., Khan, S., & Ali, F. (2024). AI student success predictor: Enhancing personalized learning in campus management systems. [HTML]. *Computers in Human Behavior*, *158*, 108301. DOI: 10.1016/j.chb.2024.108301

Shortt, M., Tilak, S., Kuznetcova, I., Martens, B., & Akinkuolie, B. (2023). Gamification in mobile-assisted language learning: A systematic review of Duolingo literature from public release of 2012 to early 2020. [tandfonline.com]. *Computer Assisted Language Learning*, *36*(3), 517–554. DOI: 10.1080/09588221.2021.1933540

Sims, S., & Fletcher-Wood, H. (2021). Identifying the characteristics of effective teacher professional development: A critical review. *School Effectiveness and School Improvement*, *32*(1), 47–63. ucl.ac.uk. DOI: 10.1080/09243453.2020.1772841

Singh, T. M., Reddy, C. K. K., Murthy, B. R., Nag, A., & Doss, S. (2025). Ai and education: Bridging the gap to personalized, efficient, and accessible learning. In *Internet of Behavior-Based Computational Intelligence for Smart Education Systems* (pp. 131–160). IGI Global. [HTML]

Sinha, M., & Srivastava, M. (2022). Augmented reality-enabled Instagram game filters: Key to engaging customers. [HTML]. *Journal of Promotion Management*, *28*(4), 467–486. DOI: 10.1080/10496491.2021.2008577

Sjödin, D., Parida, V., Palmié, M., & Wincent, J. (2021). How AI capabilities enable business model innovation: Scaling AI through co-evolutionary processes and feedback loops. Journal of Business Research. sciencedirect.com

Skemp, R. R. (2012). The Psychology of learning mathematics: Expanded American edition. In *The Psychology of Learning Mathematics: Expanded American Edition* (pp. 1–218). DOI: 10.4324/9780203396391

Smeplass, E. (2023). Investigating adult learners' experiences from using slow reading as a pedagogical approach. International Journal of Educational Research. sciencedirect.com

Song, H. G., Kim, Y. S., & Hwang, E. (2023). How attitude and para-social interaction influence purchase intentions of Mukbang users: A mixed-method study. Behavioral Sciences. mdpi.com

Sreenivasa, A., & Suresh, M. (2024). Design thinking and artificial intelligence: A systematic literature review exploring synergies. *International Journal of Innovation Studies*, *8*(3), 297–312. DOI: 10.1016/j.ijis.2024.05.001

Sreenivasan, A. & Suresh, M. (2024). Design thinking and artificial intelligence: A systematic literature review exploring synergies. International Journal of Innovation Studies. sciencedirect.com

Stanja, J., Gritz, W., Krugel, J., Hoppe, A., & Dannemann, S. (2023). Formative assessment strategies for students' conceptions—The potential of learning analytics. [wiley.com]. *British Journal of Educational Technology, 54*(1), 58–75. DOI: 10.1111/bjet.13288

Strielkowski, W., Grebennikova, V., Lisovskiy, A., Rakhimova, G., & Vasileva, T. (2024). AI-driven adaptive learning for sustainable educational transformation. Sustainable Development. wiley.com

Sudrajat. (2022). Pemahaman Relasional dan Intrumental: Bagaimana Pengaruhnya dalam Pembelajaran Matematika Ditinjai dari Pemecahan Masalah Matematis. *Elips: Jurnal Pendidikan Matematika, 3*(1), 45–52. https://doi.org/https://doi.org/10.47650/elips.v3i1.393

Sujarwo, S., Asdar, A., Sabillah, B. M., Sukmawati, S., Akhiruddin, A., & Muh. Syata, W. (2023). Innovation In English Language Learning Model Based Digital Literacy To Construct Young Learners' Character. *Ethical Lingua. Journal of Language Teaching and Literature, 10*(2). Advance online publication. DOI: 10.30605/25409190.640

Sukmawati, S., Syam, N. I. S., Jubhari, Y. J., Mardiani, M., Sasabone, L., & Sujarwo, S. (2023). Implementation of Technology on English for Specific Purposes (ESP) Students in Communicative Language Teaching Approach. *Ethical Lingua: Journal of Language Teaching and Literature, 10*(1). Advance online publication. DOI: 10.30605/25409190.566

Sulaiman, & Neviyarni. (2021). Teori Belajar Menurut Aliran Psikologi Humanistik Serta Implikasinya Dalam Proses Belajar dan Pembelajaran Sulaiman. *Jurnal Sikola: Jurnal Kajian Pendidikan Dan Pembelajaran, 2*(3), 220–234. https://doi.org/https://doi.org/10.24036/sikola.v2i3.118 Teori

Sun, Y. & Xing, J. (2022). The impact of social media information sharing on the green purchase intention among generation Z. Sustainability. mdpi.com

Sundari, M. S., Penthala, H. R., & Nayyar, A. Transforming Education through AI-Enhanced Content Creation and Personalized Learning Experiences. In *Impact of Artificial Intelligence on Society* (pp. 98–118). Chapman and Hall/CRC. [HTML]

Talaue, G. M., AlSaad, A., AlRushaidan, N., AlHugail, A., & AlFahhad, S. (2018). The impact of social media on academic performance of selected college students. *International Journal of Advanced Information Technology*, *8*(4/5), 27–35. DOI: 10.5121/ijait.2018.8503

Tammets, K., & Ley, T. (2023). Integrating AI tools in teacher professional learning: A conceptual model and illustrative case. *Frontiers in Artificial Intelligence*, *6*, 1255089. DOI: 10.3389/frai.2023.1255089 PMID: 38130325

Tang, J., & Foley, J. (2022). A Case Study on the Effectiveness of Applying Content and Language Integrated Learning in an Artificial Intelligence English Reading Course. *Arab World English Journal*, *13*(3), 236–253. DOI: 10.24093/awej/vol13no3.15

Tan, S. C., Chan, C., Bielaczyc, K., Ma, L., Scardamalia, M., & Bereiter, C. (2021). Knowledge building: Aligning education with needs for knowledge creation in the digital age. *Educational Technology Research and Development*, *69*(4), 2243–2266. nie.edu.sg. DOI: 10.1007/s11423-020-09914-x

Taub, M., Banzon, A. M., Zhang, T., & Chen, Z. (2022). Tracking changes in students' online self-regulated learning behaviors and achievement goals using trace clustering and process mining. Frontiers in psychology. frontiersin.org

Tavakoli, M., Faraji, A., Vrolijk, J., Molavi, M., Mol, S. T., & Kismihók, G. (2022). An AI-based open recommender system for personalized labor market driven education. [sciencedirect.com]. *Advanced Engineering Informatics*, *52*, 101508. DOI: 10.1016/j.aei.2021.101508

Theodorakopoulos, L., & Theodoropoulou, A. (2024). Leveraging big data analytics for understanding consumer behavior in digital marketing: A systematic review. [wiley.com]. *Human Behavior and Emerging Technologies*, *2024*(1), 3641502. DOI: 10.1155/2024/3641502

Thompson, B. S. (2021). Corporate payments for ecosystem services in theory and practice: Links to economics, business, and sustainability. Sustainability. mdpi.com

Thornhill-Miller, B., Camarda, A., Mercier, M., Burkhardt, J. M., Morisseau, T., Bourgeois-Bougrine, S., Vinchon, F., El Hayek, S., Augereau-Landais, M., Mourey, F., Feybesse, C., Sundquist, D., & Lubart, T. (2023). Creativity, critical thinking, communication, and collaboration: Assessment, certification, and promotion of 21st century skills for the future of work and education. [mdpi.com]. *Journal of Intelligence*, *11*(3), 54. DOI: 10.3390/jintelligence11030054 PMID: 36976147

Thunberg, G., Johnson, E., Bornman, J., Öhlén, J., & Nilsson, S. (2022). Being heard–Supporting person-centred communication in paediatric care using augmentative and alternative communication as universal design: A position paper. [wiley.com]. *Nursing Inquiry*, *29*(2), e12426. DOI: 10.1111/nin.12426 PMID: 34076320

Todd, E. M., & Stewart, P. (2023). Guidelines for training design thinking in organizations. [HTML]. *Industrial and Commercial Training*, *55*(3), 364–374. DOI: 10.1108/ICT-10-2022-0076

Torres-Ronda, L., Beanland, E., Whitehead, S., Sweeting, A., & Clubb, J. (2022). Tracking systems in team sports: A narrative review of applications of the data and sport specific analysis. [springer.com]. *Sports Medicine - Open*, *8*(1), 15. DOI: 10.1186/s40798-022-00408-z PMID: 35076796

Touretzky, D., Martin, F., Seehorn, D., Breazeal, C., & Posner, T. (2019, February). Special session: AI for K-12 guidelines initiative. In *Proceedings of the 50th ACM technical symposium on computer science education* (pp. 492-493). DOI: 10.1145/3287324.3287525

Tschepe, S. (April 2024). AI-enhanced design thinking. HPI d-school, www.hpi.de

Tugberk, C., & Sirin, S. (2024). *Beyond Intelligence: The Life and Work of Howard Gardner*. The Palgrave Handbook of Educational Thinkers. [HTML]

Uher, J. (2022). Functions of units, scales and quantitative data: Fundamental differences in numerical traceability between sciences. Quality & Quantity. springer.com

Ungureanu, P., Cochis, C., Bertolotti, F., Mattarelli, E., & Scapolan, A. C. (2021). Multiplex boundary work in innovation projects: The role of collaborative spaces for cross-functional and open innovation. [emerald.com]. *European Journal of Innovation Management*, *24*(3), 984–1010. DOI: 10.1108/EJIM-11-2019-0338

Uwamahoro, J., Ndihokubwayo, K., Ralph, M., & Ndayambaje, I. (2021). Physics students' conceptual understanding of geometric optics: Revisited analysis. [HTML]. *Journal of Science Education and Technology*, *30*(5), 706–718. DOI: 10.1007/s10956-021-09913-4

Valdivia, S., Backes, J. G., Traverso, M., Sonnemann, G., Cucurachi, S., Guinée, J. B., Schaubroeck, T., Finkbeiner, M., Leroy-Parmentier, N., Ugaya, C., Peña, C., Zamagni, A., Inaba, A., Amaral, M., Berger, M., Dvarioniene, J., Vakhitova, T., Benoit-Norris, C., Prox, M., & Goedkoop, M. (2021). Principles for the application of life cycle sustainability assessment. [springer.com]. *The International Journal of Life Cycle Assessment*, *26*(9), 1900–1905. DOI: 10.1007/s11367-021-01958-2 van den Adel, M. J., de Vries, T. A., & van Donk, D. P. (2023). Improving cross-functional teams' effectiveness during supply chain disruptions: The importance of information scouting and internal integration. [rug.nl]. *Supply Chain Management, 28*(4), 773–786. DOI: 10.1108/SCM-06-2022-0243

Van Laar, E., Van Duerson, A. J., van Dikk, J. A., & de Haan, J. (2020). Determinants of 21st-Century Skills and 21st-Century Digital Skills for Workers: A Systematic Literature Review. *SAGE Open, 10*(Jan-Mar), 1–14. DOI: 10.1177/2158244019900176

Velastegui-Hernandez, D. C., Salazar-Garcés, L. F., & Rodriguez-Pérez, M. L. (2023). Impact of artificial intelligence on learning behaviors and psychological well-being of college students. *Salud, Ciencia y Tecnología - Serie de Conferencias, 2,* 582. https://doi.org/DOI: 10.56294/sctconf2023582

Vergani, R., Vendraminelli, L., & Swan, K. (2021). Design thinking: Critical analysis and future evolution. *Journal of Product Innovation Management, 38*(6), 603–622. DOI: 10.1111/jpim.12610

Verganti, R., Vendraminelli, L., & Iansiti, M. (2020). Innovation and Design in the Age of Artificial Intelligence. *Journal of Product Innovation Management, 37*(3), 212–227. DOI: 10.1111/jpim.12523

Verma, A., Lamsal, K., & Verma, P. (2022). An investigation of skill requirements in artificial intelligence and machine learning job advertisements. [HTML]. *Industry and Higher Education, 36*(1), 63–73. DOI: 10.1177/0950422221990990

Vila, S., Gilar-Corbí, R., & Pozo-Rico, T. (2021). Effects of student training in social skills and emotional intelligence on the behaviour and coexistence of adolescents in the 21st century. [mdpi.com]. *International Journal of Environmental Research and Public Health, 18*(10), 5498. DOI: 10.3390/ijerph18105498 PMID: 34065560

Virvou, M. (2023). Artificial Intelligence and User Experience in reciprocity: Contributions and state of the art. Intelligent Decision Technologies. sagepub.com

Vistorte, A. O. R., Deroncele-Acosta, A., Ayala, J. L. M., Barrasa, A., López-Granero, C., & Martí-González, M. (2024). Integrating artificial intelligence to assess emotions in learning environments: A systematic literature review. [frontiersin.org]. *Frontiers in Psychology, 15*, 1387089. DOI: 10.3389/fpsyg.2024.1387089 PMID: 38966729

Votintseva, A. (2023, July). Rapid Prototyping Platform for Multi-stakeholder Involvement in the Design of User Interaction. In International Conference on Human-Computer Interaction (pp. 302-313). Cham: Springer Nature Switzerland. [HTML] DOI: 10.1007/978-3-031-35596-7_19

Wahid, A., Afni, N., & Sujarwo, S. (2025). Promoting Learners' Autonomy through Metacognitive, Higher-Order Thinking Skills and Digital Literacy of Indonesian Private Universities. *Educational Process International Journal, 16*(1). Advance online publication. DOI: 10.22521/edupij.2025.16.204

Wahyuddin, S. S., & Asfar, F. (2021). Analisis Kemampuan Menyelesaikan Soal High Order Thinking Skills Ditijau dari Kemampuan Berpikir Logis. *AKSIOMA: Jurnal Program Studi Pendidikan Matematika, 10*(2), 521–535. https://doi.org/https://doi.org/10.24127/ajpm.v10i2.3480

Wallwey, C. & Kajfez, R. L. (2023). Quantitative research artifacts as qualitative data collection techniques in a mixed methods research study. Methods in Psychology. sciencedirect.com

Walters, P. (2021). Are generation Z ethical consumers? In *Generation Z Marketing and Management in Tourism and Hospitality: The Future of the Industry* (pp. 303–325). Springer International Publishing. [HTML] DOI: 10.1007/978-3-030-70695-1_12

Wang, T., Lund, B. D., Marengo, A., Pagano, A., Mannuru, N. R., Teel, Z. A., & Pange, J. (2023). Exploring the Potential Impact of Artificial Intelligence (AI) on International Students in Higher Education: Generative AI, Chatbots, Analytics, and International Student Success. *Applied Sciences (Basel, Switzerland), 13*(11), 6716.

Wang, W. S., Lin, C. J., Lee, H. Y., Huang, Y. M., & Wu, T. T. (2025). Integrating feedback mechanisms and ChatGPT for VR-based experiential learning: Impacts on reflective thinking and Aiot physical hands-on tasks. [HTML]. *Interactive Learning Environments*, *33*(2), 1770–1787.

Wardani, D. S. (2020). Usaha Peningkatan Keterampilan Pemecahan Masalah melalui Model Problem Based Learning di Kelas V SDN Babatan V/460 Surabaya. *COLLASE: Creative of Learning Students Elementary Education*, *3*(4), 104–117.

Ward, M., Passmore, M. A., Spencer, A., Hanson, H., & Lucas, T. (2023). The effect of surface geometry on the aerodynamic behaviour of a football. [springer.com]. *Sports Engineering*, *26*(1), 33. DOI: 10.1007/s12283-023-00409-5

Weng, X., Chiu, T. K. F., & Tsang, C. C. (2022). Promoting student creativity and entrepreneurship through real-world problem-based maker education. Thinking Skills and Creativity. sciencedirect.com

Wiyono, H. D., Ardiansyah, T., & Rasul, T. (2020). Kreativitas dan Inovasi dalam Berwirausaha. *Jurnal Usaha, 1*(2), 19–25. https://doi.org/https://doi.org/10.30998/juuk.v1i2.503

Woebot Health. (n.d.). Woebot: Your mental health ally. https://woebothealth.com

Wu, H., Wang, Y., & Wang, Y. (2024). "To Use or Not to Use?" A Mixed-Methods Study on the Determinants of EFL College Learners' Behavioral Intention to Use AI in the Distributed Learning Context. *International Review of Research in Open and Distance Learning*, *25*(3), 158–178. DOI: 10.19173/irrodl.v25i3.7708

Xin, P. (2025). Ethical and Philosophical Perspectives on Human-Computer Interaction in the Design of Intelligent Products: A Comprehensive Analysis. Cultura: International Journal of Philosophy of Culture and Axiology, 22(1). culturajournal.com

Yadav, S. (2024). *Designing Effective E-Portfolios for Authentic Assessment: Encouraging Reflection and Promoting Student Ownership*. Cases on Authentic Assessment in Higher Education. [HTML] DOI: 10.4018/979-8-3693-1001-4.ch011

Yağcı, M. (2022). Educational data mining: prediction of students' academic performance using machine learning algorithms. Smart Learning Environments. springer.com

Yang, E., & Beil, C. (2024). Ensuring data privacy in AI/ML implementation. [HTML]. *New Directions for Higher Education*, *2024*(207), 63–78. DOI: 10.1002/he.20509

Ye, W. & Li, Y. (2022). Design and research of digital media art display based on virtual reality and augmented reality. Mobile Information Systems. wiley.com

Yeadon, M. R. & Pain, M. T. G. (2023). Fifty years of performance-related sports biomechanics research. Journal of Biomechanics. sciencedirect.com

Yilmaz, R. M., & Karaoglan Yilmaz, F. G. (2024). Students' acceptance of AI-powered educational tools: Exploring thc impact of metacognitive self-regulation. *Computers & Education*, *205*, 104900.

Yin, S., Chen, F., & Chang, H. (2022). Assessment as Learning: How Does Peer Assessment Function in Students' Learning?. Frontiers in psychology. frontiersin.org

Yin, C. C. (2024). Integrating or tailoring? Optimizing touchpoints for enhanced omnichannel customer experience. [HTML]. *Journal of Research in Interactive Marketing*. Advance online publication. DOI: 10.1108/JRIM-11-2023-0418

Ystgaard, K. F., Atzori, L., Palma, D., Heegaard, P. E., Bertheussen, L. E., Jensen, M. R., & De Moor, K. (2023). Review of the theory, principles, and design requirements of human-centric Internet of Things (IoT). [springer.com]. *Journal of Ambient Intelligence and Humanized Computing*, *14*(3), 2827–2859. DOI: 10.1007/s12652-023-04539-3

Yu, H. (2024). Enhancing creative cognition through project-based learning: An in-depth scholarly exploration. Heliyon. cell.com

Yu, H., Wei, W., Li, J., & Li, Y. (2022). Thc impact of green digital finance on energy resources and climate change mitigation in carbon neutrality: Case of 60 economies. [HTML]. *Resources Policy*, *79*, 103116. DOI: 10.1016/j.resourpol.2022.103116

Zaka, K. & Al Juboori, M. M. S. (2023). The Impact of Generation-Z on International Branding Strategy: An Analysis of Startup Fashion Brands: What are the possible challenges and advantages faced by …. diva-portal.org

Zhang, R. (2022). Design of an authentic project-based learning course using project management approach. [HTML]. *International Journal of Fashion Design, Technology and Education*, *15*(1), 57–66. DOI: 10.1080/17543266.2021.1992799

Zheng, F. (2022). Fostering students' well-being: The mediating role of teacher interpersonal behavior and student-teacher relationships. Frontiers in psychology. frontiersin.org

Zhou, J., Gandomi, A. H., Chen, F., & Holzinger, A. (2021). Evaluating the quality of machine learning explanations: A survey on methods and metrics. Electronics. mdpi.com

Zimmerle, J. C. (2021). Safe, sound, and private: Promoting data protection for students. [HTML]. *Computers in the Schools*, *38*(1), 1–18. DOI: 10.1080/07380569.2021.1882203

About the Contributors

Andi Asrifan, S.Pd, M.Pd, a distinguished figure in the realm of education, particularly in English Language Education, has made significant contributions through his extensive research, teaching, and leadership roles. As the Head of the Institute for Cooperation and International Affairs at Universitas Muhammadiyah Sidenreng Rappang and now a lecturer in Universitas Negeri Makassar (UNM), Dr. Asrifan's academic journey is marked by a rich tapestry of achievements, including a Doctor of Education in English Language Education. His work spans various facets of education, language, and technology, reflecting the diverse topics covered in his publications and research endeavors. These include, but are not limited to, the impact of the COVID-19 pandemic on educational practices, methodologies in English as a Foreign Language (EFL) classrooms, and the integration of technology in teaching and learning processes. Dr. Asrifan's commitment to advancing educational standards and practices is further evidenced by his active participation in international conferences, webinars, and workshops across countries like India, the Philippines, and Pakistan. These events, organized by various institutions and associations, underscore his role as a global educator and thought leader. His dedication to professional development is also highlighted through his involvement in numerous courses and certifications in personal branding, public speaking, and literacy teaching. Moreover, Dr. Asrifan's leadership extends beyond academia into organizational and educational development, where he has served in various capacities, including as an external examiner for Ph.D. dissertations and a reviewer for scientific journals. His accolades, memberships in professional organizations, and roles as an ambassador for international associations speak volumes of his influence and commitment to fostering educational excellence and sustainable development goals globally.

***

Syamsul Alam Ramli, S.Pd., M.Pd. is an academic dedicated to the fields of Early Childhood Education (PAUD) and Primary Education. He earned his Bachelor's degree in 2012 from the Primary School Teacher Education (PGSD) Program at Universitas Negeri Makassar. Pursuing further education, he obtained his Master of Education (M.Pd.) degree in 2014 with a specialization in Early Childhood Education from Universitas Negeri Jakarta. In 2015, he began his academic career as a part-time lecturer in the Early Childhood Teacher Education Program (PGPAUD) at Universitas Negeri Makassar. That same year, he was also appointed as a permanent lecturer in the Midwifery Education Program (DIV) at STIKES Mega Rezky Makassar. To strengthen his academic journey, in 2017, Syamsul Alam Ramli transitioned his academic home base to the PG-PAUD Program at STKIP Muhammadiyah Palopo, which later became Universitas Muhammadiyah Palopo (UMPalopo) in 2019. For him, education is not merely a profession but a calling — an investment for both this world and the hereafter. In fulfilling the tri dharma of higher education, he focuses on three main pillars: teaching, research (including publications and intellectual property), and community service. He is also actively involved as a speaker in various academic forums. He strengthens collaboration with lecturers from various disciplines through research and development grants supported by the Ministry of Education, Culture, Research, and Technology (Kemdikbudristek). These interdisciplinary and multidisciplinary collaborations aim to ensure that the academic theories delivered are aligned with real-world practice. The book he authored reflects such a multidisciplinary approach, bridging academic theory with practical community needs—particularly in the areas of nutrition science, counseling, and family education during critical periods of child development. Through this integrative and collaborative approach, he aspires to continually contribute to the advancement of education in Indonesia.

Asdar is a Ph. D in Indonesian Language Education from the State University Makassar, Indonesia. He has over 15 years of experience as an academic with the Universitas Bosowa, where he is currently an Associate Professor and the Dean of the Faculty of Education and Literature. His current research interest includes students' learning and development at various levels and areas of education. His publication topics include reading comprehension, online learning, learning models in language, Digital literacy, integrative approach in learning, and writing skills

Sunarlia Limbong is an English Lecturer, Associate Professor, and Head of the Language Center at the Polytechnic of Makassar Merchant Marine. She earned a Ph.D. in Indonesian Language Education from the State University Makassar, Indonesia. She has over 15 years of experience teaching as an academician. Her research interests are language learning strategies, Methods of Teaching in ELT, synchronous learning, and English for Specific Purposes

Sri Wahyuny Mustafa is a distinguished academic with extensive experience in the fields of economics and business education. Currently serving as a lecturer at the Faculty of Economics and Business, Universitas Muhammadiyah Palopo, she has held key leadership positions, including Head of the Economic Development Study Program (2018–2020) and Vice Dean for Academic Affairs, Research and Innovation, Cooperation, and Islamic Values (2023–2028). Her academic qualifications include a Master's and Doctoral degree in Economics, specializing in development and planning, from Hasanuddin University. Sri's research focuses on a broad range of critical economic issues, including labor absorption in tourism and industrial sectors, financial development, economic growth, and the socioeconomic impacts of agriculture and mining in South Sulawesi. Her scholarly work has been presented at both national and international forums, reflecting her active contribution to the advancement of economic knowledge. As a member of professional organizations such as ISEI, ADRI, and APSEP, Sri has demonstrated her commitment to academic excellence and collaboration. Proficient in statistical tools such as SPSS, EViews, and R Studio, she is recognized for her expertise in quantitative research and data analysis. Her dedication to education and research is evident in her efforts to enhance economic understanding and support sustainable development initiatives.

Yulini Rinantanti is an English Lecturer, Associate Professor, and English lecturer in Universitas Cenderawasih. She earned a Ph.D. in Indonesian Language Education from the State University Makassar, Indonesia. She has over 20 years of experience teaching as an academician. Her research interests are language learning strategies, Methods of Teaching in ELT, English Language Skills, English for Specific Purposes, and Literature

Sujarwo Sujarwo has a Ph.D in English Language Studies (ELS) from Hasanuddin University, Indonesia. He has over 11 years of experience as an Academician with the Universitas Megarezky, where he is currently an Assistant Professor and the Secretary of the English Education Department Faculty of Teacher Training and Education. His current research interest includes EFL students' learning and development at various levels and areas of education. His publication topics include translation, ESP, online learning, learning models in ELT, and Research and Development (R & D) in Education

Sujarwo Sukmawati is a Ph.D in English Language Studies (ELS) from Hasanuddin University, Indonesia. He has over 11 years of experience as an

Academician with the Universitas Megarezky, where he is currently an Assistant Professor and the Secretary of the English Education Department Faculty of Teacher Training and Education. His current research interest includes EFL students' learning and development at various levels and areas of education. His publication topics include translation, ESP, online learning, learning models in ELT, and Research and Development (R & D) in Education

Sumin Samuel Sybol is currently an assistant professor at CHRIST (Deemed to be University), Delhi NCR Campus, and has previous teaching experience as a visiting faculty member at Amity University, Noida. He has substantial expertise in analytics, Machine Learning, programming, and networking. His professional experience includes holding the position of Head of IT at Enrope Solutions and Keyfill Light, where he managed IT operations and strategies. Additionally, he has published research papers and secured a patent on improving power efficiency for wearable devices. Prof. Sumin is proficient in programming languages, including C/C++, Java, and Python, and has experience using software like Tableau, Power BI, and MySQL. He has also actively participated in various faculty development programs (FDPs) and workshops related to AI, data visualization, and IoT sensors. His work has been presented at prestigious conferences organized by IIT Roorkee and IIT Mandi.

Andi Syukriani completed undergraduate studies (Bachelor's degree) in Mathematics Education at Universitas Negeri Makassar from 2000 to 2004, followed by a Master's degree in Mathematics Education at the same university from 2007 to 2009. The doctoral degree (Ph.D.) in Mathematics Education was earned at Universitas Negeri Surabaya from 2013 to 2018. The academic career began in 2009 as a lecturer at Universitas Patompo, continuing until 2024. In 2024, [Name] transferred their home base to the Doctoral Program in Mathematics Education, Postgraduate Program, Universitas Negeri Makassar. From 2019 to 2023, She served as the Head of the Undergraduate Mathematics Education Study Program at the Faculty of Teacher Training and Education, Universitas Patompo. From 2023 to 2024, She was also entrusted with the position of Head of the Statistics Study Program at the Faculty of Science and Technology, Universitas Patompo.

Nurfaida Tasni is a lecturer at STKIP YPUP Makassar, where she has been teaching since 2012. She holds a Bachelor's and Master's degree in Mathematics Education from Universitas Negeri Makassar, and earned her Doctoral degree from Universitas Negeri Malang in 2019, specializing in Mathematics Education. Throughout her career, Dr. Tasni has been deeply involved in academic research, focusing on mathematical problem-solving and cognitive development in students.

She has contributed extensively to scholarly publications, serving as both an author and a reviewer for various national and international journals. Among her roles, she is a member of the editorial board for Jurnal Lebesgue at Universitas Bina Bangsa, and a reviewer for multiple academic journals, including PEPATUDZU and Jurnal Pendidikan Indonesia. Dr. Tasni is also an active participant in professional organizations, such as the Indonesian Mathematics Educators Society (I-MES) and the Indonesian Association of Educators and Educational Developers (APPI). Her research primarily explores mathematical thinking, problem-solving skills, and the application of cooperative learning models in mathematics education. She is highly committed to enhancing the quality of education in Indonesia, with a strong focus on integrating technology and innovative teaching methods in her field.

Hamzah Upu was born in Ciellang, Bone Regency, South Sulawesi, on August 1, 1966, the son of Upu and Muna. He completed his formal education successively at SD Negeri 72 Ammesangeng in 1977, SMP Negeri 1133 Lamurukung in 1981, and SMA Negeri 156 Watampone in 1984—all located in Bone Regency. Hamzah earned his Bachelor's degree (Drs.) in Mathematics Education from the Institute of Teacher Training and Education (IKIP) Ujung Pandang in 1988, his Master's degree (M.Ed) in Mathematics Education from Deakin University, Melbourne, Australia in 1996, and his Doctoral degree (Dr.) in Mathematics Education from Universitas Pendidikan Indonesia in 2003, graduating with cum laude honors. Prior to completing his Master's degree, he participated in the Basic Sciences Bridging Program at the Department of Mathematics, Institut Teknologi Bandung, which he completed in 1991. Hamzah has published more than 100 papers in both national and international journals, one of which is titled "The Direction of Education Quality Improvement in Indonesia."

Index

W

www.ingramcontent.com/pod-product-compliance
Lightning Source LLC
LaVergne TN
LVHW081523300926
849161LV00006B/1276